MW01119934

E. M. Forster's
Spiritual Journey
in
His Life and Works

Jeane Noordhoff Olson

"The 'Noble Peasant' in E. M. Forster's Fiction" was published by the University of North Texas, Denton, Texas, in *Studies in the Novel*, vol. 20, no. 4, Winter 1988, pages 389–403. This article has been revised and incorporated in chapter 1.

"E. M. Forster's Prophetic Vision of the Modern Family in Howards End" was published by the University of Texas Press, Austin, Texas, in *Texas Studies in Literature and Language*, vol. 35, no. 3, Fall 1993, pages 347–62. This article was reprinted in *Twentieth Century Literary Criticism*, vol. 125, ed. Janet Witalec (Farmington Hills, MI: Gale Group, 2003), 120–28.

Printed on Opus, an Espresso Book Machine located at:
Politics and Prose Bookstore
5015 Connecticut Ave NW
Washington, DC 20008

To the memory of two whose encouragement sustained me:

Lawrence Olson,

who pointed me towards Forster,

and

Carol Ohmann,

who saw publishing potential

Literature is the speech of a man which goes on living after the man has died.

The Hill of Devi

The people I respect most behave as if they were immortal and as if society were eternal. Both assumptions are false: both of them must be accepted as true if we are to go on working and eating and loving, and are to keep open a few breathing holes for the human spirit.

"What I Believe"
Two Cheers for Democracy

Table of Contents

Acknowledgments

The family is a given in novels, all too often as a dysfunctional background against which the narrative action takes place. I wanted to write about the family as a positive influence, more than just a backdrop. My own graduate curriculum included only *Howards End* as a Forster sample. My husband, who had just finished reading all of Forster's then-extant novels, suggested that Forster gave the family an active role. Over the Christmas vacation, reading the five novels then published, I knew I had found my subject. In Forster's novels the family personifying social immobility could awaken to the potential for change and growth, but only if a member (or members) were willing to take the risk. As I continued my reading of Forster's works, including many rereadings of the novels, I gradually realized the breadth of his concerns and the hidden wealth of his personal philosophy of life sprinkled liberally throughout his writings. The reflection Forster saw in the mirror he held up to life could come alive and realize his dream, at least in his novels.

I was further encouraged by my advisor, mentor, and friend, the late Carol Ohmann of Wesleyan University who, upon submitting my long paper to the graduate office with her comments, wrote that "this paper has publishing potential." Like any graduate student novitiate, I was ecstatic on reading this commendation. I should add my grateful thanks to Wesleyan University, Middletown, Connecticut, for making graduate study so easily possible for me as the wife of a faculty member.

Besides Carol Ohmann, among the English Department faculty at Wesleyan I am deeply grateful to William Stowe, whose attentive reading of my course papers and exams and his thoughtful and lengthy comments gave me solid critical suggestions—and encouragement—for improvement. The late Walter Rideout, a family friend and emeritus professor of English of the University of Wisconsin at Madison, early on took the time to read my long paper, advising a narrower focus for my first attempt at academic publication and suggesting a few presses as possibly interested in my subject. His instinct was right on target.

One does not write about Forster without writing about India. Janice D. Willis, of the Religion Department at Wesleyan University, kindly pointed me toward A. L. Basham's *The Wonder That Was India*, which provided me a rich overview of the crowded tapestry of history, art, and religion of that enormous subcontinent woven with strands from many sources over the centuries. The section on religion alone is about two hundred pages.

I must also emphasize the importance of P. N. Furbank's two-volume authorized biography—*E. M. Forster: A Life*—for its clear time line and concise identification of people important in Forster's life. Without Furbank's authoritative biography, present-day critics of Forster's life and his writings would have an onerous task of portraying Forster's background and his actions. One can only express grateful appreciation of his masterful presentation of Forster the man and author. One may assume that Forster himself was the final person to decide what should be included and what finessed.

At the University of Cambridge in England, where I spent three months reading widely in Forster's papers, Jacqueline Cox, then curator of the Modern Archives of King's College Library, and the assistant curator, Rosaline Moad, were both most helpful and efficient in providing the resource materials I requested. Even before leaving the United States, a leisurely perusal of the archive's holdings in its thorough "Hand List of the Papers of E. M. Forster" enabled me to focus immediately on what I wanted; it was an efficient time-saver. In King's College Library, Huw Thomas led me to several sources I wanted to see, and the skyscraper Cambridge University Library, alive with eager students, gave generous help whenever asked, especially in the Periodicals Division.

Three American libraries have been helpful: Dartmouth College's Baker Library (now Berry-Baker Library) in Hanover, New Hampshire, allowed me to roam its stacks and assisted with finding items in storage while Mrs. Patricia (Patsy) Carter was particularly helpful in procuring books for me through interlibrary loan. Miguel Valladares was also similarly helpful. In Washington, DC, American University's Bender Library provided easy access to its reference and periodical sections, as well as to the open stacks. George Arnold was particularly helpful and encouraging. Of the three libraries Georgetown

University's Lauinger Library has the richest selection of Forster criticism, possessing as well a large number of the seventeen volumes of the Abinger Edition, the invaluable authorized edition of Forster's works. I am deeply grateful for open access to their stacks.

Patricia A. Farrant, in 1997 president of the National Coalition of Independent Scholars, of which I have been a member, provided me with institutional identity as required for access to the Modern Archives of King's College and testified to my serious scholarly intentions. In earlier days, membership in the Center for Independent Studies, New Haven, Connecticut, a member of the NCIS, provided me with identification when I submitted my first manuscripts to academic presses in the United States. My present affiliation is with the Capital Area Independent Scholars of Washington, DC, an adjunct of the NCIS. CAIS members—Ellen Berg, Diane Calabrese, Edith Couturier, Laura Garcés, Harold Goldblatt, Diane Gottlieb, Robert Kanigel, Martha Mednick, Kay and the late Harold Orlans, Muriel Prouty, and Claire Sherman—have been warmly supportive and patient, especially Claire Sherman, whose thoughtful leadership of the core group kept it moving ahead. Her experiences with the publishing process encouraged my efforts to overcome difficulties. I am especially beholden also to Diane Calabrese who, through the years of the gestation of this book, has offered thoughtful criticism and unfailing and frequent encouragement.

A writer's friends are always called upon for reactions to various versions of a manuscript; their ideas and questions help to sharpen and tighten the work in progress. I am grateful to Bob Abernethy, Linda Abegglen, Sigrid Cerf, Gordon Epstein, the Reverend Kenneth D. Fuller, Jane Hardin, Helene Spurrier, whose invitation to join her in auditing a Wesleyan University class in nineteenth-century female British novelists' works started me on the road to an advanced degree and this book, and also her late husband Professor William Spurrier, and Nancy Zimmer and, of course, members of my family, especially my husband and our two daughters, Alix and Sally. Union Theological Seminary kindly provided me with the source of a quotation I have used. Wesley Seminary, Washington, DC, has similarly helped me find references in their library.

In the last few days of editing the Notes, I was overheard expressing my inability to obtain Forster's biography of his great-aunt in the Abinger edition, *Marianne Thornton, A Domestic Biography, 1797–1887.* Alan Hengst, Senior Circulation Manager of Pense Law Library of the Washington College of Law, affiliated with American University, offered to get it for me—and within a few days I had it, thanks to someone I had not met previously. I am most grateful to him for volunteering to help. Because it cannot be conjured up, serendipity is a miraculous gift.

There are hardly words enough—or sufficiently adequate—to describe the clear editorial eye of Jeannette Hopkins, former director and editor-in-chief of the Wesleyan University Press, a friend, and a critic par excellence. Unsentimental and direct, her queries and comments were a constant challenge, always inspiring me to greater effort and stimulating better organization and more pointed writing. I prize her penetrating insights and high standards.

As I was about to embark on what was to me the unknown challenge of marketing my manuscript, through pure seren-dipity in the person of Professor Stuart Gillmor of Wesleyan University, I met Marilyn Gaull. I cannot thank her enough for deflecting me from time-consuming dead ends and steering me toward the challenges of the publishing process. Her en-thusiasm for my subject, added to her encouragement of my efforts, permitted me to identify myself as an aspiring author.

I have had the good fortune to have the intelligent assis-tance of Elizabeth Gibbens, a young woman of many talents, who has been indefatigable in finding authorized Abinger edi-tion volumes in order to standardize the page references to quotations from Forster's novels and other works that have come out in many editions over the years. I am deeply grateful for her willingness, her youthful energy, and her clear-sighted precision—all this expressed through a charming personality. Many thanks to Bill Sosin for his expert assistance in graphic design and to Thomas S. Russell for his invaluable help in the final stages of getting the book into print.

And last, but far from least, is Aimee B. Anderson, who transformed my notes from the *Chicago Manual of Style* of ten years ago when I began my research for this book to the pre-sent-day preferred form. She has quickly and professionally done a prodigious piece of work not only with the notes but also with the selected bibliography. Because of her devotion to form as well as the logic of content, these sections are stronger and more consistent than they might otherwise have been.

Any factual errors in the notes or bibliography must be ascribed to me since I was the original note-taker.

Author's Preface

Birthdays are often the occasion for assessing earlier experiences and expressing hopes for the future. Opening the pages on a new century can stimulate a similar reckoning of accounts on a larger scale. January first of the year 1900 was both the beginning of a new century, as popular counting goes, and Edward Morgan Forster's twenty-first birthday. As the Victorian era approached its conclusion, Forster was nearing the end of his studies at King's College, Cambridge University. His great-aunt Marianne Thornton had left him the legacy that saw him through the university. But how would he support himself thereafter? The future was unclear until Nathaniel Wedd, a tutor who had become a good friend, encouraged him to seriously consider writing as a lifetime occupation. Forster eagerly grasped the idea. His first novel, *Where Angels Fear to Tread*, was published to popular approval before he was thirty years old.

Forster's first four novels, *Where Angels Fear to Tread, The Longest Journey, A Room with a View*, and *Howards End*, were all written within six years, between 1905 and 1910, with *A Passage to India* being published in 1924 and his homosexual novel, *Maurice*, seeing the light of day only after his death. All these novels were widely acclaimed when first published and are still in print.

From the age of four until he was fourteen years old, Forster lived at the house called Rooksnest near Stevenage, north of London, before the rural atmosphere was swallowed up by the inexorable spread of cosmopolitan London. Here he sent down permanent psychological roots into the land and learned to appreciate the stalwart directness of the unpretentious folk cultivating the adjacent farms. His mother from time to time would hire a neighbor boy—ostensibly to water the gardens at Rooksnest but also to provide a playmate for her young son, an only child. He attended the local grammar school for several years with these garden boys. As Forster grew older, he learned to think for himself, and he gradually began to create a personal spiritual expression for his life, starting with his roots in the countryside.

As a university student Forster rejected traditional late Victorian Christianity, but that does not mean he rejected the mystery of an unknowable God. He was searching for a god who was more human, more humane, more loving, present in all aspects of life on earth, and yet mysterious beyond human imagining. He was also gradually absorbing basic family values that he would later shape into a new definition of the family. These early roots to "place" and "history" were seminally important to Forster. His mature philosophical background was reflected in his own actions and influenced the plots of his novels; it motivated his social commentary and was the inspiration for his political actions.

Several years ago, as I was rereading *Where Angels Fear to Tread,* I realized with a sudden shock that within the violent scene I was reading was imbedded an enactment of Holy Communion, one of the most sacred rites of Christian worship. Even more surprising was that it was Forster's own interpretation of communion.

This surprising insight became questions: Were there other examples of Foster's use of Christian symbols? How did Forster employ them?

In view of the many such examples I found in his oeuvre on rereading, I wondered why there seemed to be still so little appreciation of this aspect of Forster's life experiences. In my extensive earlier reading of secondary sources of Forster criticism, I had noticed only two citations of Forster's 1959 Presidential Address to the Cambridge Society of Humanists, when he was eighty years old, recounting how he had lost his religious faith. Though the early critics understood Forster's rejection as firmly shutting the door on traditional religion, to Forster, I believe, it was the first step on his lifelong spiritual journey.

To find the text of Forster's Presidential Address to the Society of Cambridge Humanists and to see what more might be discovered, I spent three months in the Modern Archives of King's College Library of Cambridge University, where his papers are kept. When these papers became public after his death in 1970, his cogitations on spiritual matters were more easily traceable. Still, the spiritual thread remained unexamined.

Forster gave little help to searchers for he shrank from the limelight. However he was never reluctant to share his philosophical thoughts in print. He did not proselytize. Nor did he disclose any deeply personal spiritual experiences to the general reader. When at the age of eighty he publicly recounted the story of what he called his "loss of faith," it was to an audience of like-minded Cambridge Humanists.

Forster had a mind full of projects on which he lavished his energy and prescient thoughts. His homosexuality was an ever-present black cloud affecting his actions and fears. The reader who wants a deeper treatment of that significant aspect of his life should read Wendy Moffat's masterly—and graceful—volume, *A Great Unrecorded History*. Partly a biography of Forster, it is also a study of the era in which a conviction of homosexuality meant two years in prison doing hard labor. Homosexuality was also a challenge he had to confront every day.

Another constant subject was freedom of speech and the threat of censorship, often in the name of national security.

India and relations with the Empire was never out of his mind. I have included an interpretation of Mrs. Moore that brings her out from the vague shadows of her solely narrative role in *A Passage to India*. Forster also draws an understanding appreciation of Professor Godbole's traditional Hindu intellectualism. Both of these characters are important, though they exist in the background of *A Passage to India*.

Earlier in life, when film makers approached him, Forster refused to allow any of his novels to be made into movies. He did not trust Hollywood. The only performance he countenanced was a theatrical presentation of *A Passage to India* with a script written by Santha Rama Rau, daughter of an Indian diplomat, an acquaintance of Forster. Forster closely supervised the whole production. The play later had a short run in New York with some actors imported from the original London show, Forster again closely monitoring the production.

An acclaimed novelist in his own time, Forster has again become a familiar name through the superb films made of his novels in the 1980s and 1990s. Mostly produced by Merchant-Ivory, with scripts by Ruth Prawer Jabhvala, these films would have satisfied Forster's high expectations of quality and authenticity.

In his later years Forster was invited by Benjamin Britten to work on the libretto of Britten's proposed opera *Billy Budd*. Thanks to the basic structure of opera, and the true-life elements of Melville's story, Forster was able to meld in the libretto the mysterious spirituality of the unknowable God and the power and strength of hopeful human relationships.

☙ ❧

The reader may wonder at the multiplicity of footnotes. This is deliberate. Spirituality is a subject that can elicit many and diverse interpretations. The accumulated weight of Forster's own words, assembled from his writings, buttresses my conclusion far more powerfully than could any paraphrases.

Because Forster's novels have been published in a myriad of editions in the century since they first appeared, I have used the Abinger edition wherever possible to standardize references to his published works. The seventeen volumes of the Abinger edition are acknowledged to be the official version of his creative writing. *Maurice* is the principal exception to my self-imposed rule. This homosexual novel, written in 1913–1914, though circulated early among his friends, was sequestered by Forster in a desk drawer for six decades. Shortly after his death in 1970, the "Trustees of E. M. Forster," using the 1960 typescript, published the first version of *Maurice* (known popularly as the W. W. Norton edition).

Undaunted by the size and scope of the projected Abinger edition, various authorized editors over the years produced meticulously edited versions of the novels and other writings. The official version of *Maurice* apparently did not appear until 1999. The 1960 typescript, on which the 1971 Norton edition was based, has satisfied most interested readers, since the texts of the Norton and the Abinger editions are virtually identical. For purposes of this study, references in *Maurice* will be found in the Norton edition.

The 2000 edition of *Marianne Thornton*, Forster's biography of his great-aunt, first published in 1956, is even more complicated. The Abinger edition was finally published, edited by Evelyne Hanquart-Turner, eighteen years after she began her work. In this case there was no typed copy of the original text for the editor, such as the friends of E. M. Forster used in publishing *Maurice* in the 1971 Norton edition.

Forster's *Marianne Thornton* in the 2000 Abinger edition differs markedly from the text published in 1956 during Forster's lifetime. "No 'fair copy' or typescript on which the published text was based has survived." "The present text is based on the first published British edition [1956] and Forster's own manuscript amendments in the copy he prepared for an eventual second edition." Whether Forster's amendments have been used is unclear to me. But Hanquart-Turner faced a formidable task in fitting into the 2000 text pieces of information or fuller explanations that have surfaced over the decades. That it took her eighteen years to complete her work is hardly surprising. Having located an Abinger edition of *Marianne Thornton*, I was able to provide most page numbers in both editions.

E. M. Forster's

Spiritual Journey

in

His Life and Works

Part One

Roots

Chapter One

Forster's Roots and the "Noble Peasant"

Throughout his adult life E. M. Forster was frank about his dislike of the Christianity he experienced growing up at the end of the nineteenth century.[1] Even when he was eighty years old, the subject was still of some consequence to him. In his Presidential Address to the Society of Cambridge Humanists in 1959, Forster chose to speak about his spiritual journey, recounting having been taken as a child by his mother to the morning service on Sundays "when the mud was not too bad." She daily "read morning prayers to the two maids and me," but "she was never intense, and I suspect not very attentive." Of his life from the age of four until fourteen, in his beloved Rooksnest at Stevenage, a small town a few miles north of London, Forster said he remembered no religious instruction at the parish Church of England there, "and our rector . . . was not one to inflict it. He was a pleasant out of doors parson, scholarly and idle, who rode to hounds and played chess, and whose stock of sermons was scanty. . . . The rectory was no place for the Souls [sic] Awakening." "Nor was my home," Forster added.[2]

But in his second novel, *The Longest Journey*, published in 1907, when he was twenty-eight years old, Forster proposed a bolder form of worship: to Rickie Elliot religion was a "mystic communion with good; not a means of getting what he wanted on the earth."[3] What transpired on Sundays in Church of England services seemed to Forster a ritualistic ceremony embracing form over content. He sat through more sermons on practical and secular moral values than on Christianity's spiritual mysteries or the indwelling spirit. More than thirty years later, in 1938, a year before World War II began in Europe, Forster wrote of his personal beliefs in an essay entitled "Credo," published in a well-known magazine, *The London Mercury and Bookman.* Explaining his rejection of the Christianity of his childhood, he declared that whatever "influence [Christianity] retains in modern society is due to the money behind it, rather than to its spiritual appeal. It was a spiritual force once, but the indwelling spirit will have to be restated if it is to calm the waters again."[4] He did not believe such a restatement likely to occur anytime soon.

Reading such forthright comments, literary critics have generally turned away from any further consideration of Forster's spiritual beliefs. But rejection is not the end of the story. Forster's trenchant repudiation of the too-narrow confines of the traditional religious teachings to which he was exposed as a child was actually the beginning of his spiritual saga, a solitary journey in which he was very much ahead of his time. As he wrote in his private "Notebook Journal," he had no faith in "the poison of *organized* religion"[5] that was "shoved under one's nose like a plate of pudding."[6] Forster's criticism of institutional religion, forcefully articulated in his university years, is a major formative element in his adult life. An alert sensitivity to spiritual matters was constant throughout his life—but it was not the only constant value, as other factors, also dating from his early childhood, gradually added lasting details to the evolving landscape of his life.

Ministers in the traditional mold were in Forster's ancestry. His Irish grandfather, Charles Forster, chaplain to John Jebb, Bishop of Limerick, followed his mentor to England when he retired; Charles's brother, James Forster, became the Archdeacon of Killarney. Forster considered his grandfather's version of Victorian Christian theology harshly minatory. The Reverend Charles's wife was a member of the Thornton family of bankers, who were active in the Evangelical movement of the nineteenth century. In contrast with Forster's comfortable Thornton forebears, his mother's family, the Whichelos, lived a precarious economic existence. Forster's beloved grandmother, Louisa Whichelo, left a widow at forty-one with ten children to support, seized any opportunity to help herself or her children. When Forster's great-aunt Marianne Thornton took the eldest Whichelo daughter Alice, known as Lily, under her wing, Mrs. Whichelo rejoiced because of the advantages it might bring the girl. To the Whichelos, religion as a primary source of strength or guidance was, like money, largely absent from their lives. Like Forster himself, the Whichelos were quick to recognize that piety often rested on disguised hypocrisy. Their skepticism about blind devotion to traditional Christian dogma is the likely source of what Forster described as his mother's lack of intensity in religious concerns. They seemed not to care much about religion one way or the other. But both his paternal and maternal antecedents greatly influenced Forster, adding significant overtones to his unfolding life.

Family was a taproot in Forster's young life, providing comforting stability and security, along with a paralyzing rigidity that he reacted against as he grew older. His mother was a Victorian lady who could not bring herself to discuss sex with her young son, even when he was the innocent victim of a serious, if brief, encounter. Before the age of ten, the boy realized that about such "indelicate" subjects he had to take the adult role, shielding his mother from what she considered unspeakable subjects. Forster never rejected his family relationships and responsibilities, yet concerning family *structure*, he was prescient. He felt impelled to stretch the traditional shape of the family, redefining it in his novels—and his life—to reflect his own dream. Though he was writing in the first decade of the twentieth century about his dream of a new form of family, fifty years had to elapse before society began to catch up with him.

Later in his career as a novelist, feeling he had exhausted the subject of family, he switched in *Maurice* to homosexuality, reflecting on the hazardous role that society forced on gay men. Lesbians were generally ignored rather than excoriated, but the homosexual male of those days lived a precarious existence legally, socially, and economically. Written in 1913 and circulated among a small circle of close friends, *Maurice* was finally published posthumously more than a half century later.

Forster was only twenty-six years old when his first novel, *Where Angels Fear to Tread*, appeared and thirty-one at the publication of *Howards End*, his fourth novel in six years. From the beginning of his career as a novelist, his authorial voice is grounded in a view of life that remained stable, yet expansive, throughout his ninety-one years. Though flexible, his philosophy had several deep roots besides his rejection of traditional Christianity, including family relationships, the intimate connection with the land, and of course, his nascent homosexuality. These factors broadened and became more complex as he grew from childhood to early adolescence at Rooksnest. Forster's father died when his son was only a year old. As an only child the boy found companionship where he could—distant and formal with elderly aunts; easy, sometimes playful, with house servants; and spontaneous with country boys hired by his mother ostensibly to tend the flowers, who also became his playmates. Together they roamed the property of Rooksnest and explored the adjacent farm. The meadow was their playroom, where they frolicked in mounds of newly scythed hay. Folk tales were absorbed from the country people, who also delivered milk and eggs for the breakfast table. Through ten years of gradually developing deep affection for the land, in a house he dearly loved, and in daily contact with unsophisticated, direct people whose livelihood depended on unpredictable Nature, the boy Forster unselfconsciously absorbed a deep-rooted love of place and claimed values that became the building stones of his own life and the inspiration for many of the characters in his six novels.

Forster has emphasized the elemental importance of rootedness in the land in a type of character who plays a major role in all his novels. Although literary critics unfailingly acknowledge the moral dimensions in Forster's writings[7] and have isolated individual characters as Forster's moral messengers, they have not given much attention to a category of character that in all his novels consistently bears Forster's moral message. For want of a better term, I call this type of character the "noble peasant." From a simple beginning with Gino Carella, son of an Italian dentist in the first novel, *Where Angels Fear to Tread*, to its highly sophisticated final form in Mrs. Moore in *A Passage to India,* the noble peasant becomes ever more prominent as the vehicle for Forster's expression of the possibility of individual inner growth and of enriching relationships between people. That Forster's personal choice for the title of his first novel was *Gino*, the eponymous name of the Italian noble peasant in what became *Where Angels Fear to Tread*, underscores the importance to the novelist of that kind of character. But the publisher objected to *Gino* as the title, reasoning that it was not sufficiently enticing to attract prospective readers.

The term "noble peasant" suggests a dramatic contradiction. Indeed, based on traditional class distinctions, the phrase is an oxymoron. However, in his personal lexicon Forster rejects equating "nobility" with high birth; his early definition links it with an instinctive wisdom descended from a past

rooted in a specific place. Starting with a class-based definition, the dictionary also defines "noble" as "of an exalted
moral character or excellence, of an admirable high quality,
notably superior." Because Forster sees such characteristics as
universal, the noble peasant may be of either gender; any race
and class has the potential to engage in the unending effort to
sort out the mixture of "good-and-evil," to filter order out of
chaos, to strive toward "love and clear vision" in spite of
"death and decay."[8] Forster first locates such moral superiority in characters drawn from the working classes, those who
use their hands as well as their hearts and have an intimate
personal connection with the land. Only later in the sequence
of his novels does Forster confront the problem of the continued viability of the noble peasant as a moral beacon in the face
of rapid industrialization and urbanization, which relentlessly
destroy the primacy of agricultural production and attenuate
an individual's possible connection with the land. The noble
peasant carries the banner for Forster's value of "place," con-
noting both external geographical and internal psychological
roots. The noble peasant is an archetype, a catalyst whose
presence and actions are essential to the movement of the
novels. Through the noble peasant Forster celebrates the qualities that he believed were generally superior to those of the
upper middle class, which tended to become bloodlessly over-
intellectualized and to aesthetically "die away."

    Forster's life experiences are often refracted in his novels.
The unpolished Italian peasant Gino is the rudiment of an idea
that began to crystallize during Forster's first trip to Italy in

1901, where he noticed that "boys of 16 lovingly cuddled babies."[9] After Lilia Herriton, Gino's middle-class English wife,
dies bearing Gino's son, he becomes mother as well as father,
not permitting the maid to touch the child and breaking off
conversations with friends at the village *farmacia* to return
home to care for his adored son because "I like to do these
things."[10]

When Forster was contemplating his second novel, *The
Longest Journey*, he made a solitary walking trip in September
1904 near the Figsbury Rings, an Iron Age earthworks close to
Salisbury. Here he fell into chance conversation with a lame
shepherd. The young man offered Forster a smoke of his pipe,
never called him "sir," and on parting refused with dignity
Forster's proffered sixpence. Forster was deeply moved by the
youth's unfeigned simplicity and directness, his instinctive
sense of human equality, and his "enormous wisdom." In his
diary Forster enthusiastically recorded that this "incident assured my opinion that the English *can* be the greatest men in
the world: he was miles greater than an Italian: one can't dare
to call his simplicity naif. The aesthetic die-away attitude
seems contemptible in a world which has such people."[11]

As has been suggested, Forster came by his attitudes toward the middle and lower classes naturally, as a child preferring play with the neighboring garden boys to organized
games with a visiting cousin. His early companions thus were
not of the middle class like his paternal forebears, the wealthy
Thornton bankers, but closer to his mother's impoverished
Whichelo lineage, and Forster linked his later miseries in

school with social class. Referring to his schoolmates at a boarding school named The Grange, he felt that "if they were not the sons of gentlemen they would not be so unkind. If only I was at the [local] Grammar School!"[12] Very early, gentleness and the absence of wanton cruelty became synonymous in his mind with the working-class noble peasant. These laudable characteristics did not, however, disqualify an instinctive physical response in self-defense, if necessary.

Forster was by nature a modest and retiring person, shrinking from the public eye, seeking an obscure corner rather than center stage. An acquaintance of the adult Forster mentions his personal fondness for "almost aggressively dim grey clothes, wool cardigans and cloth caps" and writes that Forster—called Morgan by his friends—"felt much more affinity with the lower than the upper classes," an attitude that meshes with his complete lack of envy and snobbishness.[13] He never owned a car though he lived well into the era of the personal automobile. He even avoided taking taxis as being too ostentatious for him; he preferred public transportation. Forster deeply deplored the social forces that prevented working-class men from attending the great universities, writing that "I know so many elementary-school men who ought to have gone up [to university] twenty or thirty years ago, and who would have given as well as gained."[14] Gender equality was also important to Forster, and his dream of a classless society was firmly entrenched in his prediction that the supremacy of the middle class would finally end with new and unknown elements being introduced into society by what was called the working classes.[15]

Thus Forster realigned the relative importance of his Thornton and Whichelo backgrounds. Irascible Mrs. Failing in *The Longest Journey* is drawn from his detested Uncle William Howley Forster, while Uncle Willie's deplorable wife Emily is the inspiration for the relentlessly middle-class Charlotte Bartlett in *A Room with A View*. It was not his doting paternal great-aunt Marianne Thornton, but his maternal grandmother, Louisa Whichelo, who was the model in the same novel for Mrs. Honeychurch,[16] who fussed over puddings and applied the oil of human kindness when the social machine began to creak. As Forster once said, "In no book have I got down more than the people I like, the person I think I am, and the people who irritate me."[17]

Representing rootedness in a place, the noble peasant Stephen Wonham in *The Longest Journey* has no intention of accepting Mrs. Failing's offer of passage to one of the colonies, instinctively refusing to cut the vital link with the English soil that nourishes his spirit. Mrs. Failing has deliberately severed the connection with her roots in Nature though she resides in the country, and this casts a sadistic shadow over her manipulative caprices, while Stephen's connection with the land on which he was born and raised remains intact and gives his actions a justification that hers lack. A noble peasant of a different class is Mrs. Wilcox in *Howards End*, who, when she visits her ancestral country home, is an early riser and busies herself

with overseeing the haying or planning gardens. When she returns to her London home, neither people nor books—not
even museums—are sufficiently engaging to lure her out of
bed. That piece of soil, with its historical accretion of meaning,
is the font from which flows life's spiritual sustenance for her.
The sense of place that the noble peasant possesses is closely
connected with an awareness of the past. Of Mrs. Wilcox Forster writes, "One knew that she worshipped the past, and that
the instinctive wisdom the past can alone bestow had descended upon her—that wisdom to which we give the clumsy
name of aristocracy. High-born she might not be. But assur-
edly she cared about her ancestors and let them help her."[18]
Of the integrative role of the past in Forster's novels, the critic
George Thomson writes that

> it is the world of our ancestors which
> reaches into the present to give us
> strength and consolation. This sense of
> the past gives depth to man's experience
> of identity with nature. Moreover it im-
> plies what has taken place is the integra-
> tion into the conscious mind of ances-
> trally based unconscious elements.[19]

The noble peasant also possesses a strong intuitive sense.
Sometimes this type of character—Gino, Stephen, also Miss
Avery, a minor but not insignificant character in *Howards
End*—has little or no formal education but compensates by an
instinctive knowledge of his or her own deepest emotions and
an intuitive understanding of the nature of another person.

When for the first time she meets Margaret Schlegel, the pivotal character of *Howards End*, at the country house of the same name, Miss Avery pronounces, "You think that you won't come back to live here . . . but you will." (269) In contrast, in *The Longest Journey* Rickie Elliot's instincts are largely smothered by his years of schooling, and he is doomed to spend much of his short life peeling away layers of the English boarding school atmosphere to identify his real feelings and reconnect them with his actions. Like Rickie, some of Forster's female characters struggle to express their personal feelings in a restrictive social climate. Those rebellious heroines, Lilia Herriton (*Where Angels Fear to Tread*) and Lucy Honeychurch (*A Room with a View*), go to Italy where Lucy feels "anyone who chooses may warm himself in equality, as in the sun. . . . A rebel she was. . . who desired. . . equality beside the man she loved. For Italy was offering her the most priceless of all possessions—her own soul."[20] Though Lilia's defiance of convention was unsuccessful, Lucy manages, with help, to sort out her real Self from the Self she had perforce become through years of pinching, pruning, and shaping to which her family and society had subjected her, as if she were a topiary plant being trained to the shape of a perfect lady.

When intuition is permitted, it can bridge differences between cultures, as with the English Mrs. Moore and the Muslim Dr. Aziz in *A Passage to India*, who quickly find common ground. Ultimately such openness to others strengthens inclusive human relationships such as Forster proposes in the symbolism of the Figsbury Rings, an anthropological site employed fictionally as the Cadbury Rings in *The Longest Journey*. Rings can enclose and exclude, as Rickie's wife Agnes appreciates as she maneuvers to isolate Rickie from his college friends. In *A Room with a View*, Cecil Vyse, a suitor of Lucy Honeychurch, wishes to absorb her into his town-based family circle, transplanting her from the country and "all that she had loved in the past" (121) and excluding forever her mother and brother. Cecil's very name suggests imprisonment in an unbreachable ring or iron grip. But rings can also represent the ever-enlarging ripples of friendship, widening until they include a whole pool of friends, as Rickie finally learns. Mrs. Wilcox, too, moves beyond the consanguineous family when she chooses to bequeath Howards End, her family home, to Margaret Schlegel as her "spiritual heir." In his last novel, *A Passage to India*, Forster expands the definition of friendship to include not merely the known pool of friends and acquaintances but the unknown ocean of all humanity, regardless of race or religion.

"Heroic human quality in a working-class guise,"[21] buttressed by the spontaneous kindness that Forster attributed to the working classes, defines the character of Mr. Emerson in *A Room with a View*. The nurturing father, barely suggested in earlier novels, is assigned major significance in this work. With each succeeding novel Forster's noble peasant moves a little higher socially and edges closer to center stage. Gino is an unsophisticated peasant, pure and simple. Stephen Wonham, Forster's first full-blown delineation of an English noble peasant, grasps what life could become.[22] Though Mr. Emerson was the son of a laborer and in his earlier life a mechanic, he is now a journalist for the socialist press. Like the actual shepherd Forster met at the Figsbury Rings, Mr. Emerson is naturally kind to people and goes directly to the heart of any matter without ceremony or false reticence: "He is not tactful" and is one of those "people who do things which are most indelicate, and yet at the same time—beautiful." (10) Mr. Emerson represents an early attempt to integrate the noble peasant into the daily life of Forster's middle-class characters who populate a suburb called Sawston filled with red-brick semidetached villas. The conservative, hidebound Sawstonites define themselves—and judge others—through the lenses of Family, Property (including Money), Social Position, and Propriety, heavily influenced by the Church. Trained to suppress natural human expression, Sawstonites represent the opposite of the noble peasant in their unbending respectability and joyless insincerity. Their unthinking obeisance to accepted social standards produces widespread hypocrisy. A man like Mr. Emerson, who would go out to gather great handfuls of violets because he had overheard an elderly English tourist in Italy say how much she loved those wild flowers, was regarded as indelicately direct, lacking the required reticence and gentlemanly tact. Such a person as Mr. Emerson they considered vulgar—meaning common, coarse, boorish, and lacking cultural refinement. Forster turned this definition on its head, declaring that the Sawstonites were the ones who were vulgar because their denial of spontaneous expression of honest feelings distorted the human soul.

But the novelist had the problem of harmonizing the seeming contradiction of the rustic noble peasant with the industrialized, cosmopolitan society that he saw encroaching not only on the spirit of the noble peasant, but actually gobbling up, in spreading urbanization, the precious land in which the noble peasant had since time immemorial been rooted. In *Howards End* the novelist frontally attacks the problem of the noble peasant's position in modern life and struggles with the question of genetic versus spiritual inheritance of that catalytic role.

The character of Leonard Bast in *Howards End* is usually regarded as Forster's attack on the class system of English society. His significance for Forster, I believe, lies even deeper. Leonard is "the third generation, grandson to the shepherd or ploughboy whom civilization has sucked into the town." (113) He is Forster's noble peasant cut off from his roots in the land, his connection with Nature lost and replaced by the fragmented life of faceless metropolitan London. Like Feo in the short story "The Eternal Moment," Leonard is "the man who had no advantages, who was poor and had been made vulgar, whose early virtue had been destroyed by circumstance, whose manliness and simplicity had perished in serving the rich."[23] Forster traces the path of the noble peasant from those whose natural birthright it was, through their disinheritance due to inevitable economic/political developments, finally to the self-conscious choice of values by formally educated, city-raised people lacking any genetic connection with the land.

While over the years literary critics have uncovered much
subtle symbolism in the names that Forster chose for his characters, the crucial significance of the family name of Leonard
Bast, an important, yet frequently undervalued, character in
the category of noble peasant seems to go unrecognized. *A
New English Dictionary on Historical Principles*, published in
England in 1888, like other dictionaries, defines "bast" as a derivative of the Anglo-Saxon word for a widely used woven
matting or cordage, usually made from the inner fibers of the
lime tree. But it goes beyond this shared definition, quoting
from Gray's 1880 *Botanical Text-book*: "Bast cells. . . give to the
kinds of inner bark that largely contain them their strength
and toughness." From this one may extrapolate an intentional
value in Bast as a surname suggesting a hidden but strong and
resilient spirit. Yet there is still more to the symbolism of
Leonard's name. An American dictionary of a later date, in addition to defining "bast" as woven matting, refers the reader
to "phloem," the vascular tissue serving as a path for the distribution of food material in a plant. Clearly bast is the conduit
for transmitting the nourishment necessary for strength and
growth from the roots of the plant to its leafy extremities. By
the end of the nineteenth century, Forster recognized that the
natural noble peasant, rooted in the land and drawing his sustenance and livelihood from it, was dying out or at least becoming attenuated as shepherds and tillers of the soil were being forced from their historic place on the land into the new
industrial centers where wage-paying factory jobs were opening up. Though the town-born Leonard is a pale version of his
noble peasant grandfather, he is the all-important conduit

transmitting to his son, Helen Schlegel's baby, the elemental spiritual connection with the land that his ancestry had bequeathed to him. Forster, unwilling to allow that vital connection to disappear from the national soul without raising an alarm, fervently hoped that what was a natural instinct in those who had for centuries lived close to the land could be implanted in the psyche of intellectually trained people such as the city-born and -bred Margaret Schlegel. Margaret's connection with the land finally comes alive thanks to the house, Howards End, left her by the first Mrs. Wilcox, with its sheltering tree, gardens, and meadow, mimicking Forster's beloved Rooksnest. Ecology had not yet been named, but instinctively Forster was trying to inspire individuals to rediscover and cherish that crucial human connection with Nature, to reclaim their ancestral connection with the land, discover the clogged channels to their innate intuition, and cultivate both external and internal links, as did the archetypical noble peasants.

As an example of the regrettable tendency to regard Leonard dismissively, one may consider the 1992 *Partisan Review* article by Alfred Kazin called "*Howards End* Revisited." Kazin states that "Forster's plot depends on Leonard being discardable." To Kazin, Leonard is certainly not a pivotal character with a moral message but merely a working-class person in the background of the narrative action—this in spite of Forster's depicting Leonard as searching to reestablish his roots while clinging desperately to the edge of gentility. Forster carefully has Margaret Schlegel treating him as an equal, an attitude that emphasizes Forster's belief in classlessness. Furthermore, Kazin is confused about the origins of the sword that killed Leonard, which he describes as "the ancestral sword that has hung so long on the wall at Howards End."[24] Kazin thinks the sword is a relic of the Wilcox family of Howards End, whereas Forster clearly states that it is the German sword of Margaret's father. The Schlegel furniture had been boxed and sent down to the empty house for storage. Miss Avery had taken it upon herself to arrange the furniture as if Margaret and her husband, Mr. Wilcox, intended to live there, which was not then in their plan. Margaret was in despair at Miss Avery's unsolicited placement of the Schlegel furniture and bewildered when she saw "her father's sword... drawn from its scabbard and hung naked" on the wall among the Schlegel books. (268)

In *Howards End* the responsibility of representing the noble peasant who is still connected with the land initially devolves on the first Mrs. Wilcox. She is tugged by life in opposing directions: her heritage lures her back whenever possible to her ancestral home, but her wifely and maternal duties keep her penned up in London much of the time. To her husband and children Howards End, worthless except for its potential for development, is merely a house like so many others they have bought or rented as whimsy struck them; "they could not know that to her it had been a spirit, for which she sought a spiritual heir." (96)

The kinship that Mrs. Wilcox feels with Margaret Schlegel lies in a shared regard for "place" and for the past. Upon Mrs. Wilcox's death, though Margaret does not at that time receive the intended gift of the house from the Wilcoxes, she does inherit Mrs. Wilcox's mantle of noble peasant from the novelist. With Margaret playing the role, the noble peasant takes on a different configuration. Empathetic imagination and awareness of personal instinct and intuition now begin to assume the role that the noble peasant's direct connection with place and his or her continuity with the past had filled in simpler times.

In *The Longest Journey*, his second novel, Forster already had telegraphed a hint of this new manifestation of noble peasant in Mr. Failing, Rickie Elliot's uncle by marriage and dead long before the novel's action starts. He is described as a person who "loved poetry and music and pictures, and everything tempted him to live in a kind of cultivated paradise, with the door shut upon squalor. But to have more decent people in the world—he sacrificed everything to that." (174) He cultivated his tenants as conscientiously as he did his pastures and fields.

Like Mr. Failing, Margaret Schlegel in *Howards End* cannot lose herself in selfish devotion to cultural interests but feels impelled to try to raise the awareness of such concerns in other people. She encourages Leonard Bast in his pursuit of what he calls Romance when he goes on a night ramble through the dark fringes of metropolitan London, searching instinctively for a new bond with his long-lost country roots, a spiritual home outside his deadly round of drudgery. In spite of self-conscious efforts to revive his battered sense of Self— of connecting the inner man with his outward actions—poverty and lack of education hamper his attempts. The shifting impermanent relationships, which grow quickly and wither as fast in the concrete byways of a large city, are no compensation for the loss of connection with Nature, eternal and geographic as well as intuitive and human:

> London was but a foretaste of this nomadic civilization which is altering human relations so profoundly, and throws upon personal relations a stress greater than they have ever borne before. Under cosmopolitanism, if it comes, we shall receive no help from the earth. Trees and meadows and mountains will be only a spectacle, and the binding force that they once exercised on character must be entrusted to Love alone. May Love be equal to the task. (258)

Margaret is aware that Love unaided can hardly be equal to the task of cultivating humanity's roots; it must be assisted by willed effort. She tries to explain to Leonard that everyone must "struggle against life's daily greyness. . . pettiness. . . suspicion" and false cheerfulness by connecting mentally with friends or "some beloved place or tree." (140) As modern man becomes increasingly mobile in the "civilization of luggage," he must of necessity carry his past with him and self-consciously nourish his connection with people, if not with a place. Yet, literally by accident Margaret finds a new home and a permanent connection with Nature. She comes at last into her intended inheritance from Mrs. Wilcox, which "fit[s] into position as the headstone of the corner." (100) To the larger question posed by Forster, "Is it credible that the possessions of the spirit can be bequeathed at all? Has the soul offspring?" (96), the author answers a firm yes. Nor is *Howards End* the first of Forster's novels to mention spiritual heirship. As early as *The Longest Journey*, the phrase appears when Mrs. Failing, Rickie's aunt by blood, is reported to have called Rickie her husband's "spiritual heir" (195) because of their similar natures, though there was no genetic kinship between the two men.

While the importance to Forster of place and continuity is usually understood by critics in terms of the family as an institution defined by consanguinity, Thomson has recognized that Forster's definition of family was not limited to blood relationship; to this critic the fact that Howards End was to be inherited by the son of Leonard Bast and Helen Schlegel makes

> untenable the usual account of Forster's attitude to family. That account suggests that Forster's interest in ancestors and heirs has its basis in genetic inheritance. The truth seems rather to be that he values ancestors because they symbolize the one thing that can give stability, the collective and universal past; and he values children because they symbolize a potential hope and a potential wholeness greater than we know at present.

> Forster's interest in the living continuity
> represented by ancestors and descend-
> ants is a general rather than a particular
> interest, it is universal rather than indi-
> vidual. ... That is why it is not su-
> premely important who fathers Helen's
> child, but is supremely important that
> there be a child.[25]

Thomson's last sentence is debatable. It was, I believe, su-
premely important to Forster that the inheritor of Howards
End should have flowing in his veins the blood of the "grandson to the shepherd or ploughboy whom civilization had
sucked into the town," Leonard Bast, who still had the urge to
explore the countryside by night in a vain attempt to reconnect himself with the Romance his life craved and which the
Nature of his grandfather's roots had provided. The potential
strength of this blood connection in Leonard's son is enhanced
by the role that the house itself—in Forster's schema representing the tangible connection with the land through Mrs.
Wilcox—will play in the child's upbringing. Not only is the noble peasant a significant instrument in articulating the potential richness that Forster sees possible in the new relationships
of his dreams; Forster implies that the only hope for the future
of middle-class humankind rests in physical union with the
spiritual strength natural to the noble peasant.

As the new personification of the noble peasant, Margaret
Schlegel uneasily balances with one foot in the traditional
world of direct connection with Nature and the other in the

dawning world of global mobility and the need for portable roots. In her "integration into the conscious mind of ancestrally based unconscious elements," to quote Thomson again, Forster is creating a synthesis of old values in new forms. Fourteen years and a world war later, in *A Passage to India*, he further refines that prototype in Mrs. Moore. Unlike the failed noble peasant of *Howards End,* Leonard Bast, "one of the thousands who have lost the life of the body and failed to reach the life of the spirit," (113) Mrs. Moore has struggled to achieve—even if only partially—a new psychological reality. The essential elements in her character, in addition to her kindly nature, are implicit trust in her intuition and faith in the basic goodness of humanity. Forster's later noble peasants must depend on heart and spirit to express their values, rather than simply being rooted in a particular place. For Forster there was one great issue—"the survival and full development of the individual personality in face of a civilization increasingly urbanized, industrialized and routinized."[26] His later noble peasants cultivate and nurture inner strengths and personal relationships in order to bear the stress that once was dissipated by daily communion with Nature.

In *The Longest Journey* Rickie Elliot "could not imagine a place larger than England." (126) In *Howards End* Forster exhorts his characters and readers to "connect without bitterness until all men are brothers" (266) and proclaims, "We are evolving, in ways that Science cannot measure, to ends that Theology dares not contemplate." (238) In *A Passage to India* he expands his concept of the binding force of Love in human relations to embrace all humanity. The cosmopolitanism that in *Howards End* carries a pejorative meaning is transmuted into the equal membership of all races in the family of man. Herein lies the significance of the noble peasant to *A Passage to India*. In creating Mrs. Moore, Forster again proclaims the broader concept of spiritual heirship, depending on empathetic values rather than genetics. For Mrs. Moore has moved beyond Mrs. Wilcox's connection with a physical place; she underscores the importance of all-embracing human affection, which can be lived out wherever one finds oneself in an increasingly mobile civilization.

Forster's beliefs about human values and human relationships remained remarkably stable to the end of his life in spite of external developments. His transfer of spiritual power from Stephen Wonham, the noble peasant of *The Longest Journey*, to the educated, middle-class Margaret Schlegel, who self-consciously embraced the values inherent in the earlier instinctive native nobility of the land-centered noble peasant, was the novelist's response to the accelerating movement of population from the countryside to the city before World War I. Industrialization, the spreading stain of urbanization, increasing mobility resulting all too often in rootlessness, agricultural self-sufficiency giving way to specialization and a cash economy—all such signs of a changing social and economic order required Forster to locate another repository for those moral values he considered crucial to human relationships. The transition was chancy but imperative. Years later Forster affirmed success: "Can we combine experience and innocence? I think we can. . . . It is possible but it is rare."[27]

By the time *A Passage to India* was published in 1924, the novelist had achieved the transition. Mrs. Moore embodies the same qualities of connectedness with abstract Nature, with human nature, with the past that previous fictional noble peasants had personified but with a difference: now the connections have become intellectualized, internalized consciously, until they are once again a natural part of the being of the new noble peasant. Now transplanted, they have taken root in Mrs. Moore's mind and spirit as sturdily as once they had held Stephen Wonham to his piece of English soil. In *A Passage to India* geographical roots in England are not important; it is as if Forster had deliberately made Mrs. Moore, his noble peasant, dependent on values she could carry with her rather than on their associations with a physical place. Only as an aside does the reader learn after her death that Mrs. Moore's son proposes putting up a memorial plaque in "the Northamptonshire church where she had worshipped."[28]

The rootedness in the land, formerly so fertile a connection with the living springs of Nature, is reduced in *A Passage to India* to self-incarceration in the suffocating confines of the club, the new Sawston, as sanitarily cordoned off from the vibrancy of Indian life in the temples and bazaars as Sawston itself was hermetically sealed off from Italy in earlier novels. But for Mrs. Moore "landscape" has become an interior connection dependent on the life of the spirit rather than physical attachment to a spot of soil. From the stifling psychological atmosphere of the club where she had been watching an amateur theatrical performance in a hot room, she escapes beyond

the multiple walls of the fortified club—a transplanted Cadbury Rings now impregnable in its deliberate isolation atop an
Indian hill—to the fresher air of a nearby mosque. Here she
meets Dr. Aziz, who quickly discovers that she is not like other
English women he has met. Indeed, she doesn't particularly
like them any more than he does. She has removed her shoes
on entering the mosque, not because someone is there to
check on her but from reverence: "God is here." (15) Both have
two sons and a daughter. Neither claims to understand people
very well but only whether they like or dislike them, an intuitive approach to relationships that Dr. Aziz declares makes
Mrs. Moore "an Oriental." (17) In unconscious equality Mrs.
Moore would have invited him into the club, had she been a
member, much as she later advises her son that, instead of
withdrawing from contact with his Pleaders, his legal assis-
tants in the administration of justice, he should smoke with all
of them. Though she might have no strong roots in a particular place, she has not lost her sensitivity to natural phenom-
ena: a wasp is a "pretty dear," (29), and seeing the radiant Indian moon floods her with "a sudden sense of unity, of kinship
with the heavenly bodies . . . like water through a tank, leaving
a strange freshness behind." (24) Even the river with its dead
bodies and crocodiles is to her both terrible and wonderful. In
their similarities Mrs. Moore and Dr. Aziz surmount the cultural barriers as easily as Mrs. Wilcox and Margaret Schlegel
overcame their differences.

   But this spiritual landscape cannot, it seems, be inherited
automatically; it must be consciously cultivated and acknowledged by an act of will, which Mrs. Moore's son refuses to do,

defending his British officialdom: "We're not pleasant in India. . . . We've something more important to do." (44) That the hyena that ran into Nawab Bahadur's car is really a ghost is an intuition that Mrs. Moore could not explain, any more than she could—or would—exorcise the echo in Adela's head afflicting the young woman after her trauma in the cave on Kawa Dol. Irritated at being asked to explain the echo, the older woman only replies, "If you don't know, you don't know; I can't tell you." (190) Like Mrs. Wilcox, she knows there are no such things as "plain questions." Only when Adela looks within herself and tries painfully to understand what really happened can the young woman finally say to Mrs. Moore's son, "Ronny, [Dr. Aziz is] innocent; I made an awful mistake. . . . My echo's better." (193) Mrs. Moore's position is "of course he is innocent," (195) and she bases her defense on intuition and personal judgment: "One knows people's characters. . . . I have heard both English and Indians speak well of him, and I felt it isn't the sort of thing he would do." (196) Mrs. Moore's "refusal to trust words is . . . significant as evidence of her capacity for in-dwelling, in such contrast to the externally public world of the Club."[29]

As the connection with place and the sense of continuity that place confers become increasingly attenuated in the modernizing world, Forster sees that Nature is too easily displaced by technology, which destroys that cherished link. The "civilization of luggage" makes it possible for humankind to move farther and farther out from its geographical roots, to embrace more people within the human family—but at a price.

Ruminating on the hidden message in social contacts, in *A Passage to India*, Cyril Fielding, who has spent years as an educator in India, thinks, "It is no good. . . . We all build upon sand; and the more modern the country gets, the worse'll be the crash. . . . Everything echoes now, there's no stopping the echo. The original sound may be harmless, but the echo is always evil." The authorial voice continues: "This reflection about an echo lay at the verge of Fielding's mind. He could not develop it. It belonged to the universe that he had missed or rejected." (264) As much as he has tried to imbue his Indian students with the desire to understand, and in spite of his own feelings of equality with his Indian friends, Fielding does not qualify as a noble peasant; his intuition is insufficiently developed.

But though Mrs. Moore dies, her universal view does not. Writing to Angus Wilson more than thirty years after the publication of *A Passage to India*, Forster emphatically states that "Mrs. Moore's influence does *not* disappear . . . but reappears in the third section of the novel,"[30] and he regrets not having discussed that section with Wilson at greater length in their interview.

Others also possess a sense of the universal. Dr. Aziz continues to write poetry: "In one poem—the only one funny old Godbole liked—he had skipped over the mother-land (whom he did not truly love) and gone straight to internationality." (184) Ralph Moore, visiting India some years later with his sister, now married to Cyril Fielding, shares his mother's instinct for knowing if a person is friendly, as well as her intuitive divination of the worth of another's character. And Professor

Godbole is also, like Mrs. Moore, a sophisticatedly simple person, reverent, a mystic, a lover of Nature—he too encounters a wasp—intuitive, and appreciative of the universal point of view. The noble peasant, then, continues to live in variant forms. The thread of the noble peasant as moral exemplar runs through the intricate tapestries of Forster's novels from beginning to end, yet each such character—from Gino to Mrs. Moore—realizes only part of Forster's ideal. There are no perfect noble peasants; all are fallibly human.

The modern noble peasant is unlikely to be either highborn or a peasant; today's noble peasant must struggle to nurture that instinctive wisdom, now more remote, that alone provides entrance to the world of Forster's aristocracy:

> I believe in . . . an aristocracy of the sensitive, the considerate and the plucky. Its members are to be found in all nations and classes, and all through the ages. . . . They represent the true human tradition, the one permanent victory of our queer race over cruelty and chaos. . . . They are sensitive for others as well as for themselves, they are considerate without being fussy, their pluck is not swankiness but the power to endure, and they can take a joke . . . Their temple . . . is the holiness of the Heart's affections, and their kingdom, though they never possess it, is the wide-open world.

... The greater the darkness, the
brighter shine the little lights. ... Unquenchable lights of my aristocracy![31]

Chapter Two

Forster's Prescient View of the Family in *Howards End*

A sense of place, that deeply-rooted connection with the land, was not the only lifelong value arising from Forster's earliest childhood.[1] Family also was embedded in his character from birth, early on as a supportive nurturing environment. In spite of later manifestations of its inhibiting and distorting propensities, Forster never rejected family as a personal value but gradually recognized the need for a new configuration of the family.

That contemporaneous reviewers of Forster's *Howards End* failed to recognize his prescient image of a radically new family structure is hardly surprising. In 1910 the institutional, middle-class family in England—static, authoritarian, and based on consanguinity and primogeniture—was still assumed as a given by most readers and novelists. As a result few readers or novelists at the beginning of the twentieth century questioned the accepted institutional model of the family or foresaw the possibility of rejuvenating it to enhance individuality and equality in the family circle. Thus, D. H. Lawrence set the opening chapters of *The Rainbow* at a farm significantly called "The Marsh," but he employed the symbolism of that name narrowly, focusing on women's defiant seizure of sexual freedom rather than remolding the entire family. Expanding on the metaphor, one might say that just as a marsh is a protected nursery richly supplied with the elements necessary for the nurturance and protection of young marine life, so a more expansive and flexible form of the family could provide a richer context for human fulfillment. Forster visualized a more egalitarian, inclusive family that would be a fertile seedbed where all its members, deeply rooted in the past and securely connected with their own emotions, might be equally enriched by energizing currents from the outside.

In his massive study Lawrence Stone sees that the family was very gradually moving from "distance, deference and patriarchy" to what he calls "affective individualism."[2] Though he finds the seeds of his main features of the modern family in key segments of English society as early as 1750, in the following hundred years the development of this new family type actually regressed until the end of the Victorian period, when it began to spread slowly into other classes of English society.[3] Peter Gay's *The Tender Passion*, while focusing on examples of true love in marriage, acknowledges "the smoke screens thrown up by purposeful propriety, diligent self-censorship, and tense moral preoccupations"[4] by parents whose power over their children "often enough amounted to little more than a self-indulgent resort to superior legal privileges, emotional resources, or physical strength."[5] Even "the most affectionate and benevolent parents exercised power over their children, husbands over their wives, masters over their servants—always for their good, usually in their name."[6]

Though not a formal student of the family, Forster was a discerning observer of the social scene. More than merely recording what he saw, he pondered the common values of his society and dreamed of a family that would encourage greater fulfillment for the individual, the family, and eventually for all of human society. Gay points out that few men, and even fewer women, aspired in the nineteenth century to "unforced, unmercenary, wholly equal mutual love, of love without power."[7] Forster was one of those yearning for such family relationships; in *Howards End*, through Margaret Schlegel, he gives passionate voice to his dreams of a new kind of *functional* family, which he considered fundamental to all the other unspoken social contracts of life. In the last chapter of *Howards End*, Forster, a prophet far ahead of his time, projects an impressionistic vision of a radically different, more elastic middle-class family structure that presaged, in 1910, many of the characteristics now common to middle-class families at the beginning of the current century.

Certainly, Forster was deeply dissatisfied with the conventional family he saw in the first decade of the twentieth century. From his first novel, the reader is regaled with the horrors of the institutional family whose children are unmercifully manipulated by a domineering parent to fit his or her preconception of the fortress family protecting itself against the imagined insults of the world. Like Mrs. Herriton in *Where Angels Fear to Tread*, Henry Wilcox in *Howards End* is an unwitting captive of traditional, middle-class Sawstonite values, epitomizing in numbing detail the conventional paterfamilias of the late Victorian and Edwardian eras. His unexamined adherence to the accepted social mores inexorably leads to his collapse and his son's imprisonment and might have resulted in the destruction of his marriage to Margaret Schlegel but for her determination to nurture new family relationships based on autonomy and trust. Both Mrs. Herriton and Mr. Wilcox stand upon the foundation stones of Property, Propriety, Family Pride, and the Church. Of Mrs. Herriton Forster says, "Pride was the only solid element in her disposition."[8] Shamefaced and cautious behind a defensive facade that disguises a fear of emotion, Mr. Wilcox, like Mrs. Herriton, cares too much about apparent success and too little about the lessons of the past, is spiritually dishonest, and engages in one-upmanship for the sake of controlling every situation. Mrs. Herriton and Mr. Wilcox share with others of Sawston's stolidly conventional middle class an admiration of wealth, cleverness, and barely masked prudery, callous meddling, and a supercilious attitude toward other people. Individual members of all such families in Forster's novels are expected to sublimate their own abilities, wishes, and personalities and to defer to a hazy notion of the "good of the family" as defined by the assumed head of the family according to his or her unilateral decisions.

The later years of Queen Victoria's reign saw the beginnings of public awareness of social issues in urgent need of reform. Among those then struggling to effect changes in the social, political, and economic life of England were Beatrice and Sidney Webb; the suffragettes Emmeline Pankhurst and her daughters; Henry Fawcett, M. P., and his wife, Dame Millicent Garrett Fawcett, campaigning for equal educational opportunities for women; and Josephine Butler, whose battle for women's rights was loyally supported by her husband and sons to their professional detriment. At a time when the marital relationship was still defined by the "ancient common law concept of couveture—'the husband and wife are one and the husband is that one,' Blackstone"[9]—not one of these reformers proposed restructuring family relationships or changing the organic shape or goals of the family. All implicitly accepted the common view of the family as an immutable institution whose social, economic, and political health far outweighed in importance the personal desires of any individual member. It was the creative writer, not the social reformer, who dared to dream of personal freedom and fulfillment within the family.

Forster's authorial eye was clearly on the middle class. The various parliamentary reform acts of the nineteenth century had gradually enlarged the perimeters of the middle class until by the end of the century even a minor clerk such as Leonard Bast could be considered middle class as long as he held a position in a business office.[10] Only with Leonard and Jackie Bast did Forster attempt to describe a family that was not educated, financially secure, and socially stable. He felt the challenge keenly and, with modest pride, thought he had met it successfully.[11] Forster was more certain of his observations of the solid center of middle-class family life as he saw and experienced it. He focused on what he knew and contrasted those observations with his vision that the middle-class family could embody new definitions of such traditional values as work, property, and community.

Descended from both the prominent Thornton family of bankers and the socially and financially precarious Whichelos, Forster acknowledged that much of the freedom he achieved in his adult life was the direct result of his financial security. In the words he gave to Margaret Schlegel in *Howards End*, he was one of those who stood "upon money as upon islands,"[12] yet he was ambivalent about money. Knowing well the importance of having enough, he claimed not to like money very much,[13] and later in life ruefully admitted that "money blurs everything now, takes the edge off every character."[14] He absorbed generosity about money at his mother's knee[15] and enjoyed giving monetary gifts, which he believed "should be large so as not to be confused with loans."[16] For the latter, he expected prompt repayment. To give quiet gifts of money, Forster felt, was "an opportunity to perform acts of loving kindness,[17] exemplifying his philosophy of "athletic love."[18]

Along with money, the institutional family was linked with property in Forster's mind. Having lived in his beloved Rooksnest from before the age of four through prepuberty and establishing that connection with a place, a piece of English soil, that is so important in his writings, the boy of fourteen was traumatized "by his sudden exile from this rural paradise."[19] Years later, reading a paper entitled "Memory" at a meeting of the Bloomsbury Memoir Club, he said, "If I had been allowed to stop on [remain] here I should have become a different person, married, and fought in the war."[20] Cast out of his Eden—and paradoxically released from the prison of property—he allowed himself to express his homosexuality, and in creating for himself an extended, nonconsanguineous family with Bob and May Buckingham, he achieved a degree of hard-won personal freedom from the deadly weight of the institutional family. Forster's description of Hannah More—"childless herself, she became the family life that does not die with death"[21]—a critic suggests, can be equally applied to Forster's great-aunt Marianne Thornton, and the novelist himself.[22] Margaret Schlegel also fits the description.

Even though rigid familial boundaries were slowly eroding in his lifetime, Forster was sixty-six years old before he was his own master. As an only child he had no one to share the Victorian burden of buffering his mother psychologically from her solitary state and the disorderly demands of society. In a judicious summation of his mother's influence, Forster wrote to a friend after her death, "Although my mother has been intermittently tiresome for the last thirty years, cramped and warped my genius, hindered my career, blocked and buggered up my house, and boycotted my beloved, I have to admit that she has provided a sort of rich subsoil where I have been able to rest and grow."[23] Something of the novelist's resignation in the face of intractable societal expectations surfaces in Philip Herriton in *Where Angels Fear to Tread* when he muses that, though he can never escape his mother's demands, he is determined to carve out what limited freedom of movement he can.

Forster's prescience about the modern evolution of the family seems to have escaped his readers and critics, not only when his novels were first published but also later.[24] Neither I. A. Richards, commenting in 1927, nor Lionel Trilling in his pioneering 1943 full-scale study of Forster's novels, grapples with the radically different functional family structure that Forster depicts in the last chapter of *Howards End*. While Richards acknowledges Forster's "special preoccupation . . . with the continuance of life,"[25] Trilling is engrossed by parent-child—mainly father-son—relationships. He scarcely mentions the word "family" and perfunctorily notes that "three of the heroines are mothers of sons"[26] but complains that "they lack maternal warmth" and that "their connections with their sons are tenuous."[27] The warmer, more kindly, mainly female Honeychurch family is simply ignored, as is the male Emerson counterpart. About fathers, Trilling is equally cursory, subsuming his brief mention of male parenthood under the rubric of Forster's attitudes toward authority figures.[28] In Trilling's defense it must be recognized that the systematic study of the family only attained critical mass in the years after World War II.

Twenty years after Trilling, James Hall is one of the earliest critics to address at length Forster's theme of the family,[29] but it is George H. Thomson, also writing in the 1960s, who first identifies the nongenetic configuration of Forster's new family, observing that Forster assigns to Margaret as ancestors "ancient Danish soldiers who are not her ancestors at all."[30] Thomson also recognizes that the inheritance of Howards End is passing from the consanguineous family to a member of a more flexible and now extended family.[31]

In *Howards End*, Forster breaks with customary family values of the early 1900s and creates, however tersely, his vision of what the family might become. *Howards End* begins with an unconventional family and ends with the outline of a modern one. The unconventional family consisted of Mr. Schlegel, a widower with three children to raise; Margaret, the eldest, was but thirteen years old. When Aunt Juley Munt, their mother's sister, in accordance with the tradition of the times, offered to run the household and supply maternal affection and guidance to the children, it was Margaret who decided "they could manage much better alone." (11) At Mr. Schlegel's death five years later, the answer was the same. Mrs. Munt, the quintessential Sawstonite—though not virulent like Mrs. Herriton—gives all the wrong advice about money and would probably do the same regarding marriage, were her wisdom solicited. But the young Schlegels have learned to think for themselves, and Margaret and Helen, if not Tibby, their younger brother, have achieved some degree of self-knowledge and insight into human motivation. Of Mr. Schlegel's ample philosophical legacy to his children, his most important endowment was faith in human nature. If his trust was betrayed, his response was that "'it's better to be fooled than to be suspicious'—that the confidence trick is the work of man, but the want-of-confidence trick is the work of the devil." (39)

In contrast to the Schlegels, the Wilcox family aspires to social orthodoxy—at least Mr. Wilcox does—and vigilantly guards against investing trust in other people. Though Mrs. Wilcox might question the necessity for people with sufficient money to be working so hard to gather more, Mr. Wilcox's world is described by the accumulation of wealth. Mrs. Wilcox's faith that war would end if the mothers of various nations could meet is countermanded by Mr. Wilcox's firm belief in the idea and practice of Empire. As for religion, Mr. Wilcox, reared a Dissenter, turns to the Church of England, but not for moral or spiritual guidance. Mrs. Wilcox, of Quaker background, wants "a more inward light" than the rector's sermons provide, "not so much for myself as for baby." (88) Yet she never disputes Mr. Wilcox in anything except whether to pull down the old house and rebuild Howards End, a difference of opinion in which she carries the day. Mr. Wilcox domineers over his family. As a consequence, the children grow up in his image, not their mother's, while her life is "spent in the service of husband and sons." (71)

Though Mrs. Wilcox focuses her centripetal energies on her husband and children, Forster invests her with an important additional and private dimension. What matters to her is not intellection but connection with her own intuition and roots. In describing Mrs. Wilcox's attendance at Margaret's luncheon party, Forster makes clear that what the older woman represents is fragile, imaginative, hard to grasp, and impossible for her to articulate. Her "delicate imaginings" (71)—her experience of her inner intuitive nature at work—are destroyed by rapid-fire clever talk just as surely as Margaret's tentative connection with the countryside—her experience of external Nature—is severed by being driven through it in a motor car at high speed. Mrs. Wilcox lives "nearer the line that divides daily life from a life that may be of greater importance." (74)

Mrs. Wilcox finds in Margaret something lacking in her own offspring, a feeling of connection with the past that can, potentially, lead Margaret to the inner generative power of the human spirit. Mrs. Wilcox also senses in the younger woman what she calls, through her inability to frame a more precise definition, "inexperience," (70) a description of herself that Margaret, at age twenty-nine, finds disconcerting, since she has been the putative head of their family unit for more than ten years. Privately Margaret believes that "if experience is attainable, she had attained it." (71) But at the same time she realizes intuitively that for Mrs. Wilcox experience is a larger interior world of the heart and feelings, not just the superficialities of teacups and roasts of beef, or even concerts.

Mrs. Wilcox is like a mother to the motherless Margaret, trying to teach her something that Mrs. Wilcox's own children are not interested in, something that Margaret's own mother may not have adequately instilled in Margaret before her death. At twenty-nine Margaret is not yet sufficiently attuned to the inner life; she has so far intellectualized her life's experiences; "she mistrust[s] the periods of quiet that are essential to true growth." (77) When Margaret finally discovers the deeper vein of intuition and feeling that Mrs. Wilcox suggests she needs in order to be truly "experienced" in life, her epiphany lies in the sudden recognition of her love of the spacious land, which surprises her city-bred soul. Her newfound appreciation of the land becomes the bridge "connecting on this side with the joys of the flesh, on that with the inconceivable." (202) The novelist makes clear that this epiphany "had certainly come through the house and old Miss Avery," (202) who shared Mrs. Wilcox's deep attachment to the land and its human history.

To her marriage to Henry Wilcox, Margaret brings many of the qualities that Forster valued. Unlike the first Mrs. Wilcox, who is willing to "leave action and discussion to men," (74) Margaret never really subordinates her beliefs to her husband's. At first she makes compromises in an effort to humor her husband's ingrained attitudes, so different from hers, yet she never relinquishes her principles, and Forster tells us that in the early days of her marriage, she is undergoing a seminal change, "some closing of the gates . . . inevitable after thirty, if the mind itself is to become a creative power." (259) Thus she is adequate to the crisis as Henry's Victorian values of family privacy and superficial propriety collapse in ruins when his son Charles is charged with the manslaughter of Leonard Bast.

A careful reading of the last chapter of the novel is crucial to an appreciation of Forster's vision of the modern family. Actually he anticipates the novel's destination in the final paragraph of the penultimate chapter when he announces that "a new life began to move" (331) from the moment of Henry's disintegration. In his spiritual collapse he asks Margaret "to do what she could with him. She did what seemed easiest—she took him down to recruit [recover] at Howards End." (332)

That "recruit" in this particular context may suggest a double meaning is a safe assumption. A newness of psychological life as well as a renewal of physical strength seems not unreasonable, particularly as the last chapter of *Howards End* gives the reader a picture of that new life, those new relationships that are springing from the ground so carefully prepared by the novelist in his development of Margaret's character and equally from the collapse of Henry's life-support values: "They were building up a new life, obscure, yet gilded with tranquility. Leonard was dead; Charles had two years more in prison. One usen't always to see clearly before that time. It was different now." (334) Critics have complained that the last chapter of *Howards End* is too contrived, the characters too overtly manipulated by Forster. There is much justification for such criticism. But if this chapter is approached as a capsulated view of what family relations might be, one sees a succinct summation of Forster's vision of the family to come. Interestingly enough, it was an American reviewer in 1922 who first remarked on Mr. Wilcox's transformation: "It is at Howards End that Henry Wilcox, assured, truculent, successful when he first meets Margaret Schlegel, finally attains to something of her poise and vision."[32]

An overview of the Wilcoxes as an institutional family in the early days of the last century shows Henry Wilcox holding his children on a short rein. As thoroughly orthodox as Mrs. Herriton, he too wishes to control his sons and daughter and to use them to advance his own goals, which he thoughtlessly assumes are also theirs. Though Henry desires "no doughtier comrade" (99) when dealing with the emotions and uses his son Charles as a sounding board and coconspirator over the matter of Mrs. Wilcox's will, he can countenance no assumption of equality by Charles in the family business. While carrying out much of his father's "dirty work," Charles is kept psychologically and financially subservient. With similar lack of consideration, the second son, Paul, is sent out to Africa to run the family business there, only to be unceremoniously summoned back to England to administer the main office when Charles is sentenced to prison and Henry collapses. Paul's preferences are never asked (330); he is simply expected to accede, though it means giving up the outdoor life that satisfies him. Evie, as a daughter, is to be found a suitable husband and provided with an adequate dowry; meanwhile, to pass the time, she breeds dogs and plays tennis. The Wilcoxes might present a front of impregnable family solidarity to the world, but individually they could not endure close proximity to one another. "They had the colonial spirit, and were always making for some spot where the white man might carry his burden unobserved," (201) the burden being, in Forster's eyes, the failure to achieve family intimacy and trust.

Of the old shibboleths—Property, Propriety, Family Pride, and the Church—the last is of no help to Mr. Wilcox in his agony over Charles's imprisonment. Family Pride lies crushed and, like Propriety, in need of redefinition. As for Property—especially Money—Margaret's and Henry's views are at first widely divergent. Henry is secretive; she is open and frank about what she possesses and how to use it for beneficial purposes. To Margaret money is only "the warp of civilization"; (125) the pattern, the enrichment of the tapestry, is created by the woof "that isn't money," (127) all those fructifying ends to which money might be usefully applied to enhance the inner, as well as the external, life of humankind, not just of the possessor of money. From the time of their engagement, she urges him to be generous toward his children; she wants nothing monetary from him. But he uses money as a convenient lever of control.

Their ideas about work are equally divergent. While Henry gives his clerks "work that scarcely encouraged them to grow into other men," (179) for himself personally work is equated with money and power and is a symbol of his selfhood. Margaret looks on work as desirable and liberating, implying a certain harmony between innate ability and its expression in the workplace: "In the last century men have developed the desire for work, and they must not starve it. It's a new desire. It goes with a good deal that's bad, but in itself is good, and I hope that for women, too, 'not to work' will soon become as shocking as 'not to be married' was a hundred years ago." (108)

Given Henry Wilcox's rigidity of character, one cannot expect him to manifest major change in the fourteen months between his breakdown and the last chapter of *Howards End.* Yet he does grow. In disposing of much of his accumulated wealth to his children now they have reached maturity, Mr. Wilcox demonstrates he has learned a little bit about being a nurturing father. That he credits Margaret with the idea of sharing his money with his children while he is still alive does not invalidate the fact that he personally made that decision. Nor is he forced or cajoled by Margaret into leaving Howards End to Helen's son; in turn Mr. Wilcox asks each of his children if they want the house; only when they all reject it does he give Margaret the gift that the first Mrs. Wilcox had intended her to have.

Over the fourteen months of Henry's recruitment since Charles's prison sentence was pronounced, many changes in the Wilcox family are effected by Margaret's influence. "She, who had never expected to conquer anyone, had charged straight through these Wilcoxes and broken up their lives" (339)—broken them up and helped put the pieces back in a more modern shape. Thus, the last chapter of *Howards End* reveals the beginnings of a new, blended family: Henry Wilcox and his wife Margaret, his unwed sister-in-law Helen Schlegel (in 1990s parlance, a single parent) and her son. This is also the beginning of an extended family in which genetics is no longer the sole criterion for membership. Tom, the six-year-old farm boy, is a candidate for this extended family. He is not only present nursemaid for Helen's baby, but as Helen anticipates to Margaret:

> "They're going to be livelong friends."
> "Starting at the ages of six and one?"
> "Of course. It will be a great thing for Tom."
> "It may be a greater thing for baby."
> (333)

Here is an elliptical suggestion of the importance that Forster ascribes to the social cross-fertilization possible between
the descendant of yeoman stock (Tom) and the heir (Helen's
baby) of an intellectual family consciously making that vital
connection with the land as personified by the first Mrs. Wilcox. Here again, Forster reiterates the importance he ascribes
to the genetic union between Leonard Bast, "grandson to the
shepherd or ploughboy whom civilization had sucked into the
town," (113) a noble peasant who, though removed from his
geographic roots, has not forgotten them, and Helen Schlegel,
who has never had Leonard's visceral sense of connection with
the land but is in her own way, with Margaret groping intuitively yet deliberately toward that connection. Helen exults in
"such a crop of hay as never!" (340) just as she exults in her
son who unites the genetic strength of the noble peasant with
the intellectual vigor and sensitivity of educated people like
the Schlegel sisters. Forster "cares deeply about the Leonards
of England,"[33] just as he does about the urgent necessity for
cerebral people to forge their own modern spiritual links with
ancient long-forgotten roots in a physical place.

While the definition of the family has been enlarged to include the possibility of nonconsanguineous members, there is
no evidence of active exclusion of anyone heretofore considered a family member, as Hall suggests.[34] Mrs. Munt and Tibby
may not be the active members of the family group that they
once were—she is old, and he is launching out on his own autonomous life—but it is impossible to imagine Margaret and
Helen ever excluding either of them from their circle; even

Henry Wilcox gets along superficially well with both. Paul Wilcox may be estranged from the rest and eager to get away from them all once more by returning to Africa posthaste, but Evie has ceased being angry with her father for marrying again. Because of his trial Charles is loath to return to his home near Howards End after his release from prison and considers going so far as to change his name. But his wife, Dolly, who is not quite so vacuous as Mr. Wilcox likes to think her, defends her family identity, saying, "'Wilcox' just suits Charles and me, and I can't think of any other name." (339)

Not only is the family changing in size and constitution, and its members gaining in individual independence and equality through Henry's sharing out to his children a great deal of his accumulated wealth, but Margaret's attitudes toward the use of money are being implemented practically. Explaining that upon his death his children will receive all the rest of his estate,—"I leave my wife no money. . . . That is her own wish" (339)—Henry emphasizes Margaret's radical financial decisions. In addition to relinquishing any legal claim she had to Henry Wilcox's money by reason of marriage, she is embarked on giving away to philanthropy half of her own inheritance.

The "breakup and continuance of the family"[35] that Hall sees as a consistent theme in Forster's novels is not capricious; it has a salubrious function. The new Wilcox-Schlegel blended family has already learned how to give texture to the human reconciliation that can grow out of working through life's unexpected challenges. Not only Henry is changing. Margaret's earlier inability to forgive Henry for his treatment of Helen and her intention of leaving him have dissolved as the new life emerges that began to move and germinate during Henry's recruitment. Helen has learned to accept Henry and he, her. Helen has also discovered she has no wish to marry; she has her son. Though Helen's style of life was rare—even outrageous—in 1910, three-quarters of a century later it hardly raises an eyebrow. Margaret does not care for children, but she cares very much for adults and how they get along together in the family. Margaret has become a matriarch without ever being a mother.

Helen gives her all the credit for their "new birth": "Just think of our lives without you, Meg—I and baby [living on the Continent] . . . he [Henry] handed about from Dolly to Evie. But you picked up the pieces and made us a home." (336) Margaret acknowledges that "no doubt I have done a little toward straightening the tangle," but signifying her having learned well Mrs. Wilcox's lesson, she adds, "Things that I can't phrase have helped me." (337)

Present-day readers of *Howards End* may be excused for faulting the failure of critics of thirty or forty years ago to grasp Forster's brilliant dream of the twentieth-century family. In post–World War II days, and even into the 1960s, working mothers and nurturing fathers were the exception, unmarried mothers still a rarity, and blended families were only becoming more common. The traditional roles for women and men far outnumbered examples of equality between the sexes. From the current vantage point, with several additional decades of observing changes in the family, today's readers can better comprehend Forster's prophetic vision of a new and

more flexible form of the family; they will discern that contemporary middle-class families have advanced beyond the
families of the 1960s toward an expression of Forster's dream
of 1910. This palpable advance permits current readers to dif-
fer from Hall, who wrote in 1963 (like Trilling in 1943) that
"the ending is a *Jane Eyre* one: the offenders are punished severely and the husband is gelded, needing thereafter only a
nurse."[36]

Forster makes clear that Margaret's vision is not to be a
nurse, serving Henry's wants, but to become an equal partner
in the marriage. It can be argued that when Henry collapsed,
Margaret responded as would have been expected of the typical wife of 1910: "She did what seemed easiest—she took him
down to recruit at Howards End," giving up her intention of
leaving him in order to cleave to her sister Helen and her expected child and exile herself to the Continent to protect the
only vital family relationship she had ever had. Instead, following the ineluctable collapse of Henry's values, Margaret
seizes the chance to create a new family structure encompassing both Wilcoxes and Schlegels, in which she would be the
matriarch—not just a wife, not just an older sister, never a
mother, but sharing equally with Henry in heading an extended family. Far from searching for an ideal father figure, as
Hall implies,[37] Margaret had needed a mother figure; she
found it in Mrs. Wilcox. Margaret had a strong father, one she
admired and whose values she had thoroughly assimilated.
Mrs. Wilcox was the necessary mother figure whose example
of inner strength of intuition helped Margaret to root her

views of familial relationships—unorthodox and radical for 1910—in a new experience of intuitive visceral knowledge, not just in intellectual hypotheses.

Likewise, in nurturing a sense of spiritual kinship among very different people, Margaret goes far beyond Hall's 1963 view that "the high barriers to community of spirit remain barriers. Helen and Margaret both try to reach understanding with people of extremely different backgrounds, temperaments, and hopes. The novel yields no ground at all to this possibility."[38] On the contrary, the reader can see that the novel carefully prepares the ground for exactly this possibility, which recognizes the difficulty of the endeavor. The barriers are truly there, but Forster's sketch of the new structure of the family suggests the possibility of a community of spirit—what Hall earlier calls a "community-in-difference" among people of widely varying backgrounds.

In "Pessimism in Literature," writing of the modern novelist's search for the truth of the human condition to embody in fiction, Forster tells his audience that separation seems more truly to reflect life than does a happy ending in the form of marriage. Yet, continuing his thesis, he states that since the novelist chooses separation

> we conclude, quite unjustly, that he sees
> in life nothing but separation. The truth
> is that modern art has not succeeded in
> depicting all modern life. It has tried, it
> would like to, but it cannot. ... A man

> and an author have different aims. The
> author looks for what is permanent,
> even if it is sad; the man looks for what
> is cheerful, and noble, and gracious,
> even if it is transitory.[39]

Forster the man may be peeping through in the last chapter of *Howards End.* Is this newborn family just a passing whimsy of Forster's that is applicable in only one novel? Is it specific to *Howards End*? In the fragments of the unpublished *Arctic Summer*, we see a reaffirmation of the freer, more individualist family, where equality is valued over class and love between husband and wife includes a strong companionship. The traditional foundation stones of Property, Propriety, and Family Pride have been redefined while the Church is largely ignored.

Martin Whitby feels that his wife, Venetia, is a "comrade as well as a wife."[40] She is a working wife and a mother, autonomous, with "clear vision," (132) not a conventional woman, but one who, like her husband, hates pseudo chivalry because "it's against all true intercourse with women, and all progress." (141) The son of a manufacturer and a Quaker, Martin attended day school before going up to Cambridge. (130) He chose a bureaucratic post in the Treasury over a Cambridge fellowship. (132) Martin and Venetia share outside interests, have a healthy little son named Hugo, and like, as well as love, each other. Theirs is an "orderly love," (132) wherein reason and passion work together, (132) and they have produced wedded love, not wildly exciting perhaps, but comradely and satisfying over the long run. (133) For their child, they are anxious that he "shouldn't be taught all the rubbish about 'little girls do this' and 'little boys do that.'" (155) That Hugo should grow up liking people is what is important. And Hugo's parents make no distinction between gentlemen and other men. (155)

Thus it would seem that the new family so abruptly born in the last chapter of *Howards End* is no aberration. In Forster's new, modern, functional family, equality is basic; the idea of money as power is forsworn; individual autonomy is recognized; and class is being overcome, at least for the next generation. Women have choices regarding marriage and careers, and they work because work fulfills one part of their natures. Men, too, are liberated from the narrow stereotypes of conventional careers. Both parents are nurturers. No longer limited by genetics, families may by choice be nuclear or extended, or even blended. Working wives and mothers are becoming unexceptional. When money is regarded as a means, not an end, people are able to be more generous in spreading its benefits; within or outside the family, philanthropy is not considered extraordinary. The family that emphasizes companionship in its relations strengthens the individuality of each of its members, and this in turn strengthens the sense of community-cum-variety. Communal cohesion springs voluntarily from shared interests and feelings, not just from common bloodlines. People who are very different learn they can coexist and even come to respect and accept each other. Family relationships need no longer be the "white man's burden" (Forster's words) that forces people to flee to the ends of the earth to escape meaningless formality. Education of the young strives to be gender-free. The goal is a classless family of all humanity.

Forster unfailingly emphasized the spirit over the strictly legalistic. "A funeral is not death, any more than baptism is birth or marriage union. All three are the clumsy devices coming now too late, now too early, by which Society would register the quick motions of man." (100) What was important to the novelist was a new framework for relationships—"love without power," in Peter Gay's graceful phrase—between husband and wife, parents and children, the nuclear family and the extended circle.

Forster was indeed more prescient than he knew. Already in "Pessimism in Literature," dated 1906–7 he had written:

> Though the facts of human nature are constant, the spirit of humanity is not, but alters age by age, perhaps year by year, and, like some restless child, continually groups the facts anew.... What new and inspiring combinations it may find, no man can say; that it will find a new combination is surely inevitable, and happy the artist who records it.[41]

Part Two

Mapping Forster's Spiritual Journey

And what does the Lord require of you but to do justice, and to love kindness, and to walk humbly with your God?

Micah 6:8

Chapter Three

Family Setting

Growing Up and Growing Out

Edward Morgan Forster was born in 1879, and his father died before the baby reached his first birthday. As a child Forster inhabited a world populated largely by elderly ladies, the most significant being his great-aunt Marianne Thornton. Calling him "the Important One," she invested her affection as well as her belief in the importance of family, both past and future, in her great-nephew and closely followed his development. Forster's mother, craving a little distance from Marianne's daunting personality, leased the house called Rooksnest in Stevenage on the other side of London when the child was four years old. As an only child, he instinctively gave rein to his imagination to vivify his staid adult world with its generally conservative attitudes. More than seventy years later, in his Presidential Address to the Cambridge Society of Humanists,[1] Forster recalled that he had been fed Victorian morality stories such as *Agatha and Jessica's First Prayer* and *Precept upon Precept*, but he much preferred *Swiss Family Robinson* or astronomy or history and had invented long stories of his own. In one such "childish day-dream" he played the role of Christ. With mild self-mockery he told his 1959 Humanist audience, "My indifference towards Christ did not prevent me from usurping his position myself. . . . All I had to do was to walk about the countryside while my disciples followed me. They listened. I talked. I liked that." Another imagined story involved living among "savages" and converting them all to Christianity before leading them on imaginary adventures.

The background of traditional Christian theology continued to color the years of Forster's education, first during a brief experience as a boarding student at a preparatory school when he was eleven and later at King's College, Cambridge University. He told the Humanists that when he and another public-school student named Henson stayed home from religious services one Good Friday because they had colds, he tried to explain to Henson, who had no idea why the student body had gone to church on a weekday, what Good Friday was all about. Forster "told him about Easter and Ascension Day. He had never heard of them and he knew nothing about Jesus. He would say that Christ could not have died long ago if he had only been born last Christmas. I was very much shocked." On another occasion the headmaster, a clergyman as was usual in such prep schools then, warned the students that "in the very next road there lived a man who did not believe in God called Mr [Aldous] Huxley." Forster said the boys found the information meaningless.

Along with traditional Christian beliefs, the child Forster was also steeped in family history, especially Thornton and

Forster ancestry. In adulthood, although critical of some aspects of his family background, he never rejected his ancestors, unlike his complete break with the institutional church in which he was brought up. His paternal grandfather, Charles Forster, was the rector at Stisted in eastern England where Forster said he

> soon degenerated into a Hebrew Prophet who had nothing to prophesy about. He denounced, he exhorted, he pardoned. His sermon on the Fall of Paris was impressive rather than appropriate, and on other occasions he preached on the Errors of the Pelagians and on the Sinfulness of Hurrying from one Dissipation to Another. He was attentive to his flock, he alleviated suffering, and for this, and for the combating of Dissent and Popery, he had the full support of the Squire. ... Parson and Squire ruled unchallenged, tenants who did not vote Tory were turned out... and my grandfather got a Sunday "delivery of letters stopped."[2]

Forster's grandfather's reasoning for this ban was, presumably, the evil of working on the Sabbath.

Forster's biography of his great-aunt Marianne Thornton sketches the world of his paternal ancestors. His grandmother

was a member of the Thornton family of bankers in the eight-
eenth and nineteenth centuries who, in the Victorian period,
played a prominent role in the Clapham Sect, a group of high-
minded leaders of state and church clustered around the Clapham Common in suburban London. There the Thorntons had
built Battersea Rise, their family home. The Claphamites were
active in the Evangelical movement of the Victorian period
and were among the founders and zealous supporters of the
British and Foreign Bible Society, the Church Missionary Society, the Anti-Slavery League, the African Society, and the Society for the Conversion of the Jews. The passion that drove
the Evangelicals to work tirelessly for the abolition of slavery
in Africa also led them into a vigorous mission to spread Christianity in India, to purge the subcontinent of religious practices they considered idolatrous, superstitious, and even cruel,
and to substitute the doctrines of Christianity, about whose
superiority they had no doubts. This nineteenth-century
Evangelicalism haunted Forster in his own experience of India, and he decried its zealotry. In his novel *A Passage to India*,
he treats its twentieth-century descendants kindly yet dismissively. In later book reviews for English magazines, he
spoke with considerable vigor against the writings of those he
considered biased, dogmatic, and prejudiced against everything Indian.

The nineteenth-century Evangelical movement—not to be
confused with the more publicized faction of twenty-first-cen-
tury evangelism—was founded in 1846 to counteract "infidel-
ity [i.e., religious indifference], Romanism and ritualism, and
the desecration of the Lord's Day."[3] It sprang from fear of the

power of the Roman Catholic Church and the rigidity of Church of England practices that, Evangelicals believed, suffocated spiritual awe before the mystery of God. A direct approach to God was more vivid to them once the confining walls of an approved channel of communication had been breached. They fervently championed the right of personal judgment in interpreting the Scriptures; to them Jesus Christ was the only mediator needed between humankind and God. The title of Christian, Evangelicals felt, could not be inherited by birth simply because one was born to parents who belonged to the Church of England. Each individual must experience God personally and directly. Evangelicalism demanded rigorous spiritual effort, not mindless repetition. Prayer was more than asking for favors; it required listening to the Holy Spirit for direction on how to live life. Truth discovered through heartfelt conversations with God was what mattered, wherever it might lead. Without an established filter of received wisdom, one must think for oneself about the meaning of God in one's life and in the world. Yet escape into mysticism was no solution. While many Evangelical doctrines, such as baptism, resurrection, justification by faith, and belief in the Incarnation and the Holy Trinity, mirrored official Church of England theology, the Anglican Church considered the Evangelicals weak in theological study and personal interpretation of the Bible unreliable unless substantiated by consensus of Anglican theologians. The Church of England eventually acknowledged Evangelicalism but with considerable skepticism and institutional control.

Forster's Thornton forebears, in his portrait of Marianne
Thornton, appear as a family not pompous or rigidly orthodox, devoted to piety, duty, wise parenthood, and business.
Forster describes his great-grandfather Henry Thornton's
household as "anything but a 'Victorian' establishment.... [It
was] a blend of feudal loyalty and eighteenth-century enlightenment."[4] Children were warmly nurtured and lovingly directed into paths of probity and generous charity. Servants
were not required to forsake their own family and friends in
order to give total allegiance to their employers, as was the
custom of the times. While the family enjoyed the "soothing"[5]
sermons of the Reverend John Venn, rector of Holy Trinity
Church on Clapham Common, who elevated "a devotional
spirit" over "even the occupation of doing good,"[6] they preferred family devotions: "Battersea Rise library with the
united family kneeling seemed more sacred to them than any
consecrated edifice." "The power of the Church over the
Thorntons," Forster wrote, "was moral rather than mystic.
They were indifferent to ceremony, their references to Holy
Communion are [sic] temperate, and though they desired
sound doctrine they were not upset by deviations from it."[7]
Their personal theology was practical and moralistic. The family prayers left by Henry Thornton were written down, copied,
and repeated by friends for years and published by a relative
after his death in a volume that went through thirty-one
printings between 1834 and 1854. To Forster himself, however,
the family prayers seemed "of the usual evangelical type. They
consist of vague contrition, vague thankfulness and somewhat

precise instructions to God on the subject of His own attributes. They borrow their cadences from the Book of Common
Prayer and from unimaginative recollections of the Bible, all
the splendours and the strangenesses of sacred literature are
absent, and it is difficult to understand why their smooth rhet-
oric was preferred when so much better was to hand, and why
the use of them became in the mid-nineteenth century the dis-
tinctive sign of true Evangelism."[8] Their traditional piety
failed to recognize the divine mystery, he said; like so many
Christians, they created God in their own image. Their "indifference to the unseen seems to me the great defect of my
great-grandfather's set. . . . Poetry, mystery, passion, ecstasy,
music, don't count."[9] They disdained literature itself "unless it
was of an intellectual or formative character."[10]

Forster deplored his ancestors' pietistic gloss on riches and
charity:

> The Clapham Sect listened [to pray-
> ers], rose from its knees, ate, and then
> made money—made as much as ever it
> could, and then gave as much as it
> could away . . . and not being psycholo-
> gists they thought it would have no ef-
> fect upon their souls if they purged
> themselves promptly. The devil is sub-
> tler than that. He, like Christ, under-
> stands the deceitfulness of riches: . . .
> Wealth always fattens the person who
> swallows it, no matter how promptly

he purges, and it is significant that in spite of his fabulous charities Henry Thornton left all his nine children extremely well off, and that some of his money has even descended to myself, ... enough to remind me that there was an age when to get rich and to be good were harmonious.

A similar hope is held by the Quakers. ... They have what the Claphamites lacked: a touch of mysticism, a sense of the unseen, and a capacity for martyrdom. These impulses ... do purge the soul, in a way which almsgiving and self-examination cannot; they do lift the participant into a region outside money, whereas charity only keeps man running to and fro, from his business to his deserving cause, and then back to his business.[11]

This bulimic approach to charity, Forster seems to imply, was fed by the need to expiate a hidden sense of guilt. While praising his ancestors for their crusades against slavery in other lands, Forster condemned them and their class for failing to recognize their own role in industrial slavery of the underpaid, often underage, employees of English mines and factories. Their generous charity was dispensed not to abolish economic slavery but simply to assuage its misery, for to do more, they feared, might encourage workers to become demanding. Even his ancestors' feeble efforts at education for laborers' children seemed primarily aimed at increasing obedience and productivity.[12] Although Forster saw clearly the spiritual myopia of his Thornton forebears, he did not regard them as evil;[13] they did try to alleviate suffering, but at a safe distance from themselves. In biblical terms Forster's ancestors tried to remove the mote from their brother's eye, oblivious to the plank in their own. In contrast to this pragmatic, moralistic application of Christian dogma of the end of the nineteenth century, in a private journal entry dated April 5, 1912, Forster wrote that "Percy [Whichelo, his cousin] agrees that the english [sic] have no sense of the unseen & he is a little sorry about it."[14] This date has significance: It was Good Friday that year and only a few months after the death of Percy's and Forster's much-loved grandmother Louisa Whichelo.

Henry Thornton himself was not so much blind as myopic regarding his own shortcomings. On January 7, 1795—perhaps in the spirit of a New Year's resolution—Thornton began a diary cataloging his motives: "I think I have discovered that my religion consists too much in active duties and in efforts to edify and convert others and too little in serious self-examination and attentive reading of the Scriptures, prayer and secret self-denial." A hundred handwritten pages later he concluded, not without a whiff of self-satisfaction: "I may consider myself highly favoured by Providence, for how few can I discover round me who have half my Prosperity or who can look with

so little reason for apprehension on a numerous family of children?"[15] To the Thorntons, religion was a integral part of their
lives, unlike the recommendation of the mission from Japan in
the late nineteenth century that toured Europe when Forster
was briefly a boarding-school student. Charged with considering whether the Japanese, in an effort to modernize their nation, "should abandon their own creed and adopt someone
else's," the mission "reported favourably on the Church of
England on the ground that it aroused no enthusiasm," Forster
told his Cambridge Humanist audience some seventy years
later. Each of Forster's novels portrays characters who reflect
this lack of enthusiasm for organized religion, who find no
personal meaning in the Christian dogma and call upon institutional religion principally for rituals such as christenings,
weddings or funerals. To the Thorntons religion was more
than mere ceremony; it was energetic, and it included an element of self-criticism, though it fell short of Forster's later definition. He felt that Henry Thornton's introspection was "constant rather than painful,"[16] and secretly self-congratulatory.
Forster's personal prescription in maturity was "don't ever
shrink from self-analysis, but don't keep on at it too long."[17] In
Howards End, his fourth novel, published in 1910, when he was
becoming interested in India, he wrote that "the inner life actually 'pays,' when years of self-scrutiny, conducted for no ul-
terior motive, are suddenly of practical use. Such moments are
still rare in the West; that they come at all promises a fairer
future."[18]

Despite his criticism of his Thornton ancestors' attitude about riches and charity, Forster was a not-ungrateful recipient of their money, noting almost wistfully that wealth and goodness existed in innocent proximity then. Whether in response to his own sense of guilt or in appreciation for his good fortune—at first inherited and, as he became famous, earned by his own efforts—Forster was generous with private, often anonymous, gifts of money to friends and even strangers in need, a generosity he learned at his mother's knee.[19] In his novel *The Longest Journey,* Rickie Elliot tries to offer money to an engaged couple who must postpone marriage because of poverty, but he is sharply rebuffed by the young man, who considers the offer "unhealthy." Forster was also generous with gifts of praise and unsolicited encouragement to other writers. The American novelist Eudora Welty shared one such letter at a symposium celebrating the centenary of his birth:

28 April 1947

Dear Miss Welty: Finding myself in your country I feel I should like to give myself the pleasure of writing you a line and telling you how much I enjoy your work "The Wide Net." All the wild and lovely things it brings up have often been with me and delighted me.

I am afraid that I am unlikely to have the good fortune of meeting you

while I am over here since my itinerary
keeps me to the North and to the West.
Still there are meetings which are not
precisely personal and I've had the advantage of one of these through you,
and I would like to thank you for it.
With kind regards and all good wishes.

Yours sincerely, E. M. Forster

To her audience Miss Welty described her reaction to this
unexpected praise:

Well, it was several moments before I
was able to read the signature, partly it
was his handwriting and partly it was
my disbelief. The letter was kindness,
undreamed-of kindness. It was also
something that belongs to another
realm, another kingdom in the sense of
animal, vegetable or mineral kingdoms.
It was response. It was what I knew Mr.
Forster meant me to receive from him.
It had been received and had given
pleasure. The letter carries some marks
of tears and when I copied it off to bring
to this conference my tears came back.
This is the only time I've ever shared this
letter, mailed to me thirty-two years
ago, because it seems appropriate that I

should read it in this company, who well
know the value it had for the young
writer I was, and has for that writer today, and who can see it with me in its
lasting and undimmed light.[20]

Nineteenth-Century Winds of Change

Forster's rootedness in the land and appreciation of the character of the noble peasants; his financial security, thanks to his
great-aunt Marianne Thornton's bequest of £8,000 to him at
her death; and his rejection of Victorian religious practices are
all important facets of his philosophical legacy. But land, family, and the establishment Church of England were not the
only influences in Forster's philosophical background. The
nineteenth century was a ferment of new scientific and psychological questions that challenged traditional Christian beliefs, even the assumed dependency of humankind on a Creator. Charles Darwin's theory of evolution through natural
selection presented a major challenge to the accepted founda-
tions of nineteenth-century thought. Utilitarianism also bur-
geoned in the mid-Victorian atmosphere of new ideas and
later exerted a strong influence on the administration of the
British Empire in India.

Prominent among the philosophers of Utilitarian persuasion was G. E. Moore of Cambridge University, who in 1903
published his *Principia Ethica*, directly influencing many
young people of Forster's generation. Forster he influenced
only indirectly. In his Presidential Address to the Cambridge

Humanists, speaking of his religious beliefs, Forster clarified
the nature of his relationship with Moore: "In my second year
[at Cambridge University] . . . my Christianity . . . disappeared
. . . partly because of the general spirit of questioning that is
associated with the name of G. E. Moore. I did not receive
Moore's influence direct—I was not up to that and have never
read *Principia Ethica*. It came to me at a remove, through
those who knew the Master. The seed fell on fertile, if inferior,
soil, and I began to think for myself—that most precious experience of youth which is far from universal, and is often discouraged."

Remembered in today's parlance as "the greatest good for
the greatest number," Utilitarianism originated as a philosophy of moral and social commitment implying concern for the
well-being of a community, not just an individual: "Actions are
right in proportion as they tend to promote happiness, wrong
as they tend to promote the reverse of happiness."[21] But Utilitarianism was not a justification for selfish hedonism: "The
aim was collective happiness, it being the duty both of the individual and the state to promote the welfare of the greatest
number."[22] Implicit was an underlying love of virtue mani-
fested in a disinterested unselfishness and consideration of
the good of others. First propounded by John Stuart Mill as an
1861 essay, Utilitarianism quickly seized the imagination both
of "young thinkers at the Universities" and "young shepherds
on the mountains."[23] Mill's essay was later incorporated as
part of his volume *The Science of Logic* and eventually used as

a text at both Oxford and Cambridge universities, where it influenced graduates who went out to India as functionaries in the British raj. Unlike Evangelical missionaries with their urge to root out the indigenous religions and replace them with Christianity, proponents of Utilitarianism, though certain of the superiority of Western progress, tended to *offer* India such concepts as Western education, training in the English language, Western science and philosophy, and rationalization of the Indian practices of justice on the English model, with the goal of using Indians in bureaucratic posts in the local judiciary. These Western ideas were eagerly embraced by many Indian thinkers,[24] but when Lord Ripon, viceroy of India from 1880 to 1884, proposed in the Ilbert bill to add Indian judges to the previously all-English judicial roster in the Bengal presidency, an uproar resulted. The European business community suddenly realized that it might have to defend itself before an Indian judge without a jury, an unpalatable possibility that is eerily echoed in the trial of Dr. Aziz in *A Passage to India.*[25]

Utilitarianism emphasized the consequences of the act, not the motives of the actor. Mill, like G. E. Moore later, believed that "the goodness of a state of affairs [was] the primary ethical concept and that rightness of actions [was] a derivative concept." Orthodox Christianity, on the other hand, looked at "the rightness and wrongness of actions," considering as primary the question "What is it my duty to do?"[26] This basic difference in human motivation, helped along by the new idea of evolution, eroded the influence of traditional Christianity in many lives. Forster was sympathetic with this utilitarian concept as well as other ideas propounded in Mill's essays—individual happiness, commitment to community, responsible actions toward others, all based on "goodness" as the essential foundation for action. Forster embraced both individuality and loyalty to the larger group, whether the consanguineous family or a group drawn together by a common attitude toward life that would, in present-day terminology, be considered an extended family.

If Utilitarianism excited widespread enthusiastic discussion, the theory of evolution propounded by Charles Darwin in his *Origin of Species* (1859) exploded with the primal jolt of a volcano, affecting unexamined assumptions of the nineteenth century in every aspect of human life and thought, with aftershocks continuing into the twenty-first century.[27] Though the idea of evolution had been around for almost half a century when Forster began to publish his stories and novels, it was still a hotly discussed question, and Forster undoubtedly absorbed much from the urgent intellectual discussions of the subject in print and from the podium and pulpit. For creative writers the formal boundaries of time, sequence, point of view, and other literary devices gradually lost their old validity; uncertainty, chance, coincidence became recognized as inevitable aspects of literary and artistic expression.

The revolutionary idea of evolution through natural selection immediately ran into vociferous opposition from Christian theologians. Upsetting the myth of Noah's ark protecting two of every species from destruction by the flood was the least of it. Some thoughtful theologians of earlier centuries, among them Gregory of Nazianus, Augustine, Albertus Magnus, and Thomas Aquinas, had questioned the Noah story.[28] But Darwin in the nineteenth century was performing a service like that of Galileo in the seventeenth: "He was forcing the orthodox to revise their attitude to their sacred books."[29] No longer was the Bible the indisputable authority on scientific matters. But gradually even Victorian theologians came to see evolution as a "natural process through which God brought living beings into existence and developed them according to his plan."[30] Providence was effectively transferred from the transcendent world to the immanent world of nature.[31]

Evolution had breached the accepted boundaries not only of science and religion but of every aspect of life. Society in eighteenth- and early nineteenth-century England had been predicated on stability and continuity. Forster acknowledges as much in his biography of his great-aunt Marianne Thornton. The idea of change as an ever-present variable was not a welcome thought. Yet the theory of evolution, with its implied emphasis on individuality, forced early Victorian society to face up to change. Experimentation flourished in many areas,[32] the Industrial Revolution contributing to the unsettling atmosphere of change. Though the authorial voice was gradually suppressed by most novelists, Forster continued to speak in a strong personal voice in his novels; he also remained a firm advocate of seeing things "steadily and whole." But at the same time he accepted as inevitable the fragmentation that chance brought and sought to reconcile continuity and change in his writings and his life. Some thought he had carried coincidence a bit far in *The Longest Journey*, his second novel; both friends and critics commented on the novel's large number of sudden deaths.

Darwin objected to the unconsidered acceptance of the narrow and blinkered Christian orthodoxy of his time. In the twentieth century Forster likewise rejected traditional Christian dogma but did not deny the spiritual mystery and power of the divine, by whatever phrase it might be called. He had found the expansiveness of spirit to embrace the contradictions of life; he felt no threat from them. He accepted contradictions and inconsistencies, never regarding them as necessary evils to be eradicated or rigidly controlled. They were a normal aspect of ongoing and ever-changing life. In words Forster put into the mouth of Mr. Emerson in *A Room with a View*, "by the side of the everlasting Why there is a Yes—a transitory Yes if you like, but a Yes."[33]

"That Most Precious Experience of Youth"

Into this ferment of powerful new and evolving older ideas, Forster was born. Bereft by his father's untimely death before he was a year old, he grew up in a conservative home atmosphere, tempered by friendship with nearby farm lads. Thanks to his great-aunt's bequest, he went off to King's College, Cambridge University, where he soon discovered a larger world of friends who shared his interests. As he later told his Humanist audience, he also found religious controversy at Cambridge. The crux of the dispute was whether a proposed university-

sponsored center in London should follow a religious or a secular philosophy. Forster became involved in the argument: "A
serious minded, athletic and popular New Zealander ... was
deeply stirred by the ... controversy, and it woke up the fa-
natic in him. He realised that he was right and that everyone
else was wrong, and in danger of Hell Fire from which he must
save them." Whereupon, at his own expense, the New Zealander composed and published a pamphlet: "It was well written, its sincerity burnt." Forster saw with deep dismay the
zealotry that the controversy aroused in Christians and their
atheist opponents alike. Forster explained to the Humanists
that he was uneasy about an aspect of Jesus' character that he
saw as "so much emphasis on followers, on an elite" and as
"moving ... towards preaching and threats." Even as a child
he had felt the personal pleasure and sense of power of being
a leader pontificating to passive followers, even imaginary
ones. Only later at university, witnessing the ravages of unexamined faith in Christianity and atheism alike, did Forster recognize the potential for infection that a private agenda could
contain. Any individual, seduced by the power of leadership
and certain of the unquestionable correctness of his or her
own beliefs, might attempt to exert personal control over
trusting and unthinking followers. Forster's boyish pleasure at
talking while his imaginary followers listened later turned to
a permanent fear of the charismatic leader with a private goal
and to an equally deep distrust of the unthinking herd men-
tality that could abdicate individual responsibility to such a
figure.

A significant part of Forster's loss of orthodox Christian belief rested in his "attitude towards the character of Christ as the Gospels present it." In his own words he explained to the Humanists, "I am unsympathetic towards it. This is unusual." Even non-Christians are generally sympathetic toward Christ, he said, "and often preface their attacks on his claims to divinity by eulogising him as a man. The Christ we know is what the gospels tell us he was, we cannot see behind them or discount the misrepresentations they may contain and even in the Gospels there is much that Christ says and does that I do like and often think about." Forster suspected, but may not have precisely known, that accretions to the gospels had accumulated in earlier centuries through attempts to clarify or amplify the first Christian writings, with imperfect or partial interpretations over the centuries solidifying into dogma. While a few nineteenth-century biblical scholars were trying to separate the actual words and actions of Jesus from later interpolations and interpretations, by the end of the Victorian era such challenges to accepted teachings had not gathered sufficient credence within religious precincts to command a serious new consideration of conventional beliefs. Albert Schweitzer, whose book *The Quest for the Historical Jesus* (1922) first informed the wider public of the effort to free the real Jesus from the encumbrance of centuries of myth and misinterpretation, "showed the hero of most nineteenth-century lives of Jesus to be the Jesus wanted or needed by their individual authors."[34] Not only the character of Jesus but biblical stories were distorted to reflect commonly held myths or misinterpretations, as for instance, a sermon repeated during Forster's childhood by the Stevenage rector: "Every now and then we [parishioners] got the one about Esau and Jacob [Genesis 25:19ff]. Esau he [the rector] secretly admired, Jacob he detested and had to make the best of. ('Esau was a grand man, he was a huntsman. He was a splendid fellow. But we must never forget that Jacob was the chosen of God')." The village parson seemed to imply that God had made an inexplicable mistake in preferring Jacob. Whether Forster had ever read Schweitzer is unknown, but his instinctive spiritual values were sympathetic with the effort to resurrect historical biblical truths.

In his account of purging himself of the hidebound Christianity with which he had grown up, Forster, at the age of eighty, shared with his Cambridge Humanist audience that

> I thought first about the Trinity [God as encompassing Father, Son and Holy Spirit] and found it very odd. I tried to define it in accordance with my inherited tenets, but it kept falling apart like an unmanageable toy, and I decided to scrap it, and to retain the main edifice. I did not realise that it was a question of all or none, and that the removal of the Trinity had jeopardised the stability of the Incarnation. I began to think about that. The idea of a god becoming a man to help men is overwhelming to anyone possessed of a heart. Even at that age I was aware that this world needs help.

> But I never had much sense of sin and
> when I realised that the main aim of the
> Incarnation was not to stop war or pain
> or poverty, but to free us from sin I be-
> came less interested and ended by
> scrapping it too. . . . And so by the end of
> my third year I disbelieved much as I do
> now. . . . The debunking of Christianity
> was effected with comparatively little
> fuss.

Forster did, nonetheless, like some of the stories and parables of the New Testament, such as the parable of the hidden
talent (Matthew 25:14ff) and the one of the husbandman (Matthew 20) "with its generous defence of unfairness, and the
preference of Mary to Martha [Luke 10:38ff] which so annoyed
Rudyard Kipling, and the marriage at Cana [John 2], and the
reminder that adultery is an aspect of sex and that precious
objects must sometimes be spilt recklessly and not sold for
charity [Luke 7:36ff]—and the blasting of that sterile fig tree
[Luke 13:6-9]—in fact all the sayings and doings that move
away from worldliness towards warmth. And I am touched by
the birth stories, and overwhelmed by the death story." But
"there is so much on the other side, so much moving away
from worldliness towards preaching and threats, so much emphasis on followers, on an elite, so little intellectual power (as
opposed to insight), such an absence of humour and fun that
my blood's chilled."

Forster's short litany of what he found objectionable about the practice of Christianity in the early days of the twentieth century and what he appreciated in the biblical record of Jesus' life is full of insights into his personal spiritual philosophy. He longed for an incarnate God—a God taking on human form and nature, one who understood the sorrows of human life and accepted the fallibility of humankind. The incarnate God would be a life-enhancing God who represented what humanity yearned for in a heavenly model. In an entry in his "Notebook Journal," he expresses this dream: "The Incarnation must be a wonderful thing. Suppose I could think of Christ not as an evangelical shop walker [supervisor] but as the young carpenter who would smoke a pipe with me in his off time and be most frightfully kind. 'A man shall be a hiding place in a tempest' would suddenly mean something, and I would do all that was likely to please the fellow."[35] He was rejecting the commonly accepted nineteenth-century representation of Jesus that depicted him as remote from ordinary people and as accusatory, demanding blind obedience to a dogma that suited the requirements of Church and State more than the needs of the people. Forster yearned for a god who loved and embraced fallible humanity. In *Howards End*, describing the bustle of London with its throngs of faceless people, he remarks that "the continual flow would be tolerable if a man of our own sort—not anyone pompous or tearful—were caring for us up in the sky." (107)

Forster felt a deep revulsion against the cynicism, hypocrisy, and shallowness of most contemporary Christian worship. He wrote of his Uncle William Howley Forster:

Religion partook of the general emotional fare. "I believe in doing as your
host does" said Uncle Willie. "If you're in
a religious house, wear your trousers out
[get down on your knees] and pray like
blazes." He didn't wear out his, but he
stood no nonsense either, keeping in
with both parson and priest and re-
marking that during the hour for com-
pulsory religious instruction those little
boys who were atheist ought to do the
goose step. Aunt Emily went to church
of course—she valued her privileges.
Miss Chipman [a family friend] went too,
but separately, and in the trap; her Sunday clothes were poetic, very smartly
decorated but of sporting cut in their
fundamentals. Having left the trap in
the pub, she rejoined Aunt Emily in the
Acton pew. Aunt Emily did not think it
right to have the trap out on Sundays, on
account of the work it gave the servants.
Both ladies received the rite of Communion when it was available.[36]

In this family ceremony of the Sabbath, Forster felt no
honesty, no empathy, no humility, no sense of mystery before
the divine. He felt that form and obeisance to society's expec-

tations were of primary importance; content and commitment were lacking. Those at Sunday services were as remiss as Uncle Willie, who apparently never attended.

Origins of Forster's Personal Philosophy

Having rejected what he regarded as the static theological concepts of the late Victorian period, Forster articulated his own religio-philosophical construct. To find a thoughtfully articulated philosophy of living in one still so young is surprising, yet Forster's "contemporaries seem to have agreed he was exactly the same at twenty as he was at ninety."[37] Elizabeth Bowen expands on this idea:

> Mr. Foster, though his first novels were published when he was in the twenties, seems to have been adult when he began to write. Then he took up without hesitation, in fact with evident certainty, the position with regard to life that he has occupied since. . . . At all events, he went from that first book direct to his personal maturity. . . . The thirty-three years since *Where Angels Fear to Tread* have given him further data, but have not changed his conclusions. . . . His "development" has been a matter of equipping himself more fully, and with wider and wider reference to express what he has from the first felt.[38]

At least as early as his college years, he recognized that he "never had much sense of sin." His thoughts about sin did not emerge from a systematic study of philosophy but arose from two roots, his intuition and his belief in the essential goodness of people. In 1905, at the end of the Victorian era, when he was just twenty-six years old, Forster wrote in his "Notebook Journal," "Men . . . have not made such a mess. The conditions are appalling: poverty, matrimony, much of family life all work against love & clear vision: and to these are added the rules of the game—death & decay. Yet people contrive to get into touch—I believe because they are radically good."[39] Radically good, not radically sinful. Though "radical" is commonly associated with rejection of the traditional in favor of the new and the seemingly drastic extreme, Forster used the word in its original sense, *radix* meaning root. The generally accepted social structure of marriage and family in Victorian England denied equality and freedom to women and children, thwarting individuality and self-expression almost from the cradle, permitting wife and offspring no separate personhood; they existed legally, economically, and socially only through their husband and father. Forster boldly rejected such vitiating attitudes.

When Forster turned his back on the Christianity he had been brought up in, he did not look for a new religious home in another denomination; he walked out of the church and closed the door behind him. Undoubtedly he had been too thoroughly disillusioned to look for possible allies within the ramparts of institutional religion, for despite their name, the Dissenters shared with the Church of England many of the same theological doctrines. To Forster there was too much dogma, too little sense of the divine mystery, and too little thinking for oneself, "that most precious experience of youth which is... often discouraged." But Forster was thinking deeply. In a 1907 paper read to the Working Men's College when he was less than thirty, he spoke of three great questions that any individual might ask about life's journey, the first being how to behave toward people he or she knows, and the second how to behave toward strangers. The third question, "which some people think of supreme importance, while others neglect it entirely, is this: How shall I behave to the Unknowable? What shall my attitude be towards God, or Fate, or whatever you like to call the invisible power that lies behind the world?"[40]

In spite of his rejection of formal Christianity, Forster wrote in his "Locked Journal" on June 16, 1911, of a "growing interest in religion."[41] But it was a personal interpretation of religion, not Religion with a capital R as practiced on Sundays in most churches. In the same year, to another Working Men's College group, Forster succinctly expressed his dream for "the beauty of the unselfish action amid selfishness; the beauty of friendship amidst indifference"[42] and "the wonders, physical and spiritual, by which we are surrounded."[43] A few years later, in "Notes on Human Nature under War Conditions," written during World War I, he contended that "most men are unhappy and restless without Faith, and, to cover up the path that led them to it, give out that Faith is splendid and arduous and only fully attained by the elect. They can most agreeably believe in an enlarged and everlasting man. Hence 'God' in the past and the 'Nation' now. Either is the reflection of man; weakness upon a cloud."[44] Such faith seemed counterfeit to Forster, substituting established dogma for rigorous personal rumination and modeling God in the shape of imperfect humanity.

Yet in the 1930s Forster acknowledged organized religion as a rallying point against the growing threat of another world war: "Christianity remains untrue, and harmful as a guide in private—particularly sexual—conduct. But it has more guts in it than culture, and so can stand up to the State. Religion will be man's only defence against Totalitarianism."[45] But religious attitudes described in World War I days had not changed much by 1939 when, on the eve of the outbreak of World War II, Forster could only deplore the common religious scene again, saying that people

> listen to the religious service on the wireless, if they listen at all. Distracted by earthly chores, they hear from Broadcasting House the voice of an enlightened clergyman who tries to make religion realistic and definite and to give spiritual tips; he vibrates like a weathercock to international troubles, he grapples with daily trivialities, he enhaloes the ticket-collectors, bus-conductors, waitresses and... ambulances whom we encounter during the drab suburban

> day; he even glances at pet animals. A
> modern St. Francis, he believes in de-
> tail.[46]

This acerbic remark was made shortly after his "Credo" was published to a wide audience in *The London Mercury and Bookman*.[47]

No proselytizer—although occasionally the preacher in him broke into print—Forster did not feel the need to try to convert people to his way of thinking. In contrast to the palliative phrases dispensed by institutional religion and uncritically accepted by most people who called themselves Christian, Forster's religious vocabulary, usually reserved for his private journals, reveals his independent thoughts. Though employing the customary words, Forster's definitions provide insights into his own spiritual life. "Improvement," for example, stands for his version of "salvation." One dictionary defines salvation as spiritual rescue from the consequences of sin; another says that this rescue is wrought for man by the atonement of Christ, through Christ's sacrifice of his life on the cross for all humankind. Forster's concept of salvation is closer to the old Hebrew "to make wide" or "to make sufficient,"[48] a definition without sense of sin, rather a rescue from danger or, in the military context from which the meaning sprang, victory over evil. Improvement over the present condition of one's soul would expand the soul to strengthen its capacity as a guide through life's vicissitudes. Although the word "salvation" appears in its traditional usage in Forster's early writings, it disappears "like other absolutes" from his later writing, as he said in that important Presidential Address:

> I no longer wish to save or be saved, and here is another barrier that has interposed between myself and revealed religion. . . . What I would like to do is to improve myself and to improve others in the delicate sense that has to be attached to the word improvement, and to be aware of the delicacy of others while they are improving me. Improve!—such a dull word but it includes more sensitiveness, more realisation of variety, and more capacity for adventure. He who is enamoured of improvement will never want to rest in the Lord.

In 1930, in a private rumination, Forster says that "two people pulling each other into salvation is the only theme I find worthwhile. Not rescuer and rescued, not the alternating performances of good turns,"[49] that is, not a relationship of superiority and subservience or even of reciprocity but a search in tandem for the unique gifts of the spirit discoverable *within* each individual—in other words, self-improvement through mutual gentle encouragement, powered by hope, free from threats, coercion, guilt, and sin. Such individuals are open to encouragement and nurture their intuitive search for meaning in life. Such people, Forster insists, do not accept a "life . . . watered down by good taste,"[50] where the definition of good taste permits only the traditional conservative viewpoint.

Forster has dubbed such watered-down values "Sawstonite," after the fictional town of Sawston in his novels. Inhabiting middle-class villas, the people of his imaginary town represented a blind devotion to order in English society at the expense of individual autonomy and personal belief. Sawstonites felt deeply threatened by those who expressed personal sentiments and original speculations about such established pillars of society as family, education, the role of women, institutional religion, and the commonly accepted moral code of the day. More important than goodness or truth, order for Sawstonites was accomplished by power—social, political, economic, theological. Flouting of the church's moral posture carried with it a potent threat of ecclesiastical and social censure.

Forster's own lack of a sense of sin was undoubtedly rooted in his reliance on his intuition as moral guide rather than the external forces of church and society espoused by the residents of his fictional Sawston. Forster's kind of people were rooted not only in their own intuition and in relation to nature and the land, but they also reached out to touch the spirit within others. The "vulgar and genteel" middle class that based its values on traditional forms of marriage and family life undergirded by money lacked such meaningful connection. Forster's view of improvement strongly suggests Jesus' response in Matthew 7:1–5 to the story of the person ignorant of the plank or "log" blinding his own vision while passing judgment on his neighbor with only a tiny speck in his eye.

Jesus calls such a person a hypocrite, advising that he abstain from judging others and deal with the impediment to his own vision first.

Forster believed in a shared exploration based on equality among those who seek to improve themselves. What is required, he seems to say, is the greatest sensitivity, an acknowledgment of the variety of humanity and human experience, a willingness to try to connect with what cannot be seen. With such a sense of spiritual adventure, "he who is enamoured of improvement will never want to rest in the Lord," in the passive traditional sense in which that phrase was used, but will rather attempt an active direct involvement with the Deity in the journey of personal spiritual growth. "Worldliness" for Forster seems to be shorthand characterizing those in the middle of a spectrum extending from "preaching and threats" at one end to "warmth" at the other. The parables he liked have in common an emphasis on "warmth" in human relationships. "Warmth" suggests an inward search combined with great sensitivity in relationships. A reflective dialogue includes receptive listening among people engaged in a shared effort toward a fuller understanding of Truth. In the biblical accounts Forster refers to a movement away from commonly accepted worldliness toward the inward and outward searching for the spirit of God within each individual. Jesus preferred Mary, the thoughtful sister who wanted to converse, to Martha, the doer, who understandably felt that her efforts to put on a meal for Jesus without Mary's help was an unfair burden. Martha's "worldliness" was absorption in mundane affairs;

Mary focused on matters requiring an eager search of spirit and mind.

The marriage at Cana illustrated Jesus' caring response, this time, as the Bible says, at the urging of his mother, to a human crisis of hospitality when the wine ran out before the end of the wedding festivities at which they were invited guests. It seems likely that Forster would have appreciated the interpretation of Shusaku Endo, a Japanese Christian, that Jesus was even enjoying himself at the wedding: "It is clear from the story of Cana that in mixing socially with others, Jesus by no means wore only a grumpy face. . . . It is worth our while to compare his laughing face putting away the drinks, with the face of John the Baptist, the man . . . haranguing people forever about the wrath of God. This story discovers to us the beaming *joie de vivre* of Jesus." Endo reminds us of John the Baptist's message to the Pharisees and the Sadducees: "You vipers' brood! Who warned you to escape the coming retribution? Then prove your repentance." Jesus' message was, "The time has come; the kingdom of God is upon you; repent and believe in the Gospel,"[51] a message without menace or allusion to a wrathful or vengeful God, but instead a message emphasizing a God of love and compassion. The parable of the withered fig tree seems to represent the denial of that vital quality Forster called the indwelling spirit, without which there can be no meaningful connection with other people, much less with the Unknown. The withered in spirit rely instead on "preaching and threats." While the Jesus of the late Victorian period was usually depicted as somber, unsmiling, remote, and eternally suffering, Forster wanted a life-enhancing god figure who understood human frailties and represented what humanity yearned for in a heavenly example.

Forster was not unique in rejecting the Christianity with which he was indoctrinated at the end of the Victorian period. This phenomenon occurred almost from the beginning of the Christian era, and by the nineteenth century was not uncommon among university students. Forster's father himself rejected Christianity after university but some years later quietly began to attend Sunday services again. Nor was Forster unique in searching to fill the spiritual void. Unlike many who were content simply to remove themselves from religious practices and beliefs, Forster did not reject the idea of God but wanted a more immanent Creator who cared about humanity. From humans Forster wanted a larger sense of awe before God, an acknowledgment of a mysterious God of unimaginably generous attributes. Many of those rejecting Christianity seemed to want some spiritual element in their lives and went around and around a spiritual smorgasbord, sampling the offerings. But Forster embarked on his own search for understanding. In this pursuit he felt he had to rely on his own intellect; he could not accept secondhand someone else's ideas. It could be conjectured that this may explain why he never read G. E. Moore's *Principia Ethica*, though he averred he "was not up to that." Nonetheless, one may presume from Forster's Presidential Address to the Cambridge Humanists that he had discussions with men close to Moore, from which "the seed fell on fertile, if inferior, soil," and he began to think for himself, "that most precious experience of youth which is . . . often discouraged."

Chapter Four

Christian Symbolism in the Early Novels

I n the four novels published between 1905 and 1910, Forster rejected Christianity as practiced at the turn of the twentieth century. He rejected the Victorian dogma then current, but he could not entirely expunge Christian influence from his personal outlook on life. Though in his novels he employed Christian values that had provided so many metaphoric descriptions in Western literature, he frequently redefined them. Those values in tune with his deepest intuition, he employed sympathetically; those he disliked, he exposed with rapier wit.

Sawston Exposed—Where Angels Fear to Tread (1905)[1]

Set partially in Italy, Forster's first novel is steeped in Christian symbolism. The narrative thread of the novel delineates the efforts of English relatives to gain possession of the baby of an English mother who died in childbirth in Italy. Since her death Gino, her Italian husband, has allowed no one but himself to care for the baby. When Caroline Abbott, a friend of the

dead mother, goes to Gino's house to try to talk the young father into giving up his son to her to take back to England to
raise, she bathes the baby properly while Gino watches with
rapt attention. He kneels by the chair she is sitting in, with the
baby on her lap, to observe the process. "So they were when
Philip entered, and saw, to all intents and purposes, the Virgin
and Child, with Donor." (112)

Caroline Abbott and Philip Herriton carry most of the
weight of Forster's philosophy in this novel. Caroline is passing through a crisis of the soul as she begins to move from automatic adherence to Sawstonite social and religious mores
toward an individual autonomy more attuned to her inmost
feelings, knowing full well that flouting conventionality even
in the slightest would carry a heavy cost. Philip is caught in
the net of propriety imposed by his mother, who demands
that he go to Italy and retrieve the child. He feels "he could not
rebel. To the end of his days he would probably go on doing
what she wanted." (69)

Forster introduces the idea of prayer into his first novel. In
the cheerful bustle in the church of Santa Deodata, as the accoutrements of a religious festival are being put away, "in the
midst of this confusion Miss Abbott was praying. . . . It did not
surprise [Philip] . . . that she should greet him naturally, with
none of the sour self-consciousness of a person who had just
risen from her knees. This was indeed the spirit of Santa Deodata's, where a prayer to God is thought none the worse of because it comes next to a pleasant word to a neighbour. 'I am
sure that I need it,' said she; and he, who had expected her to
be ashamed, became confused, and knew not what to reply."

(117–18) Communication with God—at least in Forster's Italy—can go on in the midst of secular life; it does not have to wait until Sunday for expression. Nor is real prayer—from the soul—cause for shame. Philip's experience with prayer has been shaped by the Sunday formalities of the turn-of-the-century Anglican liturgy, not by response to a spontaneous expression of prayer from the heart.

After Gino's baby is killed when the carriage overturns, Philip goes to inform him that the baby, kidnapped by Philip's sister Harriet, is dead. The two men have a ferocious fight. Only Caroline's arrival prevents another death; she forces the men to stop fighting, saying, "What is the good of another death? What is the good of more pain? . . . There is to be no revenge. I will have no more intentional evil. We are not to fight with each other any more." (137–38) As Gino accepts the reality of his son's death, he clings to Miss Abbott, weeping for his loss, in a tableau that echoes Michelangelo's sculptural *Pietà* of the grieving Mary tenderly holding the body of the dead Jesus. Philip is vividly reminded by the anguish in Caroline's eyes of the many Renaissance paintings he has seen of Mary mourning the death of her own son.

Gino's baby son has his own spiritual significance. Any newborn, whether the baby Jesus or an ordinary child, epitomizes love, goodness, hope. The death of Gino's son, surrounded by evil, is the crucifixion of that innocence and love, the cause of his death the hypocrisy of Sawstonite standards. By stealing the child, the straitlaced sister Harriet denies and kills the love and hope that every newborn represents. Philip's

inanition, like that of Pontius Pilate who took no action to release Jesus when he found him blameless, contributes to the
destruction of love, hope, and goodness. Only Caroline senses
a deeper spiritual level in this scene of death and revenge.
When the maid, unaware of the tragedy, comes in with the
baby's milk, Caroline Abbott uses it as the reconciling spiritual
nourishment. In a scene that can only be called a communion
ceremony of forgiveness and atonement, she persuades the
combatants to feed each other the life-restoring milk. Though
in terrible pain from his broken elbow and the ferocious beat-
ing inflicted by Gino, Philip is so moved by Caroline's words
and actions that "there came to him an earnest desire to be
good through the example of this good woman. He would try
henceforward to be worthy of the things she had revealed.
Quietly, without hysterical prayers or banging of drums, he
underwent conversion. He was saved." (139) Caroline Abbott
is a reminder of Forster's longed-for young carpenter who
would smoke a pipe as a comrade on his break time and be
truly kind. In *Howards End* Forster writes, "London is religion's opportunity—not the decorous religion of theologians,
but anthropomorphic, crude." (107) Forster wanted a genu-
inely caring god with a human face, not a stern-faced judge.
He wanted a Jesus who would attract followers by his actions
rather than didactics and who would inspire humans to try to
emulate his example.

The final scene of *Where Angels Fear to Tread*, in the train
as Philip and Caroline leave Italy for the last time, conveys its
Christian symbolism more subtly. Philip is on the verge of proposing marriage to Caroline when she confesses to him, the

only person she can trust with her deepest feelings, that she is passionately and secretly in love with Gino, even though she recognizes she will never see him again: "I love him, and I'm going to Sawston, and if I mayn't speak about him to you sometimes, I shall die." (146) With his dream of marriage shattering about him, Philip is able "to think not of himself but of her." (146) He will sacrifice his own wishes for her good, sublimate his desires to her need. "He could even be glad that she had once held the beloved in her arms." (147) His self-denying love, of which she knew nothing—she thought it was just kindness—was a dearly-bought gift that "made her life endurable." (148)

That Philip's self-abnegation is both sacramental and intentional, Forster made clear in a letter to R. C. Trevelyan: "P. is a person who has scarcely ever felt the physical forces that are banging about in the world, and he couldn't get [become] good and understand by spiritual suffering alone. Bodily punishment, however unjust superficially, was necessary too: in fact the scene—to use a heavy word, and one that I have only just thought of—was sacramental." That Forster "only just thought of" the religious significance of the scene can be taken as evidence that his natural spiritual dimension unconsciously colored all aspects of his life and work. In his letter, Forster explains,

> The object of the book is the improvement of Philip, and I did really want the improvement to be a surprise. Therefore in chapters 1–2 I never

hinted at the possibility but at the same time did not demonstrate the impossibility, or did not mean to. In ch. 5 he has got into a mess, through trying to live only by a sense of humour and by a sense of the beautiful. The knowledge of the mess embitters him, and this is the improvement's beginning. From that time I exhibit new pieces of him—pieces that he did not know of, or at all events had never used. He grows large enough to appreciate Miss Abbott, and in the final scene he exceeds her.

All this is what I intended.[2]

In this novel Forster draws freely on religious practices as well as on identifiable Christian beliefs in prayer, communion, conversion, reconciliation, atonement, forgiveness, sin, love, salvation, self-sacrifice, but in ways radically different from traditional Anglican Christianity. For example, three times in his letter to Trevelyan, Forster refers to "improvement," his word and his personal definition of what at that time traditional Christians called "salvation." In his hands traditional principles are given new life. He uses such words as "conversion" and "saved" in the same context as the Victorian rector would use them, but with a different goal, not strict adherence to Anglican doctrine, but a larger dimension. Philip is "saved" by Caroline Abbott's example of unself-conscious prayer, her inclusive love of people, her urgent desire to heal dissension, and her refusal to accept hatred as a justification for bloodshed. She would dampen the fires of violence, creating an atmosphere that would lead enemies to make peace and extend to one another forgiveness and love and acceptance in an undogmatic way. In Forster's usage, "saved" means being freed from the human failure of *agape* love as Christ exemplified it— an unconditional, altruistic love, manifesting equal respect for all human beings—rather than "saved" from some theological definition of sin. Forster's definitions are more expansive, more enveloping of both human shortcomings and human potentiality—and simultaneously more demanding and more forgiving.

In the final scene of the novel, Philip has finally connected, from the heart, with a self-denial that must have cost him dearly. The actions of both Caroline and Philip are not driven by traditional religious teachings but unconsciously reflect Christ's example in a modern, human muddle desperately in need of the reconciliation and atonement that, in this case, only a personal sacrifice could provide.

Forster himself knew the sacrifice of self-denying love; he had learned it through his friendship with Syed Ross Masood, a handsome Muslim Indian at Oxford, who failed to respond to Forster's declaration of love for him. In *The Longest Journey* Forster depicts a similar renunciation. Rickie Elliot, who married Agnes some time after her fiancé, Gerald, died suddenly on the playing field, felt that "love desired not ownership but confidence and to a love so pure it does not seem terrible to come second." (68) Self-abnegation for the good of another or because the other could not reciprocate with equal passion was a constant theme in Forster's life.

"The Soul Has Her Own Currency"—The Longest Journey *(1907)*[3]

In Forster's second novel the focus of his antipathy shifts to English public-school education, with a few sharp sideswipes at religious attitudes. Herbert Pembroke had contemplated taking orders in the Church of England sometime after graduating from Cambridge University but had not yet got around to it. He was a housemaster at Sawston School, "and his adherence to the Church of England [was] no mere matter of form." (165) Yet "for all his fine talk about a spiritual life he had but one test for things—success: success for the body in this life or for the soul in the life to come." (166) Rickie Elliot's aunt, Mrs. Failing, was even more nonchalant about the church. She was modeled on Forster's Uncle William Howley Forster, whom he regarded as the epitome of philistinism. Mrs. Failing's appearance at church in her ordinary clothes and without a hat—her head covered only by a shawl—was intentionally insulting, as was her habitually tardy arrival. During the sermon she analyzed the dress and character of the members of the congregation and sneered at what she considered the vicar's smugness. Her supercilious patronage of the religious scene did not go unnoticed, even by the simplest of her tenants, who considered her an amusing palliative to the weekly religious ritual. (122–23) Mrs. Failing was rejecting not only the letter of the law as interpreted by institutional Christianity but, more gravely, also the spirit of universal Love as described in the New Testament.

In chapter twenty-eight, less than a page long, in which Forster philosophizes about the soul, some impressionistic outlines appear of his emerging spiritual dimensions, encompassing both the joys of earth and the promise—and what he was conditioned to see as the price—of heaven:

> The soul has her own currency. She mints her spiritual coinage and stamps it with the image of some beloved face. . . . But the soul can also have her bankruptcies.
>
> Perhaps she will be the richer in the end. . . . The face, however beloved, was mortal, and as liable as the soul herself to err. . . .
>
> There is, indeed, another coinage that bears on it not man's image but God's. It is incorruptible, and the soul may trust it safely; it will serve her beyond the stars. But it cannot give us friends, or the embrace of a lover, or the touch of children, for with our fellow-mortals it has no concern. It cannot even give the joys we call trivial— fine weather, the pleasures of meat and drink, bathing and the hot sand afterwards, running, dreamless sleep.

> Have we learnt the true discipline of a
> bankruptcy if we turn to such coinage
> as this? Will it really profit us so much
> if we save our souls and lose the whole
> world? (273)

The last sentence is an inversion of Luke 9:25, "For what does it profit a man if he gains the whole world and loses or forfeits himself?" In this poignant passage Forster records the crippling schism between the soul and the senses so long preached by the Christian church and points out the separation between worldly concerns and a spiritual life that would reject mundane matters, whether pleasant or dutiful. He cannot reconcile the joys of human life with the stern and judgmental God so commonly portrayed in the early years of the twentieth century by the Christian emphasis at that time on sin and pain. Forster recoils from the idea that the pleasures of life are not an acceptable part of Christian belief, and he questions whether Christianity has adequately considered the human cost of this long-established dogma.

Still, the penultimate chapter of *The Longest Journey* returns again to the most powerful and central Christian symbolism: Rickie Elliot sacrifices his own life to save that of his half-brother, Stephen Wonham. In a yet more direct and deeper identification of Rickie with Christ's agony in the Garden of Gethsemane the night before the Crucifixion, Forster has Rickie praying "passionately," all the time feeling that "God was beyond . . . how far beyond, and to be reached after

what degradation!" (282), echoing Jesus' sense of abandon-
ment.

In the final chapter, some years after Rickie's death, in the
dispute between Stephen and Herbert Pembroke, Forster suggests new spiritual values as he contrasts Herbert, now a
Church of England clergyman, with Stephen whose life—like
Rickie's—is intuitively based on love and respect for others—
for example, for Rickie and his creativity; for Ansell, Rickie's
intellectual friend from Cambridge days; for his own little
daughter; and also for himself. Stephen's respect extends to
the land and the people who till it. Forster contrasts Stephen's
lack of greed and his financial and spiritual honesty, his
thoughtful stewardship of the land, his true respect for
Rickie's creative gift, and his actions as a nurturing father with
the dogmatic responses of Herbert, who represents the established church and the unexamined Sawstonite values of Family Pride, Property, and Propriety.

"Deities Reconciled"—A Room with a View *(1908)*[4]

Forster fully articulates his personal spiritual philosophy in
his third novel. Though Lucy Honeychurch is the putative her-
oine and George Emerson the man she finally marries,
George's father, Mr. Emerson, is the heroic character of *A
Room with a View*. He manages to annoy the custom-bound
Sawstonites with his rough-cut spontaneous kindnesses,
which lack the suavity and convoluted diplomacy of those
who consider themselves genteel and to whom any display of
emotion is unladylike and ungentlemanly. They agree among

themselves that Mr. Emerson is "vulgar," by which they mean unrefined and indelicately direct; he lacks what they prize—the extreme reticence of the middle class. Yet Lucy intuitively defends him until her chaperone and cousin Charlotte Bartlett informs her that he is acceptable only as an acquaintance because of his lack of social graces and his lowly social standing, whereupon Lucy halfheartedly attempts to conform to polite society's expectations of her.[5]

When Forster says unequivocally that "Mr. Emerson was profoundly religious" (199), and Lucy, in her muddled despair, thought he had "the face of a saint who understood" (204), what does the author mean? Mr. Emerson had refused to have George baptized because he wanted him to be "free from all the superstition and ignorance that lead men to hate one another in the name of God." (25) George says about his father that "he is kind to people because he loves them." (24) Overhearing that one of the Miss Alans likes violets, he gathers an extravagant quantity of the wild flowers to fill her room. Her comment is, "So ungentlemanly and yet so beautiful." (114) Again it is one of the Miss Alans who remarks that "he is not tactful, yet have you noticed that there are people who do things which are most indelicate [such as offering to swap rooms with Lucy and her chaperone who lacked a view], and yet at the same time—beautiful?" (10)

Joined to kindness, active thoughtfulness, and sensitivity is Truth. In the Reverend Mr. Beebe's view of human character, Mr. Emerson "has the merit—if it is one—of saying exactly what he means. . . . It is so difficult—at least, I find it difficult—to understand people who speak the truth." (7) Mr. Emerson would have each one discover Truth, disdaining the predigested opinions dispensed by others like communion wafers, whether the subject be Giotto or Love. To Lucy, who depends on a guide to life as much as she needs her Baedeker to tell her what is important in the cathedral, Mr. Emerson's advice is to "pull out from the depths those thoughts that you do not understand, and spread them out in the sunlight and know the meaning of them." (26) To do this requires courage. Counseling Lucy in her desperation at the muddle she had made of her life, Mr. Emerson tells her that "we fight for more than Love or Pleasure: there is Truth. Truth counts, Truth does count." (204) Not only Truth but Love also counts. The driver of one of the carriages taking the English party to a scenic view overlooking Florence wants his sweetheart to accompany him. Unbeknownst to Mr. Eager, a particularly narrow-minded and obdurate clergyman, they sit on the driver's seat, personified by Forster as a Greek god and goddess, the driver with his arms around his sweetheart's waist while managing the horses. These young lovers are forced to part over strenuous objections by Mr. Emerson, whose definition of life is energized by Love: "We know that we come from the winds, and that we shall return to them; that all life is perhaps a knot, a tangle, a blemish in the eternal smoothness. But why should this make us unhappy? Let us rather love one another, and work and rejoice. I don't believe in this world-sorrow." (26–27)

Love also includes physical love, and Mr. Emerson declares that "we shall enter [the Garden of Eden] when we no longer despise our bodies." (126) At the climax of the novel, when Mr.

Emerson pleads his son's case for marriage with Lucy, he succeeds in releasing her from the sexual repression imposed on young ladies of the Victorian era. Speaking of his son he says, "I taught him . . . to trust in love. I said: 'When love comes, that is reality.' I said: 'Passion does not blind. No. Passion is sanity,'" (196) and she realizes that "he had robbed the body of its taint, the world's taunts of their sting; he had shown her the holiness of direct desire." (204) Mr. Emerson succeeds in rescuing her from her muddle and saving his son, too, about whom he has been desperately worried. He recognizes the sanctity of the human soul: "We have souls. I cannot say how they came nor whither they go, but we have them, and I see you are ruining yours." (202) He scolds Lucy: "You can transmute love, ignore it, muddle it, but you can never pull it out of you." (202) In after years she would say that she "never exactly understood . . . how he managed to strengthen her. It was as if he had made her see the whole of everything at once." (204) And "he gave her a sense of deities reconciled." (204)

The next-to-the-last chapters of Forster's four early novels are crucial to the action of each narrative, while the final chapters encapsulate vividly his dream of the Ideal. Chapter 19 of *A Room with a View* is a succinct statement of Forster's spiritual beliefs, a sermon delivered in Mr. Emerson's words. The scripture of the sermon is an all-pervasive love of humanity, an acceptance of people unadulterated by considerations of class, race, gender, or financial worth. From this arises a natural kindness, expressed directly, without subterfuge, the goal of which is happiness. Truth, too, is essential in Forster's spiritual world. Discovering Truth, Forster says, means digging deeply into one's soul. Having once uncovered Truth, one must unflinchingly acknowledge it and act upon it, knowing that doing so may lead to estrangement from society, maybe even from members of one's family. Both the exploration and the possible consequences require spiritual courage and a willingness to uphold an individual, and possibly lonely, position against accepted social dogma. Love is equally fundamental. To the inhibited Sawstonite the physical expression of sexual love was an embarrassment, contradicting the strict control over one's emotions required by English society. Women particularly had been taught to regard physical passion and pleasure as "dirty" and disgusting; men frequently were furtive about the possibility of frank sexual pleasure with their wives. But to Forster the sexual expression of Love was as important in his definition of the human soul and its spiritual dimensions as was the more abstract, generalized *agape* love. In Forster's fourth novel, *Howards End*, Margaret Schlegel wonders about her sister Helen: "Had she ever loved in the noblest way, where man and woman, having lost themselves in sex, desire to lose sex itself in comradeship?" (*HE* 309) In *A Room with a View*, Mr. Emerson, counseling the muddled Lucy, emphasizes the role of the spiritual ingredient in physical love, saying that "love is of the body; not the body, but of the body." (202)

The deeper significance of this penultimate chapter lies in the reversal of roles between the unorthodox Mr. Emerson and the ordained Reverend Mr. Beebe. Quite unconsciously Mr. Emerson has captured the high ground both physically and spiritually. While Mr. Beebe, representing the institutional practices of the Church of England, conducts his Friday service in the church for a congregation of three elderly ladies, Mr. Emerson—*in Mr. Beebe's study*—assumes the pastoral role of counselor and shepherd to a badly bewildered Lucy, meeting her very human, but very spiritual, needs with his solid advice about Truth and Love. The salvation of humanity, Forster seems to be saying, will be found in acknowledging the spiritual thirst of the human soul and trying to slake it, not in a mechanical reiteration of dogma that is unchallenged to show relevance to life's situations. Though the journey may include painful Truth, it promises liberating Truth: In Mr. Emerson's words, "by the side of the everlasting Why there is a Yes—a transitory Yes if you like, but a Yes." (27)

"Building the Rainbow Bridge"—Howards End *(1910)* [6]

The whole of *Howards End* is a disguised sermon, not a Victorian sermon but a modern one, the kind that not only explicates the text, enlarging the understanding of biblical history, but also points to ways of applying new religious insights to daily life. *Howards End* presents the clearest view so far of Forster's personal philosophy in narrative form. When Forster is "preaching" in the authorial voice, he frequently phrases his "sermon" in the plural "we" rather than in the accusatory "you," thereby identifying himself with blindly stumbling humanity; he abjures preaching *at* his readers in favor of discussing the subject *with* them. Emphasizing Forster's technique, one critic has described it as "author-and-audience collaboration"; author and readers are described as being "together in diffident bewilderment, confusion, mixed response, sentimentality, true belief."[7]

There are no clergymen in the cast of characters in *Howards End.* Absent also are visible Christian symbols such as communion or self-sacrifice for the good of others. Almost as an aside, Forster tells us that the first Mrs. Wilcox, a Quaker, wanted more spiritual substance in Sunday sermons, not for herself but for her children, while Mr. Wilcox was raised a Dissenter but as a successful businessman switched to the Church of England, needing the church only for ceremonial occasions—his daughter's wedding, Mrs. Wilcox's funeral. But in *Howards End* Forster makes abundantly clear the urgency of the individual's search for the meaning of the human spirit and its connection to the mystery of the Unknowable.

More than ten years after Forster declared at university his independence from organized religion, he had finally found his personal spiritual voice, freeing his novels—and himself—from reliance on traditional Christian symbolism. By the time *Howards End* was published, when Forster was just thirty-one years old, he had succeeded in developing his own authentic spiritual stance and in creating characters motivated by that position. He has invested daily existence with the possibility of illumination by that spark of divinity that he believes exists in the soul of every human being. He has intuitively tapped into a spiritual source that blossomed in the earliest days of Christianity, shaping the daily actions of the first Christians. The theological underpinnings for the present-day Christian social gospel point back to early Christian beliefs in respect and love for all people, freedom of conscience, communal sharing of resources as well as personal joys and sorrows, good stewardship of one's unique gifts, and a direct and humble connection by the individual with the mysterious Unknown. But Forster had no desire to proselytize; what influence he had—and over his lifetime it was considerable—was indirect and offered in his writings. In Peter Burra's words, "he has ideas. . . . He is an artist on the fringe of social reform. He is interested in causes. He has never cut himself off . . . from the political and economic questions of the outer world."[8] By 1910, when *Howards End* was published, these attributes of Christian social responsibility had become integrated into Forster's response to daily life, though he never would have labeled them "Christian." No longer self-conscious responses to situations, they had become his automatic reactions to life.

As the voice of Forster's philosophy, Margaret Schlegel speaks the important words in *Howards End,* but her philosophical roots appear earlier, when the author creates a genre of character that I call the "noble peasant,"[9] which describes a natural nobility of spirit in an individual not necessarily well educated but deeply rooted physically in the soil and equally grounded psychologically in his or her deepest intuitive feelings. The philosopher Immanuel Kant defines naïveté in fiction as "an eruption of sincerity that was natural to humanity and which is opposed to the art of dissimulation ... an uncorrupted, innocent nature, which we did not expect to find displayed ... by someone who has no intention of doing so."[10] In *Howards End*, speaking in the authorial voice, Forster says of such people, "That they were men of the finest type only the sentimentalist can declare. ... They are England's hope. ... Half clodhopper, half board-school prig, they can still throw back to a nobler stock, and breed yeomen." (320) Here Forster is predicting the union of the noble peasant and the intellectual in some form with roots in "a noble stock" and hope of well-educated progeny who, as landowners, would be yeomen, a step below gentlemen (Foster was never impressed by gentlemen) and appreciated for their integrity and thoughtful leadership in their community.

The anthropomorphic and crude extolled by Forster exemplify a way of life that could accept the direct expression of human nature uncontaminated by external social and religious strictures antithetical to the true soul of the noble peasant. The noble peasant might very well be provoked to violence, but he is not wantonly cruel. He may express raw feelings of vengeance at unjustified injury; equally, he may show rough-and-ready brotherly love, and even a generous acceptance of differences, and a principled expression of unselfish help when least expected.

In *Where Angels Fear to Tread* Gino's reaction to Philip ran the gamut from humorous male horseplay early in their relationship, to overflowing rough-and-tumble affection when Gino and his friends haul Philip up into their box at the

local opera performance, through the ferocious struggle between them when Gino's emotions at the news of the death of
his son carry him perilously close to murder, to his warm-
hearted help some time later during Philip's entanglement
with the Italian legal authorities over the baby's death. They
part fast friends, though never to meet again. Gino's actions
spring from his nature undefiled by Sawstonite repression of
emotions (though it must be noted that he possessed the restrictive Italian attitudes of the times about women, particularly his wife). In a conversation published in 1957, the inter-
viewer, an English novelist and critic, taxed Forster with "an
aspect of your work of which I'm more critical. I mean the idea
of a free natural pagan way of living which might almost be
said to be Man before the Fall. Perhaps, the Mediterranean is
the seat of this Paradise?' Forster replied, 'I let down lightly
those with instinctive moral feeling. . . . And as to the Italians.
Yes. There is a graciousness that leads to grace.'"[11]

Stephen Wonham, carrying on the line of the noble peasant in *The Longest Journey*, remained one of Forster's favorite
characters, possessing that instinctive moral feeling refined
by exposure to Truth and Beauty through his relations with
Rickie and, to a lesser degree, with Ansell. Mr. Emerson, Mrs.
Wilcox, and Mrs. Moore, whom K. W. Gransden sees in the role
of "guardians,"[12] as well as Margaret Schlegel, possess the
qualities of the noble peasant, though with an educated self-
awareness and sensitivity toward others that becomes more
pronounced with each subsequent novel. A natural connection with the land was becoming more problematic under the

relentless pressure of industrialization, the spreading metrop-
olis ever encroaching on the rural past, the growing stain of
new red-brick villas obliterating the greensward with eager
development. Margaret Schlegel had to learn the secrets of
the noble peasant's nature, self-consciously overcoming the
separation from the soil that resulted from her cosmopolitan
upbringing and her family's emphasis on intellectual, rather
than physical, ability. Encouraged by her father to think and
to feel, at last—through the house and old Miss Avery—she
recognized and claimed her dormant roots in the soil and history. Through Margaret, Forster is indirectly expressing his
belief that even educated people who have lost their physical
roots in the land and who are in danger of losing the inner
connection with their natural intuition, could, with effort, rediscover their intuitive moral compass and claim an honest, if
self-conscious, link with the land.

In their first substantive conversation Margaret Schlegel
and Mrs. Wilcox touch on the lessons that age and experience
can bring to an individual's life. Divining Mrs. Wilcox's barely
articulated thoughts, Margaret says,

> "To be humble and kind, to go straight
> ahead, to love people rather than pity
> them, to remember the submerged—
> well, one can't do all these things at
> once, worse luck, because they're so
> contradictory. It's then that proportion
> comes in—to live by proportion. Don't
> *begin* with proportion. Only prigs do

> that. Let proportion come in as a last re-
> source, when the better things have
> failed, and a deadlock—gracious me, I've
> started preaching!" "Indeed, you put the
> difficulties of life splendidly," said Mrs.
> Wilcox. . . . "It is just what I should have
> liked to say about them myself." (70)

To lift this quotation from its setting in the narrative flow does make Margaret's pronouncements seem preachy. But in the novel as a story, such philosophic statements are as natural and seemingly unremarkable as the fruit in a Christmas plum pudding, giving texture and savor to the narrative. Only re-peated readings bring them into focus as an articulated phi-losophy of life.

The potential influence of the divine on the mundane is given numerous readings in *Howards End.* Shopping for Christmas, then as now, is a clear example of the clash of the material and the spiritual:

> Margaret . . . felt the grotesque impact of
> the unseen upon the seen, and saw issu-
> ing from a forgotten manger at Bethle-
> hem this torrent of coins and toys. Vul-
> garity reigned. . . . How many of these
> vacillating shoppers and tired shop-as-
> sistants realized that it was a divine
> event that drew them together? . . . She
> was not a Christian in the accepted
> sense; she did not believe that God had

ever worked among us as a young arti-
san. These people ... believed it, and, if
pressed, would affirm it in words. . . . But
in public who shall express the unseen
adequately? It is private life that holds
out the mirror to infinity; personal intercourse ... alone, that ever hints at a
personality beyond our daily vision. (79)

Clearly, for Forster, the beginning of true spiritual expression
lies in the individual's yearnings, in honest connections with
other people, and in searching for deeper meanings.

Early in the novel Margaret advises her sister Helen,
"Don't brood too much ... on the superiority of the unseen to
the seen. It's true, but to brood on it is medieval. Our business
is not to contrast the two, but to reconcile them." (101–2) At
the end of the novel, after the vicissitudes that accompanied
Margaret's marriage to Henry Wilcox, and their emergence
into a new pattern of life and relationships, Margaret acknowledges that "no doubt I have done a little towards straightening
the tangle, but things that I can't phrase have helped me."
(337)

Awe before the inexplicable Mystery is fundamental in
Forster's spiritual profile. One way in which it can be expressed is through nature. In Helen and their father the love
of place was intuitive. Leonard Bast "was groping after it,"
driven by his genetic and spiritual inheritance as "the third
generation, grandson to the shepherd or ploughboy whom
civilization had sucked into the town." (113) Having been

brought up entirely in a town, without the direct memory of a visceral relationship with the land that his grandfather had had, Leonard goes on a nocturnal ramble through the outskirts of London, trying instinctively to recapture that historical connection with nature. The lesson of the more cerebral Margaret about the importance of place and roots in external nature comes through exposure to the house called Howards End: "An unexpected love of the island awoke in her, connecting on this side with the joys of the flesh, on that with the inconceivable. . . . It had been hidden from Margaret till this afternoon. It had certainly come through the house and old Miss Avery." (202) Perhaps underscoring his idea of spiritual inheritance, Forster stresses the importance of *through* the house and old Miss Avery: "Through them: the notion of 'through' persisted; her mind trembled towards a conclusion which only the unwise have put into words." (202) At a further depth in this rather enigmatic comment lies Forster's belief that each individual has the potential of combining the spiritual with what is natural and human—delight in "the joys of the flesh." Margaret moves beyond both Helen and Leonard as she consciously considers the link between the purely physical and the purely spiritual that her newly recognized connection with the earth provides to her.

In Forster's spiritual lexicon, "only connect . . ." points simultaneously in two directions. Inner spirituality will endow all of external daily life with depth and love, while the secular part of existence will nudge the spiritual element in humankind from abstract thought toward practical expression. As different as are Margaret and her husband, Henry Wilcox, she hopes to

> be able to help him to the building of the rainbow bridge that should connect the prose in us with the passion. Without it we are meaningless fragments, half monks, half beasts, unconnected arches that have never joined into a man. With it love is born, and alights on the highest curve, glowing against the grey, sober against the fire. Happy the man who sees from either aspect the glory of these outspread wings. The roads of his soul lie clear, and he and his friends shall find easy going.
>
> ... Only connect! That was the whole of her sermon. Only connect the prose and the passion, and both will be exalted, and human love will be seen at its highest. Live in fragments no longer. Only connect, and the beast and the monk, robbed of the isolation that is life to either will die. (183–84)

Prose and passion, beast and monk are paired to illustrate a fateful lack of connection. There are other dichotomies: "The business man who assumes that this life is every thing, and the mystic who asserts that it is nothing, fail, on this side and on that, to hit the truth. ... Truth, being alive, was not halfway between anything. It was only to be found by continuous excursions into either realm, and, though proportion is the final secret, to espouse it at the outset is to insure sterility." (192) "Prose" refers to the dailiness, the grayness of a life lived in isolated fragments. Monks and mystics might be inclined to count daily life as nothing if it is not solely dedicated to religious practice. "Beasts" are those who have suppressed their instinctive emotions, measuring life only in terms of financial or social success. Businessmen like Henry Wilcox clearly fall into this category, deliberately denying the importance of an inner life, of intuition, and of roots in history or place. They have extinguished—or at best failed to find—the vital soul buried somewhere within; overburdened with the prosiness of existence, they have not found the freedom of spirit that a passionate appreciation of life can bestow. They are fragments to whom physical existence and satisfaction of their personal wishes is everything; they recognize no unseen element, nothing beyond themselves. Unlike monks and mystics, who would ignore everything about their existence that did not directly contribute to religious devotions, Forster urges humanity to embrace the spiritual and connect it with the mundane, making continuous excursions into both realms, to eradicate the false barriers between these realms, these arches, with a love that enfolds both in its wings and carries the human spirit to exalted levels of experience.

Forster's trinity consists of Earth, Humanity, and the Unknowable. In his philosophy each human being has the power of reconciling the mundane and the Infinite in daily life. No sharper contrast with this reverent spirituality can be imagined than the trinity that Victorian English society venerated—the trinity of Family Pride, Property, and Propriety. Its raison d'être was Marriage, which requires lawyers to "tidy up Property and Propriety, reassure Theology and Family Pride." (173) With marriage, Family Pride withdraws into itself as into a fortress and hides from other people behind its ramparts. All thought is concentrated on the realization of its primary desires: How the family appears to society is what counts. Personal worth is usually expressed in economic terms, Property being the important definition. Commenting on this symbiosis, Forster, as he often does, includes himself in an authorial aside. "The feudal ownership of land did bring dignity," he writes, "whereas the modern ownership of movables is reducing us again to a nomadic horde. We are reverting to the civilization of luggage, and historians of the future will note how the middle classes accreted possessions without taking root in the earth, and may find in this the secret of their imaginative poverty." (146) The lack of a sense of roots infects all other aspects of life, Forster says, while the mere possession of things does not compensate the soul for the loss of roots and its source of inspiration. As an example of a civilization of luggage and motor cars, Mr. Wilcox changes residences with no more concern than he changes his attire as the seasons come and go. And he merely skates on the surface of the human group wherever he finds himself; he does not wish to be subsumed into the community where he is living at the moment.

To those who lived by Sawston's rules, personal worth was validated only as reflected in others' eyes. Success was the goal. In a conversation with Philip Herriton in *Where Angels Fear to Tread*, Caroline Abbott described the result as "petty unselfishness." Thinking she had misstated the phrase, Philip corrected her, but she insisted on petty unselfishness: "I had got an idea that every one here spent their lives in making little sacrifices for objects they didn't care for, to please people they didn't love; that they never learnt to be sincere—and, what's as bad, never learnt how to enjoy themselves." (60) Rejection by others was to be feared above all else; only subscription to the common social code promised the comfort of "belonging," though the intangible price to the individual soul would inevitably be enormous. Ostensibly cheerful, reliable, and brave, Henry Wilcox epitomized the meaningless fragments, the unconnected arches, the lack of sincerity, but underneath this facade "all had reverted to chaos. . . . He had always the sneaking belief that bodily passion is bad. . . . Religion had confirmed him [in this attitude]. . . . He could not be as the saints and love the Infinite with a seraphic ardour, but he could be a little ashamed of loving a wife." (183) After the argument that seemed to make their separation inevitable, Margaret conjectured that "he would soon present a healthy mind to the world again, and what did he or the world care if he was rotten at the core? He would grow into a rich, jolly old man . . . sentimental about women. . . . Tenacious of power, he would keep Charles and the rest dependent, and retire from business reluctantly." (329) Margaret assumed they would meet after death: "An eternal future had always seemed natural to her. And Henry believed in it for himself." (334) But she doubted that they would occupy the same level in the hereafter.

Henry's life mirrors a Sawstonite denial of Forster's personal dream of the all-embracing inclusiveness of nature, humanity, and the divine at work in all aspects of life. The static code of Sawstonite morality denies the thoughtful consideration of right and wrong in each situation: "Morality can tell us that murder is worse than stealing, and group most sins in an order all must approve, but it cannot group [individuals]. The surer its pronouncements on this point, the surer may we be that morality is not speaking. Christ was evasive when they questioned Him. It is those that cannot connect who hasten to cast the first stone." (309) True morality will look closely at each situation; those who are blinded to the individuality of people are the quickest to condemn others.

Forster would have people actively connect in three dimensions and celebrate "the wonders, physical and spiritual, by which we are surrounded."[13] The basic connection is upward toward the sublime Unknowable. In *The Longest Journey* he employed Demeter, the Greek goddess of the earth, to represent nurturing and protecting love and compassion for human beings. His choosing a goddess from the Greek pantheon is not surprising; Forster had read classics at Cambridge. His lifelong friendship began there with Goldsworthy Lowes Dickinson, a Fellow whose small volume, *The Greek View of Life*, first published in 1896, has been kept in print through most of the twentieth century. The Greek emphasis on beauty, both aesthetic and physical, and the ideal of "a beautiful soul, housed in a beautiful body"[14] must have appealed strongly to

Forster, as did the acceptance of passionate friendship between young men. Ideally, life was "a work of art shaped by
the man who [lived] it,"[15] the basis for which was a man's mas-
tery over himself. Lowes Dickinson saw the most ancient
Greek relationship between men and gods as external and mechanical, a contractual relationship in which there was little
mystery or inner speculation. "The conception [was] legal, not
moral nor spiritual; it [had] nothing to do with what we call
sin and conscience."[16] The gods were not considered superior
to man in spiritual or moral ways but rather in human attributes such as strength or beauty.

The statue of Demeter, guardian of agriculture and pro-
ductive nature, which Forster often visited in the British Museum, was the subject of a picture that in *The Longest Journey*
languished in Mrs. Failing's drawing room at Cadover. When
she became tired of it, Stephen Wonham appropriated it for
his quarters in the attic. Later it was the only memento in his
own home tied to his earlier life. His little daughter rever-
enced it as much as he did and affectionately said "Good night"
to the "stone lady" when she said her nightly prayers. (288)
Demeter also symbolized the continuing cycle of life and death
and rebirth. About Demeter Forster felt that "to her, all over
the world, rise prayers of idolatry from suffering men as well
as suffering women, for she has transcended sex." Demeter
continued to "touch the heart of today." Her compassion for
suffering humanity gave her, in Forster's eyes, "true immortality."[17]

Besides representing the ancient idea of the Great Mother/Earth Goddess, Forster saw Demeter as androgynous, going beyond sex to companionship, equally appealing to men and women as an object of veneration and spiritual comfort. Severely subdued by English tradition and education, the expression of emotions was considered a defect in the male character, but Forster seemed unafraid of what some might term the "female" side of the male personality. He believed that the assurance of unequivocal friendship and compassion would be likely to inspire struggling humanity's aspirations toward the Unseen. Demeter might be viewed as a female manifestation of the approachable "young carpenter who would smoke a pipe" with a workman in his break time "and be most frightfully kind." In contrast, Forster found puzzling the figures in Renaissance paintings based on biblical texts or symbolism: "They're much farther off than the Demeter of Cnidus, who's made of flesh like ourselves, though of nobler texture. These never have lived: they don't think or have desires. Yet it's difficult to explain their power if they are only a beautiful concourse of lines."[18] But he found in the Virgin Mary an understanding of suffering humanity like that of Demeter. In his address to the Humanists, he explains his feelings: "Looking at the complications and omissions of the Christ Figure, I understand why in the Middle Ages Christendom turned to the Virgin Mary. The mother gave birth to the child, saw him grow up and saw him killed. Here is something immediately comprehensible to which we can accord heartfelt pity, and the fact that Mary seldom said or did anything notable on her own account only makes her the better medium between mankind and the incomprehensible. Her seven sorrows were her own, anyhow until the theologians got hold of her, and they were not entangled with the notion of atonement."

Forster's second dimension of connection is inward—understanding that a touch of the divine Spirit is within each individual and gathering the courage to try to identify the components of such a gift and use them wisely. Forster identifies intuition and the emotions as priceless gifts bestowed freely on all human beings. He sees them as guides to learning to know the Self and to honesty in living. Forster would not deny the existence of primitive emotions such as gripped Gino on hearing of the death of his son. Rather, he saw that the first step toward controlling this kind of emotion lies in acknowledging its existence. Rickie in *The Longest Journey* is a good example of the dire consequences of denying the leadership of his intuition—in his case because he falls in love with romantic Love and is misled away from his deepest intuitive feelings. Lucy, in *A Room with a View*, succeeds in dreadfully muddling her life and the lives of several others because she has denied her own intuition in favor of acceding to Sawston's social code before she finally is freed by Mr. Emerson's private sermon to follow the truth of her heart. Forster blames the failure to develop the inward connection on the English public-school education when he writes that "it is not that the Englishman can't feel—it is that he is afraid to feel. He has been taught at his public school that feeling is bad form. . . . He must bottle up his emotions, or let them out only on a very special occasion." Public schools produce young men who "go forth . . . with well-developed bodies, fairly developed minds, and undeveloped hearts."[19]

The third dimension is outward toward other people. In addition to his coterie of English friends that grew from his King's College years at Cambridge, Forster became a dependable friend to many Indian students at Cambridge and Oxford, first through Syed Ross Masood and later because of his reputation as the author of *A Passage to India.* Forster's friendship was not given lightly, neither was it withdrawn casually. This kind of devotion to friends might be called "athletic love"[20] because it was constant rather than intermittent, not casual, but firm. The most interesting example—because it is directed to a woman for her own sake—of Forster's reaching out in devoted friendship that lasted a lifetime is to Florence Barger, wife of a King's College classmate. From World War I days Forster shared with Mrs. Barger intimate thoughts he revealed to no other person, not even to her husband, with whom he was also friendly. During World War II Forster and his mother took Mrs. Barger into their home when hers was destroyed by bombs. This friendship lasted until her death, its importance attested to by the existence of a large body of correspondence between them. A more obvious example was May Buckingham. Tempestuous though Forster's relationship was at first with May Hockey, who married Bob Buckingham, the object of Forster's own affections, over time he and May became firm friends. When she fell ill with tuberculosis and had to spend a year in a sanitarium, Forster visited her frequently. Between visits he wrote or sent books to read. Later he concerned himself with her concerns about her child and her husband. The Buckinghams' son was given the name of Robin Morgan (Forster was known to his friends by his middle name, Morgan), and as doting godfather to the child, he shared their joys over Robin's life and grief at his early death.

He took infinite pains with his friends, and when he felt he had made a mistake and wished to distance himself from a relationship, he agonized over how to do it without hurting the other person's feelings. Over time, as his novels brought him income, Forster would send money anonymously to struggling writers trying to break into print. He might direct books to them for review. His monetary gifts were always large enough to be understood as gifts; when a loan was requested, on the other hand, he expected to be repaid. Toward the end of his life, Forster gave the Buckinghams £10,000 in appreciation for the friendship and love the three of them had shared through so many years.

In his novels his more heroic characters hold similar beliefs about friends. Rickie Elliot in *The Longest Journey* agonizes over whether and how to give money to Gerald and Agnes when they are faced with a long engagement before Gerald should be able to support a wife. To Mr. Emerson in *A Room with a View,* kindness is as natural as breathing, while in *Howards End* Margaret is able to convince Henry to give his children substantial gifts of money in his lifetime when they need it for their growing families. At the same time Margaret herself arranges to give away much of her own small personal income to philanthropy.

Toward friends and family Forster had a strong sense of duty as well as responsibility. Interfering though his mother might be, Forster's sense of responsibility and loyalty toward her never wavered. His personal preferences were never allowed to overpower his commitment to other people, and this reaching out was blind to class or social position. His inner life was rich in personal spiritual resources; he was unafraid of differences; and over time he found spiritual connections with other religions, notably those of India.

Part Three

A Passage to India

Chapter Five

Mrs. Moore's Role

India: Chance or Karma

F orster and Syed Ross Masood met when the handsome Muslim Indian arrived in England to enter Oxford University. He lived temporarily with English friends, next-door neighbors of Forster and his mother; when she learned that Masood needed coaching in Latin, she volunteered her son as tutor. How assiduously the Latin study was pursued is uncertain, but through Masood Forster was introduced to Indian history, culture, and thought, an interest that possessed him the rest of his life. In the years between 1906, when his eyes were first opened to India through Masood, and 1912, when he experienced the subcontinent directly, Forster read extensively about all aspects of Indian culture and even learned some Urdu. By July 1912, when his friendship with and love for Masood had been growing for six years and he had already published four novels, Forster could note with satisfaction, "Have caught on to the Bhagavad Gita at last. It's [a] division of states into Harmony Motion Inertia. (Purity Passion Darkness). Can also think about Karma."[1] In *Howards End,* published in 1910, Forster had already begun to incorporate some Hindu ideals into his characters: Margaret Schlegel's father is described as being a soldier who fought "without visualizing the results of victory," (267) a philosophic principle stressed by the god Krishna in his tutelage of the warrior Arjuna in the Bhagavad Gita, one of the great texts of Hinduism. In 1912 Forster wrote a short essay, "Hymn before Action," concerning an episode in the Bhagavad Gita in which Krishna replies to Arjuna's question about why he should fight when he had friends and relatives on both sides of the struggle. Krishna's second injunction—Duty—must have mattered greatly to Forster, as did the god's insistence that looking for a reward could lead only to spiritual death. One does the right thing because it is right, not for hope of reward or recognition, always remembering "the fortunes of men are all bound up together, and it is impossible to inflict damage without receiving it."[2]

A three-cornered conversation among Forster, no longer a conventional Christian, Masood, a Muslim, and a third man Forster calls "Masood's queer Indian," possibly a Hindu, is enlightening about Forster's personal assessment of his spiritual location in April 1911, more than a year before he experienced India for the first time:

> [Queer Indian]: What are you, as regards religion?
> [Forster]: If you want to label me, an agnostic.
> [Queer Indian]: If you do not mind, will

you describe how you lost your faith?

[Forster]: It is difficult to describe how, but I can tell you when—at Cambridge.

[Queer Indian]: How old were you then?

[Forster]: 20.

[Queer Indian]: Ah, a dangerous age. What were you reading at the time?

[Forster]: Classics.

[Queer Indian]: Not Huxley? Rationalistic publications?

[Forster]: No, neither science nor philosophy. First the doctrine of the Trinity upset me—like so many other Christians—then the study of History—I saw that other creeds believed as firmly in God as Xtianity [Christianity] & there was also the example of my friends.

[Queer Indian]: I think you are a Deist— that is better than an Agnostic.

[Masood]: *Better?*

[Queer Indian]: I will not say that, but he knows there is a God.

[Forster]: I do not, but I should say that I have more sense of religion now than in the days of my orthodox Xtianity. Do you say that unless one believes in God, one has no religious sense?

[Queer Indian]: Yes.

[Masood]: I disagree.[3]

Later the same year Forster again privately acknowledges his own "growing interest in religion."[4]

Forster's intense belief in the importance of personal relations and his intuitive sensitivity toward other people made him open to the human situations he hoped to encounter on his first visit to India in 1912. In contrast, the goal of one of his traveling companions, his good friend Goldsworthy Lowes Dickinson, was pragmatic—to visit jails and schools, factories and religious establishments, expecting to come quickly to some practical conclusions about the state of the subcontinent. Though he could engage in deep discussions of Greek philosophy with the Maharajah of Chhatarpur, Lowes Dickinson was lost in the Indian culture. He was searching for an accessible enumeration of facts and was not able to cope with all the contradictions that comprised India. He "could make no sense of it and felt that no Westerner could."[5] With considerable relief he went on to China, his main goal of the trip. Forster's own goal was simply to be immersed in Indian life in order to begin to experience the Indian soul. He went admirably equipped to attempt it. He had learned in his young life to trust instinct about what was most complete and unique in himself—and in others—and to protect it from the suppression that lurked in the social conventions of the day.

Unlike those not willing to take the risk, Forster did not seem to fear this daunting search into the unknown recesses of his soul. What he was interested in was an inward and sympathetic connection with the inner spirit of another person—what Jung called the collective unconscious. Something

greater than a surface relationship, the desired spiritual connection was an inward oneness with others, both known and
unknown, an acknowledgment of membership in the Family
of Man, the opposite of alienation and loneliness. But he believed that community alone "cannot satisfy the human
spirit." Forster felt that English people, weak in inspiration
and spirituality, needed to engage in "a struggle for truer values, a struggle of the individual towards the dark secret place
where he may find reality."[6] In many of his contacts with Hindus and Muslims, Forster found this kind of instinctual relationship. To his joy he also discovered in India a natural openness to the spiritual side of life and an easy integration of the
mundane and the divine in daily actions. He discerned a vital
and unapologetic spirituality, lacking the shame and hypocrisy he often felt in English religious observance, that informed the individual's daily life and actions, a dimension of
religious practice quite outside his experience in England.
Daily devotions—*puja*—are usually performed at home, but on
occasion worshippers also go to a local temple. Whereas in
Christianity, Islam, and Buddhism, worship is usually a congregational affair requiring a large meeting space, Hindu worship, even at the temple, is mostly an individual matter. So,
Forster wrote, "however large and elaborate the Hindu temple
is outside, the inner core of it is small, secret, and dark . . .
where the individual is at the last resort alone with his god."[7]

Hindu Spirituality in Daily Life

Early in his first trip to India, Forster found himself in "a long talk about religion" with Sir Tukoji Rao III, raja of Dewas Senior:

> Indians are so easy and communicative on this subject, whereas English people are mostly offended when it is introduced, or else shocked if there is a difference of opinion. ... He believes that we—men, birds, everything—are part of God ... When I asked why we had any of us ever been severed from God, he explained it by God becoming unconscious that we were parts of him, owing to his energy at some time being concentrated elsewhere. Salvation, then, is the thrill *we* feel when God again becomes conscious of us, and all our life we must train our perceptions so that we may be capable of feeling when the time comes.[8]

Forster met Sir Tukoji through his friend Malcolm Darling, previously tutor to the raja, and spent Christmas week of 1912 in the tiny kingdom of Dewas Senior with the raja and his court, together with the Darlings and another English couple. In a letter home Forster wrote that Sir Tukoji refused to believe that God had deliberately created suffering and sin. In this he was not far from the ancient gnostic sect which, differing from the orthodox group in the young Christian church, questioned "whether all suffering, labor, and death derive from human sin."[9] Sir Tukoji's religious practice, continued Forster, "is inspired by his belief in a being who, though omnipresent, is personal, and whom he calls Krishna. [Sir Tukoji] is really a remarkable man, for all this goes with much practical ability and a sense of humour. In the middle of a chat he will suddenly pray, tapping his forehead and bobbing on his knees, and then continuing the sentence where he left it off; 'On days when one feels gratitude it is well to show it,' he said."[10]

About a month earlier, Forster had had "a Krishna conversation" with the maharaja of Chhatarpur in which he asked the ruler whether he meditated: "'Yes—when I can for two hours, and when I am busy for forty-five minutes.' 'And can you concentrate and forget your troubles?' 'Oh no, not at all, they come in with me always unless I can meditate on love, for love is the only power that can keep thought out. I try to meditate on Krishna. I do not know that he is a God, but I love Love and Beauty and Wisdom, and I find them in his history. I worship and adore him as a man. If he is divine he will notice me for it and reward me; if he is not, I shall become grass and dust like the others.'"[11]

Krishna is one of the most important and venerated of India's abundance of gods and goddesses. Historians of Indian philosophy agree that at first there was no concept of a creator

god, but by the first millennium BCE the idea of an all-pervad-
ing god had developed. The name given to this creator god is
"Brahman." Not so much a personage as a spirit, Brahman is
transcendent, the Supreme Being, the Unknowable One. Brahman is never personified—there is no picture of Brahman—but
represents the perfection to which humankind aspires. To emphasize how impossibly far beyond human qualities Brahman
is, Hindus often call this Creator God "Neti, neti"—a negative
phrase meaning "Indescribable" or, in an approximate translation, "Not this, not that." Three subsidiary gods—Prajapati,
Vishnu, and Shiva—representing differing and more accessible aspects of the Supreme Being, are generally accepted as a
triad of equal importance, but Hindus stress that they are not
to be confused or compared with the Christian Trinity.
Krishna, an avatar of Vishnu the Preserver, came down to
earth in bodily form as an incarnation of that god to represent
to humans the qualities of Vishnu. Incarnation also exists in
Christianity through the figure of Jesus. Krishna is worshiped
as a heroic protector, a god who loves music and little children
and whose erotic side is celebrated in age-old stories. Cow-
herds especially venerate Krishna because he was one himself
in the early years of his earthly existence. From his earliest
days on Indian soil, Forster was learning firsthand about the
Hindu pantheon of gods and religious concepts such as meditation, prayer, love, beauty, wisdom, sin and suffering, salvation, joy and pleasure, and humanity's connection with the Inconceivable. The vocabulary is familiar to Christians, but the
expression of these concepts is Indian, not Western. Although

Hinduism seemed to answer many of the religious shortcomings that Forster felt so poignantly in the Christianity with which he was indoctrinated as a child, he would never become a Hindu or follow a guru or a philosophical school as did some of his younger friends, like Christopher Isherwood, decades later.

One of the shortcomings, vivid by its absence from the Christian experience that Forster absorbed as a child, was joy as a religious value. Joy and humor are, however, important characteristics of Hinduism. In a review of the sixth century Sanskrit drama *Sakuntala*, Forster called it "august" and an "unlikely home for jokes and sentimentality." Yet with its august tone, "it was also humorous, enchanted, gracious." Even when the action moved beyond the earthly, it "did not leave fun" behind.[12] Had Forster searched, he might have found a few theologians and lay critics of Christianity who had, even in the late Victorian period, approached in all seriousness the question of humor in the Bible and its specific importance in Jesus' actions and sayings.[13] Even in the late twentieth century only a few scattered references can be found that mention Jesus' humor. In the 1960s an American theologian, Elton Trueblood, wrote:

> The widespread failure to recognize and appreciate the humor of Christ is one of the most amazing aspects of the era named for Him. ... We are so sure that He was always deadly serious that we often twist His words in order to try to

> make them conform to our precon-
> ceived mold. A misguided piety has
> made us fear that acceptance of His ob-
> vious wit and humor would somehow be
> mildly blasphemous or sacrilegious. Re-
> ligion, we think, is serious business, and
> serious business is incompatible with
> banter.[14]

In an essay on "Humour and Faith," Reinhold Niebuhr, the eminent twentieth-century theologian, agreed that "there are many sayings of Jesus which betray a touch of ironic humour. . . . Humour is, in fact, a prelude to faith; and laughter is the beginning of prayer." But, Niebuhr added, in the most intimate relationship with God, "laughter is swallowed up in prayer and humour is fulfilled by faith."[15] This statement undoubtedly goes further than Forster would venture. Jesus employed the full armory of humor, depending on whether his audience was shepherds, fishermen, and unlettered villagers, on the one hand, or scribes and Pharisees highly trained in the accepted religious interpretation of the Hebraic law of the Old Testament. Trueblood wrote that "there is good reason to suppose that Christ *meant* His words to sound preposterous."[16] Jesus employed humor purposefully to reveal "some facet of truth which would not otherwise be revealed."[17] In 1924 L. M. Hussey had written, "Jesus was a teacher with a twinkle in His eye" but later "in the hands of Holy Church all the humanity was squeezed out of Jesus as a high symbolic divinity was pumped in."[18] Forster would have agreed. As he told his humanist audience in his Presidential Address, "I don't desire to meet Christ personally, and, since personal relations mean everything to me, this has helped me to cool off from Christianity. If the religion of my fathers (i.e., C. of E.) [Church of England] had provided me with a more satisfactory father-figure, brother-figure, friend, what you will, I might have been more tempted to stay in it. It contained much that I respected and respect, but too little that I could care for."

Absent also from Victorian religious practice was an appreciation of human physicality. Although the renown of India's Khajuraho temples among Westerners generally rests on the explicitly sexual sculptures, such panels occupy only about one percent of the surface of the structures. In its totality the sculpture, covering almost every square inch of the temples, suggests a symbiosis of the sacred and the secular. Forster's understanding of the Khajuraho temples developed from active dislike in his 1912–13 visit to a recognition in 1920–21 that they expressed all aspects of human experience, of which physicality was only one facet. But Forster did not fully appreciate Khajuraho's spiritual values until 1940, when he visited a London exhibition of Indian photographs that he described as "a spiritual exhibition" aimed at "interpreting the Hindu tradition." He confessed the impact of this exhibition on him when he wrote that "if I ever get back to Khajuraho again . . . I shall look at it less stupidly."[19]

For all Forster's self-education in England, he still expected to be surprised and baffled by the complexities of India.

In his first exposure to India, he often used Western comparisons to describe Indian scenes, as when he described the hill of Devi as "the sacred acropolis with the rakish cap." He continued, "Devi (or Devivasini, the Goddess' Residence) probably gave Dewas its name. It rose about three hundred feet about the level. Some steps led up to the dark cave of Chamunda on the top. She was a barbaric vermilion object, not often approached by us. . . . Who was Chamunda, and how long had she resided up there? I never found out, but it was agreed that she had been around longer than anyone else." And he finished his description thus: "She concludes the curiosities of Dewas."[20] The slight tone of flippancy suggests that Forster did not know then whom he was describing. Most of the bewildering plethora of Indian gods and goddesses are expressions of some specific aspect of a more complex god or goddess such as the Great Goddess Devi, whose roots go back four thousand years to the Mother Goddess of the protohistoric culture of the Indus River valley. Chamunda gained a place in the Indian pantheon because Devi, in the guise of the goddess Kali, who represented the darker side of Devi's power, defeated and beheaded two demon generals, Chanda and Munda. From this mythical encounter arose the goddess Chamunda, another aspect of the great Goddess Devi.[21] Of little significance to Forster, "the barbaric vermilion object" to Sir Tukoji was a potent symbol of Devi's protective power.[22] Such flippancy may appear to be disrespectful, but Forster was trying to describe what he was seeing in terms understandable to people thousands of miles away and mired in prejudicial ignorance about

India. In addition he was struggling with his own mystification at the complexity of Hindu religious philosophy and practice.

At first Islam seemed more intelligible to him than Hinduism, perhaps because superficially it is like Christianity in some attitudes and beliefs, such as belief in one God, solemnity of liturgical ceremony, and a dogma depending on a single holy text. While sensitive to the Hindu's sincerity, Forster could not surmount the assault on his aesthetic sense by the garishness and jumble of Hindu ceremonies. In a mixture of respect and irreverence, he could write home about a Hindu religious ceremony that "it is difficult to make vivid what seems so fatuous. There is no dignity, no taste, no form, and though I am dressed as a Hindu I shall never become one. I don't think one ought to be irritated with Idolatry because one can see from the faces of the people that it touches something very deep in their hearts. But it is natural that Missionaries, who think these ceremonies wrong as well as inartistic, should lose their tempers."[23] Standing before the awe-inspiring beauty of the Taj Mahal, listening to a muezzin "with a most glorious voice" giving the call to evening prayer, Forster contrasted the strong aesthetic sense the Mughal emperors brought to India from Persia with the more exuberant indigenous Hindu practices: "I do like Islam, though I have had to come through Hinduism to discover it. After all the mess and profusion and confusion of [a festival], where nothing ever stopped or need ever have begun, it was like standing on a mountain."[24] Yet he was naturally humble, not arrogant, about another's religious expression and gradually understood that Hindu religious pageantry expressed a breadth and depth of spiritual feeling, a sense of awe and wonder before the mystery of "the One that could not be described" that he had found neither in Christianity nor Islam.

Although there are numerous references to Islam in *A Passage to India*, in the opinion of G. K. Das, expressed in his penetrating study of Forster's relationship with India and its people, "nowhere in the accounts of his personal experiences in India does he attempt to approach the subject of Islam as deeply, or in the same proportion, as he has dealt with Hinduism."[25] Even as Forster was puzzled by Hindu religious expression and aesthetically offended by the garishness of religious ceremonies, he sensed the broader spiritual embrace of Hindu worship. The eminent Indian scholar of Hinduism, K. M. Sen, compares the development of Hinduism to "a tree that has *grown* gradually" rather than "a building that has been *erected* by some great architect at some definite point in time."[26] Underscoring the wide-ranging nature of traditional Hinduism and its natural growth and development over the centuries, he writes, "Hindu society is a product of many races and many cultures. It is necessary to recognize this fact to appreciate the complexity of the Hindu society and religion."[27] Thus Sen draws attention to the syncretic nature of Hinduism, its expansive, inclusive quality that, over the centuries, has selectively incorporated features of others' religions into Hindu practice. Sen is also subtly emphasizing the fact that religion

in India is entwined with society in all its activities, making the
secular and the religious impossible to separate.

Whatever Forster's motivations for his first trip to India, a
religious pilgrimage was not among them. He must have been
intensely surprised—and not a little happy—to find a culture
where daily life was suffused with the sacred. As Das writes,
"He can see that there is in Hinduism the possibility of a spiritual meaning which, it seems to him, Christianity as well as
Islam lacked. . . . Hinduism presents religion as 'a living force,'
by conceiving of God as an immediate reality apprehensible by
man."[28] But Das warns against any tendency to view *A Passage
to India* as an objective study of Hinduism and Hindu life:

> The novel is not to be read as a system-
> atic exposition of the Hindu and the
> Muslim ways of life, or as an account of
> the author's own formulated opinions
> on these two religions. . . . Yet it will be
> seen that in significant ways the novel
> reflects on some main questions con-
> cerning the two religions, and also
> throws light on an interesting stage in
> the author's intellectual confrontations
> with these two religious beliefs of India.
> . . . Scrutinising the possibilities of a
> value in the spiritualism of India, which
> might be tenable for him personally, he
> seems to have seen in Hinduism, rather
> than in Islam, such a possibility.[29]

After his first visit to India, during which he met both Muslims and Hindus, Forster commented in a 1915 article on Hinduism's embrace of variety within unity:

> It is true that Hinduism emphasizes the fact that we are all different. But it also emphasizes the other side of the human paradox, the fact that we are all the same ... and these two contradictory beliefs do really correspond to two contradictory emotions that each of us can feel, namely, "I am different from everybody else," and "I am the same as everybody else." ... Hinduism ... does reveal a conception of Man's nature, and in consequence always has appealed and will appeal to souls who are technically outside its pale. It may not intend to proselytize. ... But it gains proselytes whatever its intentions, because it can give certain types of people what they want.[30]

While Forster's response to India was primarily in the spiritual realm, he was also alert to the powerful ferment bubbling around Indian-British political relations. Because this important subject was not directly examined in *A Passage to India* except in terms of individual personal relationships, some Indian critics have complained that Forster deliberately

avoided the political scene. M. M. Mahood rebutted their accusations in an article linking Forster's writing and the action
at Amritsar in April 1919, when General Dyer ordered his
troops to fire on a peaceful assembly in the town square, kill-
ing several hundred Indian civilians and wounding many others. This action at Amritsar may have been little noticed at
first in England, but Forster, soon to make his second trip to
India, was paying attention.[31] Forster later commented that *A
Passage to India* is about "something wider than politics, about
the search of the human race for a more lasting home."[32]

Spiritual Elements in A Passage to India

In *A Passage to India*, Forster invests Mrs. Moore and Professor
Godbole in heavy theological robes, Mrs. Moore, in the manner of Forster, questioning her quasi-orthodox Christian faith,
while Professor Godbole symbolized what Forster found in
Hinduism that filled the lacuna in the traditional Christianity
of his youth. As a minor theme Dr. Aziz, an amateur poet, represents Forster's partial understanding of Islam and the novelist's great appreciation of Mughal art and literature.[33] When
Aziz stops to rest in a small mosque close to the English civil
station, inspired by the beauty of the night, he unbridles his
imagination and begins to invest the mosque with romantic
notions of beauty, love and death, "meanings the builder had
never intended."[34] Mrs. Moore has fled to the mosque for her
own reasons, away from the English club and the boring amateur performance there. Dr. Aziz, shocked and angry when he

discovers a foreign woman in the mosque, shouts that the mosque is a holy place for Moslems and that she should have removed her shoes. When she explains that she has left her shoes at the entrance, he apologizes, explaining that "so few ladies take the trouble, especially if thinking no one is there to see." "That makes no difference," she replies, "God is here." (14–15) Forster is signaling that Mrs. Moore is not the usual Christian.

Some eminent Indian critics believe that Forster presents the Muslim Dr. Aziz as the hero of the novel and deliberately makes Professor Godbole, a Hindu Brahman, an object of derision. Their interpretation is understandable, springing, as it must, from the bent of mind with which India's history and their Hindu heritage naturally tinges their interpretation of all of life, this novel included. But far from making Professor Godbole an object of derision, Forster respects the deep spirituality that infuses the remotest corners of his life with sacred meaning. In a personal interview with the Indian critic V. A. Shahane, Forster emphasized his "artistic earnestness" and lack of intention "to convey comic impressions" of the Hindu ceremony in the Temple section of *A Passage to India*. In Shahane's words, though "scenes of Godbole's Temple ceremony seem farcical in one way, yet in my view, they have a deep symbolic meaning."[35]

An educated high-caste Brahman of Aryan ancestry, Professor Godbole illumines some of the positive spiritual attributes that Forster found congenial in the Hinduism he experienced at the court of Dewas Senior in 1921–22. His expression of the Hindu belief that everything about life is sacred—that there is no division into divine and secular—is contrary to the religious practices of many Western Christians. What makes them awkwardly self-conscious, to a Hindu would seem merely natural. To a Westerner such simplicity may seem like oversimplification or naïveté—hard to comprehend or accept. The residents of the British civil station considered that Indian people who "spent their lives in knocking two sticks together before a scarlet doll" represented "humanity . . . drifting beyond the educated vision." (32) Though at the time in which the novel is set most Indian people were far outside the Western bounds of accepted religious expression, Forster respected the unself-conscious spirituality he experienced in his contacts with the maharaja of Dewas Senior and other Indians.

Gokul Ashtami

In the kingdom of Dewas Senior, the annual August festival of Gokul Ashtami, honoring the god Krishna, who supposedly was born in nearby Gokul, was the most important religious activity of the year for Sir Tukoji and the people of his small domain. This festival was first recorded in the Bhagavad Gita. Gokul Ashtami was celebrated mainly out of doors. It was not a priest-led worship because to its participants *bhakti*, the direct contact with their god through Love, not ritual, was what mattered; emotion was the basis of their festival. To a Westerner like Forster, with his highly developed sense of Western aesthetics, it was a painful pandemonium of "noise, noise, noise" and decorations piled willy-nilly upon decorations. Participants smeared each other with butter and threw red powder at one another until the air turned crimson. Viewed from Western standards of dignity, taste, and form, only one thing about the whole affair was beautiful to Forster, "the expression on the faces of the people as they bow to the shrine."[36] Yet Forster continually found similarities with Christianity. Sir Tukoji danced before the altar where the tiny Krishna figure lay; King David in the Old Testament danced before the ark. (64) Krishna shared with Jesus a threat to his life as a baby. Each child had to be hidden to escape being killed, and when Krishna was not found, the Indian king, like Herod, ordered the massacre of all the children in his kingdom. Because the final climax of the Indian festival comes when the baby Krishna is born, Forster confessed, "Why, since he had been listening to hymns for eight days, he was now to be born was a puzzle to me. . . . Of course the Festival is no more illogical than Christmas, though it seemed so owing to its realism." (65) This comment is a strong reminder of the episode many years previous when Forster was trying to educate a fellow schoolboy about Good Friday and Jesus. Years later in India, as ceremonial games were played before the altar, Forster remembered that "there were games of this sort in the Christian Middle Ages and they still survive in the Cathedral of Seville at Easter." (66) The Gokul festival also reminded him of the Greek "Adonis festival, where the God is born, dies, and is carried to the water, all in a short time." (68) Likewise, on the final day of the festival, the baby Krishna is born and carried to the water where the miniature village of Gokul is sunk, symbolizing Krishna "who cannot of course be drowned." (68)

Beyond aesthetic criticism, Forster was sensing a deeper aspect of Hinduism. He wrote that "I am very much muddled in my own mind about it all, for [Sir Tukoji] has what one understands by the religious sense and it comes out all through his life. He is always thinking of others and refusing to take advantage of his position in his dealings with them; and believing that his God acts similarly towards him." (64) In describing the influence of religion in Sir Tukoji's life, Forster wrote, "The unseen was always close to him, even when he was joking or intriguing. Red paint on a stone could evoke it." (70) Though Sir Tukoji had a framework of belief and behavior, he could be inconsistent, a human trait Forster accepted with equanimity. Nor did he subscribe to asceticism; matter and spirit were both important. Above all, Forster declared, "he believed in the heart. . . . Affection, or the possibility of it, quivered through everything, from Gokul Ashtami down to daily human relationships." In the same passage he quoted a message from the raja—"Tell him from me to follow his heart and his mind will see everything clear"—Forster responding that "as phrased [it] is too facile: doors open into silliness at once." But the underlying meaning of Sir Tukoji's message and his approach to life was "to remember and respect and prefer the heart, to have the instinct which follows it wherever possible—what surer help than that could one have through life? What better hope of clarification?" (70–71) Writing much later of Sir Tukoji, Forster noted that he was "never deaf to the promptings which most of us scarcely hear. His religion was the deepest thing in him. It ought to be studied—neither by the psychologist nor by the mythologist but by the individual who has experienced similar promptings. He penetrated into rare regions and he was always hoping that others would follow him there. He was never exclusive. . . . To recall the conversation that we had forty years ago in an upper room at Delhi, he was hopeful that we should all be recalled to the attention of God." (113)

During the Gokul Ashtami festival, Forster found Sir Tukoji "as always, successful in his odd role. I have never seen religious ecstasy before and don't take to it more than I expected I should, but he manages not to be absurd." (64) While not denying his personal dismay at the lack of aesthetic sensibility in the festival described in the third section of the novel, Forster recognized as infinitely more important the potent spiritual bliss on the faces of the assembled worshippers. Here for a fleeting moment these devotees of Krishna felt at one with the spark of the Hindu *atman* (the human spirit aspiring godward) within themselves.

Mrs. Moore

Mrs. Moore reflects much of Forster's own childhood religious exposure and his later mature thought.[37] Like Mrs. Wilcox in *Howards End,* Mrs. Moore's life has been spent in attentive devotion to her family. Unlike Mrs. Wilcox, whose life was mainly spent in the cocoon of English suburban society and culture with occasional visits to her ancestral country home, Mrs. Moore's experience of India deeply upsets the tenor of her life and her philosophic underpinnings. Though she was brought up in the Church of England, she retains a direct connection with her own intuition, which nudges her spirit with a nagging suspicion of the inadequacy of her traditional Christianity. In India she experiences a deep connection with Nature, "caught up in the shawl of night together with earth and all the other stars" and feels "a sudden sense of unity, of kinship with the heavenly bodies" that, as quickly as it had come, departs from her, "leaving a strange freshness behind."[38] These feelings are reinforced when later she catches a glimpse of the Ganges in the moonlight. Informed that in that luminous beauty lurked crocodiles along with the ashes of devout Hindus who had gone to Benares, upriver, to die in that holy city and be "buried" in what Hindus believed was the holiest of rivers, she could embrace what other Westerners might consider contradictions. She comments, "What a terrible river! what a wonderful river!" (26) Later, as she is preparing for bed, she discovers a wasp on the peg where she had intended to hang her cloak. Respecting the insect's equal right to that space, she does not brush it away but murmurs acceptingly, "Pretty dear." (29)

On another occasion, accusing her son, the city magistrate, of acting like a god and asserting that "Englishmen like posing as gods," she delivers an emphatic sermonette:

> "India is part of the earth. And God has
> put us on the earth in order to be pleas-
> ant to each other. God . . . is . . . Love. . . .
> God has put us on earth to love our

neighbours and to show it, and He is omnipresent, even in India, to see how we
are succeeding. . . .

"The desire to behave pleasantly
satisfies God. . . . The sincere if impo-
tent desire wins His blessing. I think
everyone fails, but there are so many
kinds of failure. Good will and more
good will and more good will. Though
I speak with the tongues of . . ." (45)

Her homily trails off into silence. Forster tells us that
"Ronny approved of religion as long as it endorsed the National Anthem, but he objected when it attempted to influence
his life." (45) Mrs. Moore is finding God "increasingly difficult
to avoid as she grew older, and he had been constantly in her
thoughts since she entered India, though oddly enough, he
satisfied her less. She needs pronounce his name frequently,
as the greatest she knew, yet she had never found it less effi-
cacious. Outside the arch there seemed always an arch, beyond the remotest echo a silence." (45–46) Yet already Forster
has subtly hinted at a divine mystery: "Beyond the sky must
not there be something that overarches all the skies, more im-
partial even than they? Beyond which again . . ." (34) Forster
leaves the suggestion hanging.

What happens in the Marabar caves, outside Chandrapore,
is the fulcrum of the narrative action. Having gone to India as
chaperone for Adela Quested, Mrs. Moore is somewhat over-
shadowed by the younger woman. The two women are invited

by Dr. Aziz to go on an elaborate picnic-cum-exploration to see the caves. While she is exploring Kawa Dol, the most prominent of the caves, with Dr. Aziz as her guide, Adela has a sudden and shocking insight into the impossibility of marriage to Mrs. Moore's son, leading to her frantic rush down the thorny hillside and her hysterical accusations of molestation by Dr. Aziz, resulting in his arrest and subsequent trial. In the plot these developments divert attention from Mrs. Moore's experience of her own truly frightening spiritual epiphany in the first Marabar cave.

On entering that cave earlier in the day, Mrs. Moore is followed by the entourage that the picnic expedition has accumulated along its path from the railway. Crammed into the dark, smelly, suffocating cave, slapped in the mouth by a baby's diaper, hitting her head in the low-ceilinged narrow tunnel, she panics and struggles to regain the larger outside world. Against the crush of other bodies crowded round her, she finds herself in a situation with no power to act independently, every action and sound magnified by the "oumboum" of sound caroming wildly off the walls of the cave and the wiggling flickers of the reflected light from matches running up and down the polished walls like worms in a chaotic frenzy. Suddenly "the echo began in some indescribable way to undermine her hold on life. . . . It . . . managed to murmur: 'Pathos, piety, courage—they exist, but are identical and so is filth. Everything exists, nothing has value.'" (140)

Why does she panic? Once free of that claustrophobic hole, she is momentarily more concerned that Dr. Aziz should be happy with the success of the entertainment he has provided for his foreign guests than with her own psychological anguish. But in just a brief moment her life has been assaulted, its ramparts breached, its raison d'être swept away. Is it claustrophobia? Pitch darkness? Temporary insanity from the heat of the pitiless sun? A sense of being physically and psychologically trapped? Does she feel a sudden loss of individuality, that she is only an anonymous speck in a flood of people who perhaps regard her as not different from an inanimate object such as a stone or a tree branch? Something else? Whatever the cause of her panic, the shocking experience in the cave destroys her spiritual connection with her Christian God, leaving her comfortless, vulnerable, and abandoned. Like a cave, the soul is dark, hidden, and there is little to see until something external and hard strikes fire in it.

The symbolism of caves in *A Passage to India* is ambiguous, and it is that double nature of a cave toward which Forster points the reader, as womb and tomb, the beginning of life and its mysterious end. It may also stand for the self-conscious journey of the person into the hidden recesses of his or her soul. It can objectify humanity's search for the mysterious divine, a search that must forsake the familiar guideposts of custom and logic for the uncertainty of faith and intuition. Or the cave might represent disorganized chaos. Mrs. Moore trusts her instincts about people. Does her devotion to personal relationships depend on a one-to-one situation? In the mosque she quickly finds rapprochement with Dr. Aziz, while in the crowded Marabar cave she panics; in the mosque she has a strong sense of God in a holy place, but in the cave her sense of the divine presence abandons her. She is at the mercy of a ragtag crowd of strangers; perhaps she senses chaos, disintegration, an assault on her personal individuality. Furthermore, the dark confusion of the cave may have led to a premonition about death.

Although the Marabar caves were not considered holy but merely a secular tourist attraction, in their physical arrangement they were not unlike a Hindu temple—small, dark, internal—each one a place for private meditation, a small space sufficient for a searcher and the Unseen. But Mrs. Moore does not find such an ambience at Marabar. To enter a cave is to leave certainty behind. Gone are the familiar guideposts of mundane life—work and productivity, money, pleasure, the warmth of human relationships. One takes a risk on entering. What is lurking there in the dark? Wild animals? Bats? Rushing underground streams with no discernible source or end? Rifts and tunnels in the seemingly solid rock that may lead nowhere or cause the unwary to lose the path and be entombed forever? Or something even more frightening and ephemeral—wriggling reflections of lights and eerie echoes? Plato's cave is filled with indistinct shadows that have only the feeblest correspondence with reality. But a cave can also be a place of refuge, a safe isolation that offers the possibility of contemplation free from the distractions of daily life. To enter a cave may require a leap of faith, hope that one can regain, or at least reapproach, the child's instinctive spiritual trust, now overgrown with layers of adult caution and rationality and the all-too-human desire for control of one's life and environment. The mysterious lure of a cave may lie in the possibility of new insights, greater understanding of the self, a quietude that opens the soul to larger possibilities than one has dared to imagine. Or a cave might seem to be a place of retreat, a safe place to hide and defend oneself from the assaults of the world.

Like Adela Mrs. Moore suffers a sudden descent into spiritual darkness. For Adela it is a psychological darkness full of distorted shadows of the psyche, mixed up with love, sexuality, and marriage; for Mrs. Moore the frightening darkness represents the sudden collapse of her traditional Christian security. Described by an Indian critic as one "who lives in the other universe . . . of the religious consciousness," Mrs. Moore is "left for a time with nothing."[39] As does Adela later, Mrs. Moore tries to find a human cause for her inner turmoil, examining each person emerging from the cave, but she quickly realizes that among the crowd of simple peasants there is no villain. Her anguish has deeper roots. Confronting psychic wreckage within instead of religious certainty, she feels the approaching end of life as suddenly tumultuous rather than undergirded by a calm spiritual framework. Traumatized by the sudden blind chaos of the cave, she retreats in terror to the world of pitiless light and heat where she tries to identify the elements of her nightmarish experience, but the memory has undercut her inherited Christian beliefs and weakened her hold on life. Should the sound uttered in the cave be majestic poetry or the vilest thoughts, the echo would be identical. And "suddenly, at the edge of her mind, Religion appeared, poor little talkative Christianity, and she knew that all its divine words from 'Let there be Light' to 'It is finished' only amounted to 'boum.'" (141)

This absolute negation of her Christian heritage haunts
Mrs. Moore through her remaining days in India, filling her
with an almost unbearable lethargy and apathy. If all that she
believes to be good is accorded only the same regard as supposed evil, her existence is founded on nothing more solid
than sand. She cannot bring herself to visit Adela, feverish
from the cactus spines that had to be extracted from her flesh
one by one. She even loses interest in Dr. Aziz and "didn't want
to communicate with anyone, not even with God," (141)
though she does assert Dr. Aziz's innocence when pushed to it.
She did not feel the presence of her Christian God in the cave,
but she does recognize that "nothing evil had been in the
cave." (139) To try to reestablish her connection with that
Christian God, does she perhaps silently say, as Godbole once
sang, "Come, come, come, come" and, like Godbole, receive no
answer? The sound of the echo—"boum" or "bou-oum" or
"ou-boum"—as Forster transliterates it is not quite the three-
syllable mantra—"a-u-m" or "o-u-m"—often chanted in Hindu
worship, immediately bringing to the worshiper's mind the
Sacred Mystery. Indeed, Forster's interpretation seems a deliberate devaluation of that holy sound, a primal scream that
only confirms the absence of any kind of god or spiritual comfort for Mrs. Moore. She is shaken to her roots. Nothing is
worth any effort anymore because there is no longer any certainty in her spirit. She feels comfortless, vulnerable, abandoned.

In *Howards End,* published fourteen years earlier, in the
description of Beethoven's Fifth Symphony, Forster had suggested "panic and emptiness" and the presence of goblins who

"merely observed in passing that there was no such thing as splendour or heroism in the world." But Beethoven in the end "took hold of the goblins and made them do what he wanted." Helen Schlegel wonders whether those goblins had really been there at all or whether they were only the phantoms of cowardice and unbelief. She ponders whether one healthy human impulse could dispel them. Forster puts into Helen's thoughts his interpretation of the music:

> "Beethoven knew better. . . . They might return. . . . It was as if the splendour of life might boil over and waste to steam and froth. In its dissolution one heard the terrible, ominous note, and a goblin, with increased malignity, walked quietly over the universe from end to end. Panic and emptiness! Panic and emptiness! . . .
>
> "Beethoven chose to make all right in the end. . . . He led his Fifth Symphony to its conclusion. But the goblins were there. They could return."
> (*HE*, 31–32)

To most Western Christians the idea that pathos and courage and filth could all be found on the same side of the ledger is antithetical; the Hindu belief in the unity of all life—of whatever form—contrasts starkly with the Judeo-Christian penchant for separating things, sheep from goats, good from evil, heaven from hell, the elect from all the unelect. Forster recognizes the Christian's difficulty with the concept of unity and equal value of all aspects of life in a brief mention of two Western missionaries in *A Passage to India*:

> In our Father's house are many mansions, they taught. . . . Not one shall be turned away by the servants on that verandah, be he black or white. . . . And why should the divine hospitality cease here? Consider, with all reverence, the monkeys. May there not be a mansion for the monkeys also? . . . Young Mr. Sorley . . . saw no reason why monkeys should not have their . . . share of bliss, and he had sympathetic discussions about them with his Hindu friends. And the jackals? . . . He admitted that the mercy of God, being infinite, may well embrace all mammals. And the wasps? . . . And oranges, cactuses, crystals and mud? and the bacteria inside Mr. Sorley? No, no, this is going too far. We must exclude someone from our gathering, or we shall be left with nothing. (32)

What her Victorian Christian upbringing has inculcated in Mrs. Moore is that duty is paramount. Her "appropriate life" is synchronous with helping others. Once her son and Adela are engaged, she would be free to "go home and help the others, if they wished. . . . Her function was to help others, her reward to be informed that she was sympathetic. Elderly ladies must not expect more than this." (86) (Forster made Mrs. Moore about fifty years old.) In this modern restatement of the biblical Mary/Martha dilemma, Mrs. Moore faithfully discharges her Martha duties, apparently unaware that Mary potentialities lurk unfulfilled in the inner recesses of her psyche. Like the Marabar Hills, altered over the eons by geological forces, her own spiritual landscape has been drifted over with the silt and detritus of unexamined existence. Forster asks, "What had spoken to her in that scoured-out cavity of the granite? . . . Something very old and very small. Something snub-nosed, incapable of generosity—the undying worm itself." (198) The "undying worm" that so tormented Mrs. Moore after her hideous epiphany in the cave is her belated recognition of that part of her soul that has been stunted by the Christian emphasis on duty: "Most of life is so dull that there is nothing to be said about it. . . . Inside its cocoon of work or social obligation, the human spirit slumbers for the most part, registering the distinction between pleasure and pain, but not nearly as alert as we pretend." (125)

Such a dichotomy of spirit between duty and the yearnings of the innate soul is not exclusive to Mrs. Moore. Fielding feels it, too; his professional life is his duty. He has tended to suppress the contemplative aspect of his spirit by the denial—or neglect—of beauty and art as important to the human psyche of either gender. Of an evening as the stars began to appear, that "lovely, exquisite moment . . . [passed] the Englishman with averted face and on swift wings. He experienced nothing himself; it was as if someone had told him that there was such a moment, and he was obliged to believe." (181) Still, his emotions are not so dulled that he is unable to feel suddenly discontented "and wondered whether he was really and truly successful as a human being. After forty years' experience, he had learnt to manage his life and make the best of it on advanced European lines, had developed his personality, explored his limitations, controlled his passions—and he had done it all without becoming either pedantic or worldly. A creditable achievement, but as the moment passed, he felt he ought to have been working at something else the whole time,—he didn't know at what, never would know, never could know, and that was why he felt sad." (181) In many ways Forster makes it clear that Fielding—dedicated though he is to the laudable goal of improving the world through education, believing firmly in equality among people, and working for the spread of universal brotherhood—is a failed person psychologically because his reliance on intellectual clarity and logic denies any role to feelings and intuition. Where heart and emotion should be there is only an empty space, a lacuna in his soul.

The first chapter of part 2, the cave section of *A Passage to India*, parallels the opening chapter of the novel in setting the physical scene, except that chapter 12 goes literally deeper than the surface description of chapter 1, with its geologic description emphasizing the prehistoric creation of the land and the caves, underscoring the timeless and primeval. Forster is perhaps forecasting his intention to excavate more deeply

into the emotions and primal sources of action in his characters. In spite of eons of slow change, the caves and the Marabar
Hills appear the same as ever. So, too, the deepest recesses of
the human spirit retain the primal force the soul has always
had in spite of society's relentless pressure to shape the human spirit to accord with its rules and regulations. In Mrs.
Moore's dilemma we see the god-given human psyche terribly
misshapen by decades of social admonitions yet still replete
with its fundamental force. To recognize that withered spirit
within herself and know that she personally has to bear by de-
fault part of the responsibility for its paralysis and distortion
is a devastating realization. Too late to repair the damage, she
is left with remorse for what might have been. She has wanted
to be at one with the universe, caught up in the shawl of night
with the moon and the stars, "but there was always some little
duty to be performed first ... and while she was pottering
about, the Marabar struck its gong." (198) The gong spoke of
mortality, of lost opportunity, of an unfulfilled life, of her undeveloped self. In her agony, experiencing the sudden collapse
of her Christian faith structure, lacking a personal identity independent of duty, she calls on her intuition, which has not
the strength of mature development. She is in the depths of
"spiritual muddledom": "Oh, how tedious ... trivial. ... Her
mind seemed to move towards [Adela and Ronny] from a great
distance and out of darkness. 'Oh, why is everything still my
duty? when shall I be free from your fuss? Was he in the cave
and were you in the cave and on and on ... and Unto us a Son
is born, unto us a Child is given ... and am I good and is he bad
and are we saved? ... and ending everything the echo.'" (195)

Previously venerated religious concepts have lost their accepted meaning. All she wants is to be free of duty to others and retreat into a cave of her own (191), a hiding place from the demands of others and the chaos that life suddenly seems to be. Fretfully, Mrs. Moore says that "relationships are not important." She may be painfully recognizing the deeper level of self-knowledge and unique abilities that have lain dormant all her life beneath duty's more strident demands in the ever-present relationships of family and society. This muddle may even have clogged the channels of her innate relationship with the Divine.

As a young Kingsman at Cambridge University, surrounded by sympathetic, searching fellow students, Forster had, with facile philosophical logic, purged himself of the moribund Christianity of his youth. Shedding his Christianity freed his soul. But for Mrs. Moore, alone and suddenly facing the imminence of death, the wrenching loss of her religious support is a devastating experience; in a single lightening strike of emotion, her mind and soul are thrown into severe trauma. She has never learned the lesson that informed much of Forster's own adult life: "Death destroys a man; the idea of Death saves him." (236) Sustained proximity to one's possible demise often results in a radical readjustment of values as each day becomes a precious gift, time to be spent more deliberately than in the days of blissful disregard of the fragility of life. Forster intuited this lesson early. Mrs. Moore learns it too late to do her much good.

Not until Mrs. Moore's train trip to Bombay to catch the steamer home can she find any stable spiritual ground. She sees that her personal values of inclusive acceptance and generalized Christian love toward those she meets are insufficient to the situation in which she found herself in India. Off she goes, alone by choice, on the long train trip to Bombay, winding through the vast heart of India, viewing "the indestructible life of man and his changing faces, and the houses he has built for himself and God." (199) They remind her of the universal cycle of life and death and rebirth as well as the individual's sometimes tenuous bond with the place of his or her origin. Though crushed in spirit she finds comfort in the thought of her personal experience as a continuing process, moving onward like the train. Her renewed sense of the importance of place and one's roots is tinctured with her wistful acceptance of a deep regret for lost opportunities. She has achieved a new appreciation of the importance of the inner life and the possibility of various roads to Truth, and her courage is beginning to reassert itself. As the train approaches Aligarh, she sees the city's fortress with the mosque to its right. Ten minutes later the city reappears, but this time the mosque is to the left of the fort's bastions. The train has inscribed a semicircle around the city. Even an incomplete circle suggests such concepts as perfection, the integration of all existing life forms into a seamless whole, the continuity of life. Of equal importance is the deeper perception that there are numerous points of view from which to approach Truth, all of them partial, but still valid—partially. There are various paths toward the Divine. Though individuals may not live to see the perfection of the circle, even the partial view—the semicircle—holds out hope.

Chapter Six

The Wider Spiritual View

Professor Godbole's Religious Significance

While Mrs. Moore can easily accept the spiritual ambience of the mosque where she first met Dr. Aziz, she has had little personal exposure to any manifestations of Hinduism. Her ephemeral acquaintance with Professor Godbole at Fielding's tea party, where they only perfunctorily addressed each other, offered no opportunity to learn about Hinduism since the professor took his tea apart from the others and spoke very little, though he did sing a religious song imploring the god to "come, come, come, come," but the god did not come. Mrs. Moore did not meet Professor Godbole again. Professor Godbole only begins to assume dimension after Dr. Aziz is accused of assaulting Adela, when he and Fielding have a long and tortured conversation, their minds eluding each other, slipping and sliding past a mental meeting because of the different cultural conditioning molding them as children. Forster implies his own difficulty in understanding an Indian like Professor Godbole, but he can accept even while he cannot understand: "No eye could see what lay at the bottom of the Brahman's [sic] mind, and yet he had a mind and a heart too, and all his friends trusted him without knowing why."[1]

Wanting Professor Godbole's candid opinion as to Dr. Aziz's guilt or innocence, Fielding asks him bluntly whether Dr. Aziz would do such a thing as he is accused of. Professor Godbole avoids a direct answer; considering the whole situation in a larger philosophical context, he replies that "I think you are asking me whether the individual can commit good actions or evil actions, and that is rather difficult for us." Fielding misunderstands, thinking that Professor Godbole is equating good and evil. Professor Godbole protests: "No, not exactly, please, according to our philosophy. Because nothing can be performed in isolation. All perform a good action, when one is performed, and when an evil action is performed, all perform it. . . . When evil occurs, it expresses the whole of the universe. Similarly when good occurs." Again Fielding misunderstands, muttering, "And similarly when suffering occurs." But Professor Godbole charges him with changing the direction of the discussion: "We were discussing good and evil. Suffering is merely a matter for the individual. . . . [Good and evil] are not what we think them, they are what they are, and each of us has contributed to both." When Fielding objects that he is "preaching that evil and good are the same," Professor Godbole explains again: "Oh no, excuse me once again. Good and evil are different, as their names imply. But, in my own humble opinion, they are both of them aspects of my Lord. He is present in the one, absent in the other, and the difference between presence and absence is great, as great as my feeble mind can grasp. Yet absence implies presence, absence is not non-existence, and we are therefore entitled to repeat 'Come, come, come, come.'" He goes on to recount an ancient legend—a story that to Fielding is apropos of nothing and, as often happens with Professor Godbole's conversations, "culminate[s] in a cow." (168–70)

The story, involving a murder, a dagger, good and evil, a thirsty Hindu raja, and an equally thirsty cow, epitomizes Professor Godbole's understanding of the Hindu concept of good and evil, as well as the universality of all beings, when the raja gives the cow the water he is about to drink himself. Ever deepening bafflement seems to be all that Fielding can glean from such an abstruse philosophical conversation in which the basic assumptions are torn loose from his accustomed definitions. Yet both men are dealing with the concept of Love, Professor Godbole's Hindu interpretation emphasizing universality, Fielding's Christian expression of Love directed toward the suffering of an individual.[2]

Forster sees the punkah wallah at Dr. Aziz's trial as another example of traditional Hindu values unself-consciously integrated into daily life. In his diary from the 1912 trip to India is the entry, "Punkah boy, seated at end of table, had the impassivity of Atropos."[3] In Greek mythology Atropos is identified as the Fate who cuts the thread of life, the Fate that cannot be avoided, a definition that brings to mind the Hindu idea of karma, a concept that has been appropriated, in superficial meaning at least, by the Western vocabulary. Karma represents the effect that deeds committed knowingly or unwittingly in one's present life will have on one's situation in the next. But in Hinduism the next life is not the static heaven or hell of Christianity; it is rather another chance to live physically again on earth in another status, which may or may not be human. In *A Passage to India* the novelist writes that because of his physique, the punkah wallah "stood out as divine" and "seemed to control the proceedings. . . . He seemed apart from human destinies, a male fate, a winnower of souls" yet "he scarcely knew that he existed." In spite of implied beauty and power, this servant of all was just a lowly citizen of Chandrapore, "its garbage had nourished him, he would end on its rubbish heaps." (207) Beauty and pathos and filth—all exist in the punkah wallah; all these constituent parts are identical and have equal value. Yet in some elusive way he is aloof from such definitions.

Forster explains the presence of the Hindu temple in part 3 of *A Passage to India* as "architecturally necessary. I needed a lump, or a Hindu temple if you like—a mountain standing up."[4] Like the mosque and the cave, it is space-enclosed, small, sacred, internal—where the soul may privately meet its god. But whereas the mosque was no longer used for religious services and the caves had no well-defined spiritual purpose, the Hindu temple of the third section is a fully developed, robust, and deeply spiritual place. Not that it fits Forster's description of the small dark room at the center of a Hindu temple, a retreat for private meditation and worship. This time it is the backdrop for congregational worship in an exterior setting, a spiritual festival full of vitality, joyous worship, intense spiritual concentration accompanied by much clamor, color, and action, all spiritually directed. In the words of a present-day interpreter of India, community festivals employ rituals that emphasize the role of religion in the celebration of ordinary human life: "For Hindus, the activation of icons makes present the power of the various deities represented. This presence is transmitted to festival sponsors and audience by . . . viewing the icons, by . . . worshipping the deity, by eating . . . food permeated with the god's power, or by love or service to the god as indicated by singing his praises, dancing, engaging in a drama, or other means. By participating in this way festival-makers and -goers are marked by the presence of exemplary figures, becoming more like gods and goddesses and hence better people."[5]

The Gokul Ashtami festival, celebrating the birth of Krishna, which Forster experienced during his stay at the court of Dewas Senior, was inspired by Tukaram, a local seventeenth-century poet and saint. "For [Tukaram], love was supreme and it is through love that he identifies God's nature in verse":

> This thy nature is beyond the grasp of the mind
> or of words,
> and therefore I have made of devoted love a
> measure.
> I measure the endless by the measure of love.
> He is not to be truly measured by any other
> means.

This Hindu articulation of the Creator as Love is a recognition of the godly spark (atman) in the human spirit that can lead to self-transcendence, a devotion to his or her god that carries the human being beyond personal self to a unity with all of creation. It is not an intellectual approach to worship but an emotional one, from the heart, extending respect to other religions and celebrating diversity, reconciling differences through divinely inspired Love. And it is a self-directed worship without need for priestly intervention between humanity and the spirit of the god. The similarity with early Christian practices is not lost on Forster as he makes Professor Godbole the symbol of this aspect of Hinduism and a bridge between Forster's personal spiritual beliefs and what he discovered about traditional Hinduism during his stay at Dewas Senior.[6]

Professor Godbole's importance to Forster in *A Passage To India* becomes clear in the opening words of "Part III: Temple," placing the action squarely in the spiritual realm: "Some hundreds of miles westward of the Marabar Hills, and two years later in time, Professor Narayan Godbole stands in the presence of God." (274) He takes his role in the festival celebrating the birth of the god in the form of Krishna, and in Professor Godbole's mind tiny slivers of dissociated images bob to the surface—first of "an old woman he had met in Chandrapore days," then "a wasp seen he forgot where. . . . He loved the wasp equally." (277) The old woman, whose name he does not remember, is not important to him. What links Mrs. Moore to Professor Godbole is the wasp. In her brief Indian experience two years previously, "a little, little wasp" preempted the peg where she intended to hang her cloak. Of such a private and ephemeral episode Professor Godbole can have no knowledge. By delicately—and deliberately—connecting two such disparate characters, Forster subtly underscores their shared role as exemplars, Mrs. Moore's feeble Christianity contrasting with Professor Godbole's indefatigable expression of Hindu spirituality. Though of different religious traditions and in vastly different stages of understanding the Infinite—Professor Godbole stands in the presence of God while Mrs. Moore is trying to find that presence—they inhabit the same spiritual landscape, each seeking reconciliation of the many confusing, and often seemingly opposing, aspects of human life.

Forster describes this spiritual landscape through the actions of the crowds of worshippers: "The assembly was in a tender, happy state unknown to an English crowd, it seethed like a beneficent potion. . . . A most beautiful and radiant expression came into their faces, a beauty in which there was nothing personal, for it caused them all to resemble one another during the moment of its indwelling, and only when it was withdrawn did they revert to individual clods." (275) Similarly "the singers' expressions became fatuous and languid. They loved all men, the whole universe." (276) Forster does not deny the difficulty of retaining that fleeting state of spiritual union with the Incomprehensible. Yet even as they failed, "all sorrow was annihilated, not only for Indians, but for foreigners, birds, caves, railways, and the stars; all became joy, all laughter. . . . The human spirit had tried by a desperate contortion to ravish the unknown, flinging down science and history in the struggle, yes, beauty herself." (278) To the Hindu all life is included in the act of worship. Some who share in the spirit and joy of creation are quite incapable of expressing their joy, yet they, too—caves, railways, and stars, even foreigners with their stunted spirituality—are considered equally worthy to share in the joy of Infinite Love that the ceremony vivifies.

Equally important in the religious celebration is joyous humor. In his 1959 Presidential Address to the Cambridge Humanists, Forster says: "It may seem absurd to turn from Christ to Krishna, that vulgar blue-faced boy with his romps and butter-pats. Krishna is usually a trivial figure. But he does admit pleasure and fun and jokes and their connection with love." That Krishna was a prankster conferred divine approval on including games and jokes in this particular worship experience. "This worship achieved what Christianity has shirked: the inclusion of merriment. All spirit as well as all matter must participate in salvation, and if practical jokes are banned, the circle is incomplete." (279-80) Long after Forster's second trip to India, in preparing *Hill of Devi* for publication, he reiterated Krishna's significance: "One was left ... aware of a gap in Christianity: the canonical gospels do not record that Christ laughed or played. Can a man be perfect if he never laughs or plays? Krishna's jokes may be vapid, but they bridge a gap."[7]

About the same time Forster reviewed a book about Krishna for the BBC's *The Listener*, which sums up his understanding of the god, beginning with a chatty listing of his "encounters" with Krishna; it is worth quoting at length:

> The present reviewer has encountered
> Shri [Lord] Krishna once or twice in a

casual way: has attended his birth and
festival at Dewas; has seen his palace
dances at Chhatarpur; has read the
Bhagavad Gita and the tenth book of
the Bhagavata Purana; possesses a picture by Jamini Roy of a young farmer
claiming distant cousinhood; is indeed
on nearer nodding terms with Krishna
than with any other god. This is not
saying much, for to what god does one
venture to give a nod? Jehovah's awful
one certainly invites no response.
"Down on your knees!" is the more
usual injunction. Krishna inclines to
gaiety. Even if he kills a dragon he
dances on its teeth, which St. Michael
would not do. He is gay to the point of
silliness. . . . Discrepancies have to be
faced. How is it that the warrior who
drives Arjuna into battle and lectures
him *en route* on the nature of the universe is also a dark-skinned cowboy
who seduces hundreds of cowgirls?
The answer is that there must have
been two deities who coalesced. The
earlier one, the warrior, fits neatly into
the Indian cosmogony as an incarnation of Vishnu. The later one began as
a godling of a group of cattle-keepers

in the Jumna valley, was cheerful, disrespectful to the priesthood and to his elders, scandalously amorous, and he needed tidying up. He was tidied up in two directions—one social, the other mystic. Socially he became a king, who was legally married to hundreds of queens and was consequently respectable. Mystically, his "amours"—or rather the longings that were felt for him—symbolised the longings of the soul for God. The famous round dance, in which each girl believes that she, and she alone, dances with the beloved is ridiculous in terms of the body, possible in terms of the spirit. The infinite has enough to go round—enough and to spare.

Warrior, counsellor, randy villager, divine principle, flautist, great king: these are some of Krishna's aspects, and to them must be added the destroyer of dragons, the Hercules-Siegfried hero who makes the earth habitable for men. It is no wonder that in India so varied a deity exercises a wide appeal. Hindu religion has the high distinction of being non-propagandist. But if it abandoned that distinction ... and competed with Christianity and Islam as the unique representative of Truth, it might well push Krishna forward as its champion. There is no one in its contemporary pantheon, neither Siva nor Durga, who would function nearly as well.

... On the whole our Blue Boy comes out well. Some imaginative legends attach to him, some profound thoughts, some tenderness, and his birth story (where the Wicked King massacres the Innocents in the hope of destroying the God) evokes unexpected echoes. The present reviewer feels it however his duty to conclude with a word of warning to prospective worshippers: Krishna can be appallingly silly. His sense of fun makes the heart to sink. He adores practical jokes. When his mirth is at its height he steals the cowgirls' dresses while they are bathing; and hangs them on a tree. As an alternative, he steals butter.[8]

As Forster notes, along with his widespread penchant for tricks and jokes, Krishna's actions often were vehicles to reveal some facet of Hindu truth. During the festival depicted in *A Passage to India*, a deeply significant game played by the adults objectified Krishna in a child chosen randomly from the crowd at the festival. The chosen child is carried around: "All stroke the darling creature for the Creator's sake, and murmur happy words. The child is restored to his parents ... and another child becomes for a moment the World's desire. And the Lord [Krishna] bounds hither and thither ... irradiating little mortals with His immortality." (280) The game praises ongoing life and emphasizes the importance of the whole community in loving and nurturing all children spiritually as well as physically. In this gentle game, as in Jesus' injunction, "Suffer the little children to come unto me for of such is the Kingdom of Heaven," is reflected the gift of the divine atman, the spirit implicit in each human soul, that impels the individual to seek a connection with the divine Source. An unknown Hindu expressed the importance of atman succinctly in doggerel:

"Money lost, nothing lost
Honour lost, much lost
Courage lost, more lost
Soul lost, all lost."[9]

At each step of Forster's account in *A Passage to India* of the birthday of the Lord Krishna, he juxtaposes references to the story of Jesus' birth. Bethlehem is linked with the model of the village of Gokul; mention is made of "King Kansa, who is Herod, directing the murder of some Innocents, and in a corner ... stood the father and mother of the Lord [Krishna as well as Jesus], warned to depart in a dream." (278) Another connection with the Christian Good Friday story occurs in the release of a prisoner during the celebration of Krishna's birth. With the greatest finesse, in an almost offhand manner, Forster links Jesus' concern for the lowly and oppressed—"the least of these"—with Hinduism's ancient belief in the equality of all people whatever their status, at the same time pointing the reader's attention to the echo at the Marabar caves that murmured to Mrs. Moore, "Pathos, piety, courage—they exist, but are identical, and so is filth." Everything must be included in salvation, else the unity of all life is not complete. So it is the turn of the sweepers, who perform the lowliest and most menial tasks, to take part in the festival: "The Sweepers' Band was arriving. Playing on sieves and other emblems of their profession, they marched straight ... with the air of a victorious army. This was ritually the moment of the Despised and Rejected; the God could not issue from his temple until the unclean Sweepers played their tune, they were the spot of filth without which the spirit cannot cohere." (295–96) Only when every part of creation is accounted for is the full measure of the love of the Creator God realized.

Summing up in *A Passage to India* the effect of the festival on the worshippers, Forster wonders if their individual attempts at worship of the God have been successful. He answers yes but grants that the experience cannot be proven: "Not only from the unbeliever are mysteries hid, but the adept himself cannot retain them. He may think, if he chooses, that he has been with God, but as soon as he thinks it, it becomes history, and falls under the rules of time." (278) The experience becomes distorted by attempting to articulate it; felt in the soul, it is not easily translated into the solidity of words. Forster is aware of the multiplicity of interpretations of Hinduism but reiterates that "religion is a living force to the Hindus, and can at certain moments fling down everything that is petty and temporary in their natures. The festival flowed on, wild and sincere, and all men loved each other, and avoided by instinct whatever could cause inconvenience or pain. Aziz could not understand this, any more than an average Christian could." (294–95) But this vital quality of his religion is the bedrock of Godbole's life. He moved more easily than most between the physical level of melting butter and red powder and the spiritual realm wherein "he had . . . again seen Mrs. Moore, and round her faintly clinging forms of trouble. He was a Brahman, she Christian, but it made no difference. . . . It was his duty, as it was his desire, to place himself in the position of the God and to love her, and to place himself in her position and to say to the God, 'Come, come, come, come.' This was all he could do. How inadequate! But each according to his own capacities, and he knew that his own were small. 'One old Englishwoman and one little, little wasp. . . . It does not seem much, still it is more than I am myself.'" (281)

Here in one succinct paragraph Forster touches on many of his own beliefs—trust in individual intuition, *agape* love for all humanity, respect for the stranger one may meet in life's journey, awe before the divine mystery, acceptance of human flaws, duty (and desire) to try to emulate the god, willingness to take private action on behalf of another ("Come, come,

come, come") as well as acknowledgment of human imperfection. All this Forster finds in the Hinduism he saw in practice around him in his days at the court of Dewas Senior; all this Forster had found sadly lacking in the Christianity he knew. In the figure of Krishna he perceives a figure of worship for Hindus that shows signs of what Forster had vainly looked for in Christianity—"a man of our own sort," not pompous or tearful, but someone who would listen to one's woes, someone caring and encouraging.

Had Hinduism and its applicability to daily life been nothing more than an attempt to bring verisimilitude to the novel, one might have expected it to disappear with Mrs. Moore's death and the conclusion of the annual festival. Reintroducing the subject via the unlikely vehicle of three English visitors—Fielding, returned to India, now married to Mrs. Moore's daughter Stella, and her younger brother—signals Forster's sustained interest in the subject. Ever the logical, rational man, Fielding remains skeptical, and in asking the Muslim Dr. Aziz for advice, approaches the wrong counselor: "It is useless discussing Hindus with me. Living with them teaches me no more," (310) sums up Dr. Aziz's reaction. Fielding is no more interested for himself than he was when he left India two years before; now he wonders why his wife and her brother, who had never previously been in India, should "like Hinduism, though they take no interest in its forms? They won't talk to me about this. They know I think a certain side of their lives is a mistake, and are shy." (310) Stella, he admits, has found "something soothing, some solution of her queer troubles here." (309) Perhaps it is the "something in religion that may not be true, but has not yet been sung . . . something that the Hindus have perhaps found," as he himself had once earlier explained it. In a devastating comment reflecting his own spiritual deafness, Fielding adds, "Hindus are unable to sing." (265)

About Professor Godbole's origins Forster was frank. In a conversation with G. K. Das, he said, "I never met anyone like him. Professor Godbole was mainly constructed by me."[10] Professor Godbole is based on Forster's observations of Hinduism in a limited setting and is, therefore, in the eyes of Indian critics, partial. Yet Forster's experience of Hinduism was vital in relieving an ache in his own life that his experience of Christianity could never assuage. Though neither Professor Godbole nor Hinduism, as reflected in *A Passage to India*, is presented as a definitive view of Indian spiritual and secular life, Forster realized that an understanding of Hinduism could not be extracted by logic and rational analysis: "No man could say where was the emotional centre of it, any more than he could locate the heart of a cloud." (*PI* 306) "Godbole . . . becomes the character-equivalent of the Forsterian voice. . . . For him, as for the Forsterian voice, a full perception of the transcendent reality is impossible, as is a full awareness of the unity within the physical world; but his achievement, though partial, though won only by renunciation, is still a victory."[11] Professor Godbole is not intended to be an accurate or complete reflection of India but an instrument by which Forster expresses his hope for Universal Love within the Family of Man and his vivid appreciation of the Hindu spirituality, which attempts to reach out to what is godly in others and to look within to discover one's intrinsic spirituality.

That a religion could possess the vitality of traditional Hinduism, based as it is on an unabashed spirituality integrating the secular and the divine, was a welcome revelation to Forster. The concept of doing right simply because it was right (*dharma*), without expectation of reward, resonated with his ingrained sense of duty. Neither for the Hindu responding to the demands of the situation with dharma nor for Forster with his sense of personal responsibility was there need of a group of followers to strengthen personal resolve or provide an aura of validity. Lacking a single founder and a single accepted canon of belief and refusing to personify the god/spirit of creation, Hinduism emphasizes the direct contact of the person with his or her god. The individual or the family stands in private reverential awe before the mystery of the Creative Spirit, thankfully acknowledging the divinity within each human soul. All life is unified in the spirit (atman) of god and equal before it; within that unity wide variety is accepted. Syncretism, eclecticism, assimilation, tolerance are all traditional Hindu values that spoke to Forster's soul. Each of the multitudinous gods and goddesses of India is only a manifestation in human form of one or a few attributes of that "personality beyond our daily vision" that cannot be defined by finite human understanding. The earthy humanity of these godly figures makes them more readily accessible to ordinary people. In its ample dimensions Hinduism therefore provides expansive space for joy and humor and unashamedly embraces the physical side of life, including the sexual. In consequence there is little sense of sin or guilt; suffering is not from god. The individual's wrongdoings will be recorded in his or her karma.

What Forster found personally incompatible in historical Hinduism is more quickly listed: Asceticism to him denied the physical side of life with its joys and pleasures. He found the caste system unacceptable for the same reason that he struggled against the English class system: It denied the unique gifts and abilities of each human being and would relegate the individual to plodding through life instead of taking a chance based on private intuition to try to fulfill individual potential. And to him the deplorable lack of aesthetic sensibility was a personally insurmountable obstacle to his wholehearted emotional participation in Hindu religious festivals, although he accepted what discomforts he might have to endure in taking an active physical part in those festivities. In his own mind Forster was clear: he remained true to his definition of humanism. Yet Hinduism's values corresponded with many of his own spiritual beliefs and confirmed his personal philosophy of life.

"Invisible Power That Lies beyond the World"

Of course Forster was not the only English novelist to feel alienated by the narrow definition of acceptable religious practice in the Victorian period. By the time he appeared on the literary scene in the first decade of the twentieth century, his contemporaries who questioned the established order had gained recognition for their ideas, if not acceptance in public forums. But earlier novelists found public acceptance elusive, particularly where established religion was concerned. In the early days of the nineteenth century, the Brontë sisters— Charlotte, Emily, and Anne—daughters of an Anglican rector, knew from personal experience the bitterness of doctrinal differences between Anglican churchmen and their dissenting (non-Anglican) neighbors who, dissatisfied with the religious atmosphere they found in the Anglican church, broke away, some as early as the 1600s, to form their own independent denominations. In an 1840 letter to a friend on the public resentment of Dissenters forced to pay the state-imposed church-rate—a levy on all for the maintenance of the state-sanctioned Anglican church only —Charlotte Brontë ardently described the "noble, eloquent" sermons by two Anglican curates who attacked their audiences of Methodist and Baptist Dissenters for defying established religious authority, but she could not agree with the Anglican churchmen "either in all or in half their opinions." She considered them "bigoted, intolerant, and wholly unjustifiable on the ground of common sense." If she had been a Dissenter, she said, she would have "horsewhipped, or at least kicked" the curates "for their stern, bitter attack on my religion."[12]

Charlotte Brontë's first novel, *Jane Eyre,* was generally greeted with scathing reviews in religious publications, where it was called a "heathenish doctrine of religion," "pre-eminently an anti-Christian composition," that "violated every code human and divine." For depicting the destitution of the poor and "murmuring against the rich," Brontë was accused of flouting "the God-given order" with "a proud and perpetual assertion of the rights of man ... at once the most prominent and the most subtle evil ... [that] civilised society ... has at the present day to contend with."[13] Another reviewer accused the novelist of trying to show "how impossible it is to reconcile religion with love of mankind" and declared that Brontë "could not understand 'the pure ennobling influences of true Christianity.'"[14] While reviewers in religious journals were highly critical, individual clergymen sometimes expressed more complimentary views, praising *Jane Eyre* or recognizing that Brontë "draws the principal characters of the clerical class in a manner that makes you respect them."[15]

Like her sister, Anne Brontë had a clear-eyed view of Anglican clergy. In her novel *Agnes Grey* she contrasts a worldly rector's vengeful God, demanding the strict formalities from his village congregation, with his young curate's compassionate God as he visited the poor parishioners in their impoverished homes, commiserated with their ailments, and left them solaced in spirit by his nonjudgmental kindliness.[16]

Emily Brontë, best known as the author of *Wuthering Heights*, a powerful novel of love and hate and misshapen family relationships, also left a substantial poetic legacy. Even as a child, she was retiring and unsociable and considered brusque and "peculiar." Like Charlotte and Anne, she loved the Yorkshire moors surrounding their village of Haworth, where she felt in tune with Nature whether beneficent or wild and stormy. Rarely did she leave Haworth, usually only when driven by economic necessity. That she differed from her sis-

ters in her religious beliefs is made clear in her novel and confirmed in her poems. The local chapel in *Wuthering Heights* is
described in the opening pages of the novel as situated in a
hollow of the hills near a swamp, not a salubrious location, but
at least its roof is intact. There is no role in the novel for a clergyman of any kind, and the main characters, flouting social
mores and religious conventions, live lives as turbulent as the
storm clouds over the moors. Joseph, a servant, depicted as a
self-righteous pharisee who searches the Bible for passages fa-
vorable to himself and other verses threatening punishment
on everyone else, occasionally dragoons the youth of the
household to serve as unwilling congregation while he delivers a hellfire-and-brimstone sermon three hours long. In the
closing lines of the novel, only seven months later in narrative
time, the chapel is again brought to the reader's attention,
now in an advancing state of decay, with broken windows and
a leaking roof, a fitting symbol for Emily Brontë's disillusion-
ment with the Christian church, which seemed unable to provide the *Wuthering Heights* characters—or indeed, Emily herself—any protection against the harshness of life or any solace
or hope. Though she could laugh with family and a trusted
friend, her view of life was very largely informed by death,
loneliness, disappointment, and a longing for freedom. Substituting for dogma in Emily's philosophy were faith in her own
imagination and intuition, a passionate love of Nature in all its
moods, and a strong element of occultism from her childhood
exposure to the fantastic folktales of the country people of
Yorkshire. Her poems express the lifelong pain that her soul

endured and the heroic effort she continually had to make to
live with that pain:

> Riches I hold in light esteem
> And Love I laugh to scorn
> And lust of Fame was but a dream
> That vanished with the morn—
>
> And if I pray, the only prayer
> That moves my lips for me
> Is—"Leave the heart that now I bear
> And give me liberty."
>
> Yes, as my swift days near their goal
> 'Tis all that I implore—
> Through life and death, a chainless soul
> With courage to endure![17]

Twenty-two years of age when she wrote this poem, she died
at thirty.

The Brontës never openly turned away from the church,
not even Emily. In a letter to a friend dated December 1847,
Charlotte Brontë wrote that "I love the Church of England. Her
ministers, indeed, I do not regard as infallible personages. I
have seen too much of them for that, but to the Establishment,
with all her faults—the profane Athanasian creed *ex*cluded—I
am sincerely attached."[18] In his own time Forster had opinions
on Athanasius and Arius, two early Christian thinkers, and
their dispute, with its consequences troubling centuries later
to Charlotte Brontë—and to Forster himself.

Because of the narrow confines of the Brontës' lives and the short span of their existence in the first half of the nineteenth century—none of them reached the age of forty—the sisters had little exposure to the intellectual circles of their generation; most of the seminal ideas of evolution and utilitarianism appeared on the intellectual scene after Charlotte, the last surviving sister, died in 1855.

George Eliot, though born in the same decade as the Brontës, lived until 1880. She was brought up an Anglican, became briefly an ardent Evangelical, finally rebelling against the church in her early twenties, and turned toward German theologians whose new thoughts about Christianity were challenging accepted Victorian beliefs. From at least 1841 Eliot had been exposed to the English intellectual avant-garde of the mid-century and also to new religious thoughts from Auguste Comte, as well as German philosophers such as David Friedrich Strauss and Ludwig Feuerbach. Eliot spent several years in the decade of the 1850s translating Strauss's iconoclastic *Life of Jesus, Critically Examined,* followed later by her translation of Feuerbach's *The Essence of Christianity.* She also translated or reviewed other books on religious and philosophical subjects.

Unlike the Brontës, Eliot's rejection of the institutional church was complete. Her "love of the beauty of holiness" was expressed in striving for a "Moral Perfection" that would result in a broader sympathy for others, a goal suggesting comparison with Forster's belief in mutual improvement among friends as a substitute for the traditional notion of salvation. Like Forster, Eliot yearned for a "comprehensive Church whose fellowship consists in the desire to purify and ennoble human life,"[19] and where, she hoped, "the best members of all narrow churches may call themselves brother and sister in spite of differences." In an 1873 conversation reported by a friend, commenting on the traditional usage of the words "God," "immortality," and "duty," she "pronounced, with a terrible earnestness, how inconceivable was the *first*, how unbelievable the *second*, and yet how peremptory and absolute the *third*."[20] This statement, indeed, seems much more unequivocal than Forster's phrasing and completely lacking in his sense of mystery and awe before the divine, though, in the later years of her life, she did not deny a personal inner life: "Hardly anything could have happened to me which I could regard as a greater blessing, than the growth of my spiritual existence when my bodily existence is decaying."[21] Forster did not wait so long to embark on his spiritual journey.

Whatever George Eliot may have felt personally about organized religion in the nineteenth century, in *Adam Bede* she realistically portrayed both the Methodist woman preacher, Dinah Morris, and the Anglican rector, the Reverend Adolphus Irwine, with sympathetic understanding rather than ridicule or comedy, without ignoring the shortcomings of their theology or human relations. In contrast with some Methodist preachers who were described as the "ecstatic" type or the "bilious," Dinah spoke quietly and persuasively from the heart. Perhaps "witness" is a better description as she exhorted rather than threatened. About Mr. Irwine, speaking in the vernacular of the village of Hayslope, Adam defended him as being free of didacticism: "Mester Irwine's got more sense nor to meddle wi' people's doing as they like in religion. That's between themselves and God, as he's said to me many a time."[22] The difference between Dinah Morris and Mr. Irwine is clearly defined at the death of Adam Bede's father when Dinah walks several miles to console the widow Bede while the rector, whose congregation included the Bedes as faithful communicants, only presides at the funeral at the parish church. Later, suspecting that Arthur Donnithorne, scion of the landowning family, might be seducing Hetty Sorrel, the lovely farm girl, Mr. Irwine does not attempt to "preach" to Arthur about moral issues.

Eliot devotes a whole chapter to explaining why she, as a novelist, should not—indeed, could not—repaint the social scene at the beginning of the nineteenth century to conform with later zealous ideals. She has an imaginary conversation with Adam Bede about the virtues of the more traditional Mr. Irwine, kindly and understanding, who respected all his congregants regardless of their station in life, opposing to him another Anglican rector who was called a "Ranter," a pejorative usually applied by Church of England believers to Dissenters such as Methodists for their hellfire-and-brimstone sermons. Eliot has Adam stoutly defending the Reverend Mr. Irwine. Acknowledging that Mr. Irwine is not an inspired preacher and is more interested in practical than spiritual matters, Adam insists that he "said nothing but what was good, and what you'd be the wiser for remembering."[23]

Still another novelist and social commentator on the last half of the nineteenth century scene, Anthony Trollope wrote, in his Barchester novels, about the deep divide between pastoral ministers who were truly caring shepherds of their flocks and those more interested in personal advancement to positions of visible power in the church hierarchy. Commenting on the common use of the curate as ill-paid underling, Trollope wrote that "it is notorious that a rector in the Church of England, in possession of, let us say, a living of a thousand [pounds] a year, shall employ a curate at seventy pounds a year, that the curate shall do three-fourths or more of the work of the parish, that he shall remain in that position for twenty years, taking one-fourteenth of the wages and doing three-fourths of the work, and that nobody shall think the rector is wrong or the curate ill-used!"[24] The Reverend Josiah Crawley in Trollope's *The Last Chronicle of Barset* was a curate of this sort. No longer a newly anointed clergyman but matured by many years of service, the Reverend Crawley had been shunted into a permanent curacy with an income hardly sufficient to support his family in the most meager fashion. His professional "failure" lies in choosing to devote himself to the spiritual lives of his small and impoverished flock at the expense of his advancement up the hierarchical ladder.[25]

While these and other Victorian novelists inveighed against the rigid dogmas of the institutional church, they were powerless as individuals to effect any change; the Church-State connection then seemed unassailable. Weak though their individual voices may have been, the narratives of their novels and poems spoke over the decades in a clarion voice; their influence lay in inspiring a potent cumulative sympathy in their readers for feelings expressed in their novels, an influence greatly feared by still another Brontë reviewer, who felt that Charlotte Brontë "had not faced up to the novelists' 'responsibilities as potentially influential directors of moral behaviour.'"[26] Forster shared with such nineteenth-century novelists a belief in the importance of human relationships, respect for the individual regardless of class or gender, devotion to the Truth that resides in the mind and the heart, and a passionate wish for more fulfilling life. Forster's advantage lay in his era; as the Victorian age moved inexorably toward the turn into the twentieth century, discussion of new ideas helped to diminish the power of previously unquestioned institutions to impose a set of rigid standards on society as a whole. People felt freer to speak and act. Some of the previously unassailable attitudes disappeared or were quickly adapted; others, such as religion, were harder to change. But at least dissenting voices were being expressed more clearly, and in greater numbers and volume, than before, and Forster was not reluctant to speak his mind.

That the social climate had changed markedly in the century since the Brontës and George Eliot is evidenced by the *Twentieth Century* magazine's invitation to Forster to comment on his personal spiritual beliefs and his eagerness to reply. He began by defining humanism in terms covering both his religious and political response to life: "If I say I am an atheist the obvious retort is 'That sounds rather crude,' if I say I am an agnostic, the retort is 'That sounds rather feeble,' if I say I am a liberal, the answer is 'You can't be: only Socialists and Tories [can claim to be liberals],' and if I say I am a Humanist, there is apt to be a bored withdrawal. On the whole Humanist is the best word, though. It expresses more nearly what I feel about myself, and it is Humanism that has been most precisely threatened during the past ten years. Humanism covers my main belief and my main disbelief." His firm belief is "in the individual and in his duty to create and to understand and to contact other individuals. A duty that may be and ought to be a delight. ... Whatever his own ... weaknesses, he himself is here, is now, he must understand, create, contact."[27]

While Forster's explanation of humanism seems subjective and personal, the dictionary definition is diffuse, covering everything from literary culture and classical learning to a "way of life centered upon human interests or values." Literary culture and classical learning were among the values he espoused. Other humanistic values in Forster's philosophy included individualism, as well as community, the potential for achieving self-fulfillment; a thoughtful, critical eye; the basic equality, dignity, and worth of humankind, to which he added the element of awe before the mystery of creation.

In contrast to Forster's belief in the most inclusive definition of humanism, he is strikingly focused, even adamant, about his disbelief: "I disbelieve in spiritual authority, however sincerely expressed and however nobly garbed. It is right to be respectful to other individuals and indeed to certain institutions, and to listen to what they have to say, one knows little enough and must seize every opportunity. But to believe anything *because* someone has said it or *because* some institution has promulgated it seems to me dead wrong." Continuing, he wrote: "My attitude towards religion may seem... very foolish. I like or anyhow tolerate most religions so long as they are weak, and I find in their rites an acknowledgement of our smallness, which is salutary. But I dread them all without exception as soon as they become powerful. All power corrupts. Absolute power which believes itself the instrument of absolute truth corrupts absolutely." These sentiments echoed Forster's younger reaction to the Cambridge University New Zealander's unquestioning certainty that he knew Right and Wrong and that others had only to follow his leadership.

In his letter to the *Twentieth Century*, using examples he saw about him to illustrate his point about the danger of institutionalized religion to the individual, Forster contrasted what he considered the more moderate Catholicism he saw then in English universities, where it was exposed to competition, with Irish Catholicism, which in that day was "strong and unchecked." Dr. Billy Graham's Protestant evangelism seemed less threatening to Forster than the fact that it had been given the Church of England's stamp of approval, which Forster feared could lead to "authoritative fundamentalism." A third example of unchecked religious power was "the protean movement which has been successively known as Buchmanism, The Oxford Group, and Moral Rearmament," whose founder once exclaimed, "Thank God for Hitler!" Forster linked these examples with "the religious aspect of Marxism, which tolerates no rival once it is established," as illustrations of religious and anti-religious absolutes, both absolutes equally heinous to his way of thinking. The antidote, Forster maintained, is humanism, yet organized religion is slanted against humanism: "Its conception of human nature, and its hopes for it are implicitly denied by emphasizing the arbitrary theory of Original Sin." Writing of his own life, he adds, "I have found it [humanism] something more positive than this, something life-giving, something which has made the work of the past seventy years exciting and valuable and sometimes comprehensible." And he concludes by listing simple ways in which humanistic virtues could be honored: "by reciting a list of the things one has enjoyed or found interesting, of the people who have helped one, and of the people whom one has loved and tried to help. The list would not be dramatic, it would lack the sonority of a creed, but it could be recited without any humility, for here speaks the human spirit." Forster sees no need to defend or apologize for holding humanist views.

Today most men and women would likely find this list of virtues insufficient inducement to practice a humanist ethic. But beneath such seemingly weak reeds proclaiming humanist ideas is a steely faith that hope will continue to grow like an arctic flower and bring forth blossoms of Love and Beauty in human relations in the most hostile environments. In his deliberately naive language, Forster stresses an *agape* love of humankind and life-enhancing relationships between modern-day people, similar to the practices of the early Christians who, in emphasizing equal respect for all and sharing with others, underscored the sanctity of the individual spirit and the importance of mutual improvement. Striking by its absence in Forster's philosophy is any inclination to form a group larger than those one has helped or been helped by; individual responsibility to act is what matters. Forster exhorts his readers to have the courage to be themselves and do what they enjoy doing and study what they are interested in, not what accepted canon tells them is required. Forster's concept of intuition is not a synonym for self-indulgent sybaritism; rather, it demands devotion to Truth as a spiritual rudder. Forster never pretends that a life guided by the humanistic values he revered is easy or simple; he knew the solitary commitment demanded and the psychic energy required to sustain a liberal position.

By the time he was eighty in 1959, Forster shared with the audience of Cambridge Humanists his adolescent announcement to his family—as he put it, his "rather pompous" announcement—that he had lost his faith: "It so happened, though I did not know it, that my father had lost his about 30 years previously and had recovered it after a short interval. My family assumed that I should follow the paternal pattern. They did not worry, and when time went on they got used to my having no faith, and so it has gone on since. I have been spared the trials of Ernest in *The Way of All Flesh*." In rejecting the traditional definition of God propounded by the Anglican church, Forster called himself an agnostic, not an atheist. At another time, in a conversation with an Indian scholar, he referred to himself as an unbeliever, amending that after a moment's consideration to "non-believer perhaps—a better description."[28] This self-definition brings to mind Professor Godbole's statement in *A Passage to India* that "absence implies presence, absence is not non-existence." Nonbeliever implies the possibility of belief, though not in the commonly accepted religious coin.

Agiornamento (Renewal)—Vatican II

Forster's spiritual philosophy was remarkably consistent throughout his long life, and clearly he was far in advance of his time. Forster was, after all, eighty-three years old when Vatican II began its discussions and had lived his own brand of spiritual life for more than sixty years. The conclusions of that momentous council could not have represented any new values to him. Vatican II was, actually, catching up with his prescient spiritual philosophy. The surprising call convening the Second Vatican Council in 1962, promulgated by Pope John XXIII over the negative reaction of his closest counselors, electrified Catholics around the world, and even motivated various Protestant denominations to look critically at the condition of their faith. In his opening speech the Pope called for the restoration of "the simple and pure lines that the face of the Church of Jesus Christ had at its birth."[29] The deep fissures between the conservative faction prevailing at the Vatican and liberal voices scattered through the worldwide Catholic church made every session of the council contentious; every word and nuance of its pronouncements were the result of fierce verbal battles, both on the floor of the council and behind the scenes; and differences were never entirely reconciled or eliminated over the four years of deliberations.[30] But the final decisions opened the Catholic church to new practices that reflected some of the attitudes of the early Christian churches and, incidentally, approached closer to Forster's lifelong beliefs and actions.

Besides proclaiming the importance of humanizing the Church of Rome and the person of Jesus (which, as has been noted, had been distorted by centuries of accumulated myth, careless copying of scripture, and fallible human interpretation), Vatican Council II is notable for empowering the Catholic laity to participate actively in the life of the church, including the ceremony of communion; instead of being merely passive spectators, they were acknowledged as "the people of God" and "a royal priesthood," both terms taken from the Bible. Individual personal dignity and freedom of conscience were proclaimed. That human dignity extends equally to all people was formally acknowledged, as was the belief that the Holy Spirit was indwelling in all people—though Vatican II seems to imply that "all people" means all Christian people, that somehow the Spirit is a monopoly of the Christian church. In addition to the traditional emphasis on salvation of souls so that they might enter Heaven, the mission of the church was expanded to address social issues of human life on earth. The separation of church and state was accepted, and the old practice of branding non-Christian religions "heretical communities" abandoned. That other religions were recognized as equally concerned with the question of humanity's relationship with the divine, though by other paths,[31] did not cause the Church of Rome to forswear proselytizing.

Vatican II validated for Catholics beliefs and attitudes that Forster had reached in early maturity and had been practicing privately for more than half a century. His lifelong religious expression had always been much closer to the values of liberal Protestants and Catholics, as well as the Quakers, Unitarians, and Humanists, than to institutions such as the Roman Catholic Church and the Church of England or, indeed, certain Protestant denominations. Yet he would have been happy to read the post-Vatican II statement of Hans Küng, a noted liberal Catholic theologian, that

> Jesus has often seemed to be "domesticated" in the Churches, turned almost into the representative of the religio-political system, justifying everything in its dogma, worship and canon law: the invisible head of a very clearly visible ecclesiastical machinery, the guarantor of whatever has come into existence by way of belief, morals and discipline. What an enormous amount he has been made to authorize and sanction in Church and society in the course of Christendom's two thousand years! ... For what odd ideas, laws, traditions, customs, measures he has had to take the blame! Against all the varied attempts to domesticate him, therefore, it must be made clear: *Jesus did not belong to the ecclesiastical and social establishment.*[32]

Forster would have been even more cheered to read that "Jesus ... was not an ascetic. ... Sour-faced piety he found repulsive. . . . He shared in the ordinary life of men. . . . Jesus' message appeared in many respects to be one of joy and liberation,"[33] and "it was addressed particularly to those who were not an elite and knew it."[34] It would surely have warmed Forster's heart to read the statement of such an important theologian that "Christianity and humanism are not opposites."[35] But I found no evidence that Forster expressed any interest in the discussions of Vatican II or recorded any comments on it. He certainly never felt the need for any outside approval of his personal philosophy. Indeed, he died in 1970, four years before Küng's voluminous book appeared in its original German; the English version came out two years later.

The works of the small number of scattered biblical scholars who, over the nineteenth and twentieth centuries, had each embarked on the long search for the "real" Jesus became more visible with the opening of public discussion during Vatican II. Present-day scholars who had also been pursuing the subject of the historical Jesus in lonely separateness finally came together in 1985 to organize the ecumenical Jesus Seminar. Using historical sources dating from the first three centuries of the Common Era, the Jesus Seminar fellows have applied the sum of their individual research to try to extract what in all likelihood Jesus actually said from the volume of words attributed to him in the gospels. Twelve years of discussion resulted in the publication in 1993 of *The Five Gospels: The Search for the Authentic Words of Jesus*. One of the concepts guiding the discussion of the Jesus Seminar is "beware of finding a Jesus entirely congenial to you." The fellows state that they continually ask themselves "whether the Jesus we have found is the Jesus we wanted to find. The last temptation is to create Jesus in our own image."[36] No individual names are given as authors of this volume since the fellows of the Jesus Seminar agreed early on that the results of their deliberations would be the product of the group, not individuals. The fifth gospel referred to is the Gospel of Thomas, written in the Coptic language and discovered at Nag Hammadi in Egypt in 1945. It consists of 114 sayings attributed to Jesus, half of them with parallels in the synoptic gospels of Matthew, Mark, and Luke. Interestingly, one of the earlier scholars to whom the Jesus Seminar dedicated *The Five Gospels* is David Friedrich Strauss, "who pioneered the quest of the historical Jesus" with his *Life of Jesus*, first published in 1835, translated into English by George Eliot in the middle of the nineteenth century. Strauss lost his teaching post at the seminary in Tübingen, Germany, because of his book. Almost 150 years later some fellows of the Jesus Seminar also were punished by their institutions because of their relationship with the seminar. Marcus Borg, a Protestant biblical scholar and fellow of the Jesus Seminar, in his volume *Meeting Jesus Again for the First Time*,[37] draws a picture of Jesus that coincidentally iterates many of Forster's beliefs. But Borg's lucid study was not published until 1994, twenty years after the publication of Küng's massive work and almost a quarter-century after Forster's death. The Jesus Seminar members agree that Jesus' actions focused on people, not doctrine or ritual procedures. Because his disciples were hungry, Jesus, believing in a compassionate God, told them to pick

ears of corn from the field on the Sabbath, in direct contraven-
tion of Old Testament law. He healed the sick on the Sabbath,
again intentionally breaking Hebraic law. He touched the unclean and ate with tax collectors and other "unsuitable" people and even talked with and counseled prostitutes, deliberate
actions that were assiduously avoided by the Pharisees. Not
fully comprehended during his lifetime, Jesus' radical rejection of the traditionally accepted code of conduct in favor of a
more compassionate attention to people faded in importance
over the centuries as organizational liturgy gradually usurped
a larger share of the worship service and the life of the growing Christian church. As has been mentioned before, had Jesus'
emphasis on people, rather than rigid rules of conduct largely
devised by fallible humans, been given adequate attention
over the centuries in Christian pulpits in England, it is reason-
able to believe that Forster would not have rejected the figure
of Christ as an exemplar.

"Breathing Holes for the Human Spirit"

Hopeful though Forster personally was of humanity's *potential* for improvement, he was yet realistic about the desperate
"muddle"—to use a favorite expression of his—in which the
world was floundering. While recognizing the disheartening
conditions of the human struggle, Forster wrote that "the people I respect most behave *as if* they were immortal and *as if*
society were eternal. Both assumptions are false, both of them
must be accepted as true if we are to go on working and eating
and loving, and are to keep open a few breathing holes for the

human spirit."[38] Forster was not one to formulate a lofty goal for everyone else while excusing himself from engaging in a personal struggle toward that goal. Burdened with a difficult relationship with his mother, occasionally disappointed in friends, often frustrated in his love life, full of dread about the state of the world, Forster refused to give in to such daunting public or personal realities, preferring to meet the problems and dangers of life *as if* they did not count. They were there, but they were not to be allowed to shape life's destination. Claude J. Summers, in his deeply researched and insightful critique of Forster's work, quotes a lengthy passage from Christopher Isherwood; referring to Neville Chamberlain's trip to see Hitler in Munich in 1938, Isherwood describes Forster as more representative of Isherwood's definition of England than was Chamberlain: "Well, *my* 'England' is E. M. Forster: the antiheroic hero. . . . He advises us to live as if we were immortal. And he really does this himself, although he is as anxious and afraid as any of us, and never for an instant pretends not to be."[39] Forster—and the people he admired—would go on about the business of life, forever trying through all its burdens and uncertainties to keep alive even a tiny sense of hope, as a "breathing hole for the human spirit." The present could never replicate the past; change was inevitable. But curiosity and imagination, the courage to explore what was new and strange, and a willingness to take risks—these were qualities of Forster's character that emboldened him to live as if the world were stable and predictable when he knew it was quite the opposite.

For his times Forster was a radical, rejecting the leadership of both religion and science in his own instinctive search for the spirit that informs life. In his "Letter to *The Twentieth Century*," he wrote in 1955 about the individual: "The human race to which he belongs, may not survive, but that should not deter him, nor should he be deterred by minatory theories about its origin, nor by recent evidence that he, the individual, may after all be divisible." Forster's urgent charge to his readers bears repeating: "Wherever our race comes from, wherever it is going to, whatever his own fissures and weaknesses, he himself is here, is now, he must understand, create, contact."[40] To try to prepare "for all the emergencies of life beforehand" would mean equipping oneself "at the expense of joy." (*HE*, 57) As Alan Wilde writes, Forster believed that man must "give what meaning he can to his chaotic, orderless world, through his own, unaided efforts.... Such an effort will never be easy; the forces of disorder are powerful and persistent, but they can be fought against and partially subdued, if not conquered."[41]

During World War I, when Forster was with the Red Cross in Egypt, he read widely about influences of various religions in the history of Alexandria, especially about the struggles of the early Christians to define themselves. One argument was between Athanasius, who believed that God and Christ, being of the same substance, are therefore equals, and Arius, who believed that since Christ is the Son of God, he had to be younger than God and, though *like* God, is not of the same substance. Esoteric as this dispute may seem now, it was of vital importance to the early church and was finally decided at the Council of Nicaea in CE 325, when Athanasius's view prevailed, and reaffirmed in the First Council of Constantinople in 381. Forster preferred Arius's position: "It is easy to see why Arianism became popular. By making Christ younger and lower than God it brought him near to us—indeed it tended to level him into a mere good man and to forestall Unitarianism. It appealed to the untheologically minded, to emperors and even more to empresses. But St. Athanasius ... saw that while it popularised Christ it isolated God, and he fought it with vigour and venom. ... But the strife still continues in the hearts of men, who always tend to magnify the human in the divine, and it is probable that many an individual Christian today is an Arian without knowing it."[42]

From Egypt Forster corresponded regularly with Florence Barger, wife of a friend from Cambridge University days, the one person Forster trusted implicitly with his most intimate thoughts and feelings. From Egypt, probably in the summer of 1917, Forster wrote that, while her husband's example as a private student of Latin did not "inspire me to study the Synoptics [Matthew, Mark and Luke], yet I have been with them all day (Sunday), fearsomely examining the psychology of Christ, whom I am told I resemble."[43] From this offhand remark, shared with no one else, it is clear that Forster's response to life was already recognized by an unidentified person as closer to the historical Jesus than to the current practices of the Christian church he had disavowed.

Throughout his life Forster reiterated his view of Christianity in numerous book reviews, discussions with the BBC on the bias he perceived in their religious broadcasts, and in articles and letters in prominent journals of the day on subjects of current interest. He was never timid about expressing his opinions;[44] though politely phrased in beautiful language, his comments were often devastatingly ascerbic. While most critics simply accepted Forster's rejection of the traditional expression of Christianity, R. N. Parkinson, in a chapter called "The Inheritors," in Das and Beer's *E. M. Forster: A Human Exploration*, recognizes that Forster, as a novelist, is articulating his own spiritual journey:

> In some respects *Howards End* is Forster's symbol of God and his expression of religious feeling. This should come as no surprise, in spite of Forster's attitudes to organized religion. He has faith—the humanist faith in higher human possibilities—and he needs in this novel a way of expressing it. . . . If Forster rejects the particular system of Christianity, he accepts its results. His "aristocracy of the sensitive, the considerate and the plucky" has classical roots and it also has Christian ones, but he seems to want to go back to an archetype behind both. The house (the home of traditional wisdom), the wych elm

(superstition on its way to faith) and the
meadow (the beauty, joy and dignity of
labour) are his attempt to embody them.
He professes to be interested not in the
Ideas or the gods but in human witnesses to their reality.[45]

Though Parkinson did not carry forward his idea into a
consideration of Christian symbolism and Forster's own beliefs expressed in his other novels, this forthright acknowledgment of the Christian roots of Forster's spiritual dimension
stands in contrast to Wilfred Stone's interpretation in *The
Cave and the Mountain*, still a milestone in Forster criticism.
Stone's view of Forster is that "art is an *idea* of wholeness. . . .
Art . . . is a humanistic surrogate for God or the Divine Idea."[46]
This view is far from Forster's sense of awe before the mystery
of the Unknowable. For Forster Art is an avenue of communication between humankind and the divine. Forster is not looking for a surrogate god; he senses something larger than human imagination can provide as a sign of the "invisible power
that lies beyond the world." Before this mystery, not Art, he
stands in awe. Stone approvingly quotes Forster when he
writes that "higher pleasures [art, beauty, culture] . . . rather
resemble religion, and it is impossible to enjoy them without
trying to hand them on. . . . This 'passing on' impulse takes
various forms . . . but it is essentially a glow derived from the
central fire, and to extinguish it is to forbid the spread of the
[cultural] Gospel."[47] Perhaps Stone was not aware of Forster's
1959 Presidential Address to the Cambridge Humanists when

The Cave and the Mountain was published in 1966; whatever the reason, he fails to realize that this "passing on" is not merely a "glow" but an active impulse related to Forster's emphasis, stated in his Presidential Address, on "mutual improvement" between friends as preferable to the traditional means of salvation.

Stone further quotes Forster as saying, "I do not believe that this art business can be swept aside. No violence can destroy it, no sneering can belittle it. Based on an integrity in man's nature which lies deeper than moral integrity, it rises to heights of triumph which give us cause to hope."[48] Stone's response is, "Surely this argument, in the age of Hiroshima and Buchenwald, is mistaken."[49] Stone seems not to grasp that with Forster, beyond his disavowal of the Christian dogma of his childhood, there was a subliminal sense of hope and a personal integrity, deeper than just a moral response, that taps into the most basic religious response to the unknowable omniscience of a Creator. Forster also held the belief that a bit of that spirit of creation is present in each human soul, only awaiting the individual's urge to connect with it. Not easily accomplished, this tapping into the sublime spirit of the Divine is hardly a topic for table conversation. Those Western characters in Forster's novels who do possess it—Mrs. Wilcox, the mature Margaret Schlegel, Stephen Wonham, Mr. Emerson, Mrs. Moore—are usually quite unable to articulate the connection, but their muteness does not deserve Stone's too-clever characterization as "spiritual autism."[50] In *Howards End* For-

ster comments that "some closing of the gates is inevitable after thirty if the mind itself is to become a creative power."
(259) Only thus could Margaret develop her inner life. Stone
sees only the surface result of such quietude, but that inartic-
ulateness is just the outward evidence of a strenuous attempt
to bring the inner being into connection with the infinite creative force. What Stone sees as muteness can be interpreted as
simply an effort to allow the intuition to function unimpeded
by society's rules or institutional religion's dogma.

While Stone quotes Forster about "the lower personality,"
he fails to accept his argument that "each human mind has
two personalities, one on the surface, one deeper down. The
upper personality has a name. . . . The lower personality is a
very queer affair. . . . Without it there is no literature, because
unless a man dips a bucket down into it occasionally he cannot
produce first-class work. . . . It has something in common with
all other deeper personalities, and the mystic will assert that
the common quality is God, and that here, in the obscure recesses of our being we near the gates of the Divine."[51] Stone
too glibly dismisses Forster's personal views of undogmatic
Christianity, a free-flowing stream of faith before its flow became confined in more narrowly defined channels over the
centuries by canonical proclamations and obstructed by perceived political urgencies. The unintended result is that the
individual worshiper was distanced further and further from
the source of belief, and obstacles of hierarchy and dogma
were interposed between the worshipper and his or her God.

In contrast to his myopia about Forster's use of Christian
symbols in earlier novels, Stone is enthusiastically articulate

about Hinduism's importance in Forster's spiritual philosophy, and his insights are significant:

> [Forster] honors the Hindu way in par-
> ticular because it is the least resistant to
> the unconscious and the instinctual, the
> least dogmatic and theological, the least
> appalled by the vision of the shadow.
> Shadows and their echoes are not good,
> any more than death is good; but to be
> unable to acknowledge and be in touch
> with such facts of life, whether out of
> fear or fastidiousness or obtuseness, is to
> fragment life, to render it sterile, joyless,
> and fundamentally unreal.
>
> Hinduism, therefore . . . is valuable
> in that it restores those things that the
> West (and some of the East) has most
> repressed and forgotten. The book ex-
> horts our spiritually impoverished,
> symbol-less age to connect the con-
> scious and the unconscious sphere of
> our being.[52]

Readers will perceive similarities between Forster's spiritual
position and the theories of C. G. Jung, the Swiss psychiatrist
who stressed the importance of the spiritual in the human
soul. Born in 1875, Jung was of the same generation as Forster,

but an examination of Forster's journals, though not deliberately searched for mention of Jung, found none. It is probable
that in pursuing his own spiritual path, Forster independently
developed a personal philosophy resonant in accidental ways
with Jung's teachings.

Forster comments in 1914 on his perception of the difference between religion as commonly practiced in England and
the Hindu religion in India, writing shortly after his first trip
to India in 1912:

> Religion, in Protestant England, is
> mainly concerned with conduct. It is an
> ethical code—a code with a divine sanc-
> tion it is true, but applicable to daily life.
> We are to love our brother, whom we
> can see. We are to hurt no one, by word
> or deed. We are to be pitiful, pure-
> minded, honest in our business, reliable,
> tolerant, brave. These precepts . . . lie at
> the heart of the Protestant faith, and no
> accuracy in theology is held to excuse
> any neglect of them.
>
> . . . The code is so spiritual and
> lofty, and contains such frequent ref-
> erences to the Unseen, that few of its
> adherents realise it only expresses half
> of the religious idea. The other half is
> expressed in the creed of the Hindus.

The Hindu is concerned not with conduct, but with vision. To realise what
God is seems more important than to
do what God wants. He has a constant
sense of the unseen—of the powers
around if he is a peasant, of the power
behind if he is a philosopher, and he
feels that this tangible world, with its
chatter of right and wrong, subserves
the intangible. ... Hinduism can pull
itself to supply the human demand for
Morality just as Protestantism at a
pinch can meet the human desire for
the infinite and the incomprehensible.
But the effort is in neither case congenial. Left to itself each lapses—the
one into mysticism, the other into eth-
ics.[53]

Looking beyond ritual, doctrine, and religious hierarchies,
Forster approaches what seem to others to be irreconcilable
opposites. His desire is to try to embrace seeming contradictions, to bring differing points of view together in a harmony
that is inclusive rather than divisive. In *Howards End* Forster
states his conviction succinctly: "Truth, being alive, [is] not
halfway between anything. It [is] only to be found by continuous excursions into either realm." (192) Unity, not dichotomy,
is his goal. Unity, reconciliation, inclusion, incorporation of
differences—all would demand change by everyone involved;

but the synthesis, if practiced, would not mean giving up something to achieve compromise but would result rather in a more fully realized human spirit. This is Forster's dream. But he sees this dream accomplished not by an institution but by individuals for "any human being lies closer to the unseen than any organization." (28) Individuals are likely to be engaged in a personal spiritual search that is far removed from the dogma of "institutional religion's three R's—ritual, rules, and wrath"[54]—experienced by those who accept without question the teachings of an institution, exemplifying Martin Buber's comment that theology is talking *about* God while religion is *experiencing* God.

At least one friend felt that Forster was a person who experienced God. W. H. Auden wrote to Christopher Isherwood, "As I see him, Morgan is a person who is so accustomed to the Presence of God that he is unaware of it: he has never known what it feels like when the Presence is withdrawn."[55] Earlier, in 1934, Auden wrote of Forster's "sense of the mystery of life," and "called him one of the 'examples permanent and alert' of those who believed that the fight to save humanity can be won by mental action."[56]

Even those close to Forster disagreed about his spiritual life. Isherwood, who was hostile toward religion, thought that Auden's comments were colored by Auden's "distinct Christian leanings."[57] Though Auden and Isherwood argued fiercely about religion, they united in acknowledging Forster's strong influence on them professionally and personally. Auden wrote a sonnet "To E. M. Forster" that he and Isherwood used for the dedication of *Journey to a War*, their brief experience of the 1930s war in China.

Some years later Isherwood's curiosity was still nagging him about Forster's religious attitudes. In a 1944 letter to Isherwood, Forster writes in obvious answer to a question, "Yes, I'm aware of something in myself at times which isn't myself. ... I don't like to call it God nor do I think it wisely so called, for the reason that the word 'God' has kept such bad company and hypnotizes its users in wrong directions. I even queried your saying that it was infinitely *greater* than oneself; *different*, yes, but one hasn't the apparatus for measuring size."[58] Furbank, Forster's chosen biographer, relegated Auden's comment to a footnote and invoked Isherwood's doubts about Auden.[59] With Furbank, Stone, and other critics of that period, could there have been a personal antipathy toward established religion that colored their interpretation of Forster's personal spirituality?

How to account for Forster's idiosyncratic spiritual dimensions? He was brought up like thousands of other children of his generation, baptized in the Church of England, taken to services "when the mud was not too bad" by parents more likely to be nonchalant than devout, to listen to sermons long on duty and short on awe, and exposed to little or no religious instruction from either church or family. Few felt, and fewer followed, the spiritual urge to which Forster seemed naturally attuned. Yet he absorbed enough of the traditional teachings of the Church of England in his early years to try to enlighten his fellow student at boarding school about Easter and Pentecost and Christmas. Undoubtedly the absence of strong pressure to conform was an advantage; it left room for Forster's unsullied spirit as a child to search on its own terms for what it could not articulate but only feel. Forster's great-grandfather Henry Thornton believed that imagination was something to be actively extinguished in children, describing it as "'that foggy region' which makes many . . . 'err long and much from the truth.'"[60] Thornton worked assiduously to do so with his own offspring, while allowing them amusements such as puppet shows or amateur theatricals with moralizing scripts. He even considered such diversions necessary "to enable us to perform our duties."[61] And duty was the primary motivation and goal of life then. Leaders of the succeeding generations, while still inclined toward conformity, admitted art and science into the list of acceptable influences and began to see foreign countries as interesting in themselves rather than merely as fields for missionary enterprise and economic exploitation.

Forster's mother was not so heavy-handed a parent; indeed, it could be said that she was rather distant in many respects, whether from choice or example or ignorance. Instead of the prevailing Victorian model of deliberate parental molding—or suppression—of childish impulses, Mrs. Forster's apparent lack of interference may have allowed the boy to define his own values, to trust his natural instincts and feelings, and to develop self-direction. She was not without sensitivity to the problems her child experienced in his formal education; she dismissed the tutor when she perceived that her son was not flourishing as she had hoped. Similarly, she later found a day school for him to attend when boarding school caused him great unhappiness, and she never inhibited the growth of his vivid imagination, an ineluctable factor in his lifelong openness to new, or previously unacceptable, ideas. In his later years Forster would describe thinking for oneself as "that most precious experience of youth which is far from universal, and is often discouraged."

Fortunately his family desisted from active discouragement. As he grew older his spiritual philosophy never flitted from one faith pattern to another. The mature religious framework he created for himself was consistent and discerning, open and sensitive to other people, embracing both the human and the sacred. Forster was alert to the possibility of finding in other religions some beliefs or actions that echoed his personal spiritual practices and filled lacunae that he deeply deplored in the traditional forms of the faith of his forefathers.

Part Four

Wider Circles

Chapter Seven

Homosexuality: Mother, Church, and Society

Maurice

Forster's novel *Maurice* mirrors the threatening world that faced homosexuals in 1913 England. Until 1861 male homosexuality had been punishable by death, and though the death penalty was abolished in that year, penal servitude remained. The "Criminal Law Amendment Act of 1885," also called the Labouchère Amendment—under which Oscar Wilde was charged—increased the penalty for relations between consenting males to a criminal offense punishable by as many as two years' imprisonment "with or without hard labour."[1] Lesbians were generally legally ignored.

Oscar Wilde's imprisonment in 1895 hung like a roiling thundercloud over homosexual men who were branded "unspeakables," "perverts," "sodomites." Sometimes they called themselves such opprobrious names: At one point in the early pages of *Maurice*, Clive Durham describes his attraction to the eponymous Maurice Hall as "my criminal morbidity."[2] While it can be argued that this novel is as carefully crafted, psychologically sound, and beautifully written as the earlier ones,

Forster's comic spirit is clearly missing; the subject was too threatening to joke about, and the position of homosexuals too precarious, too vulnerable to economic pressure and social ostracism, even to rejection by the family. But to Forster, "a happy ending was imperative." He was "determined that in fiction anyway two men should fall in love and remain in it for the ever and ever that fiction allows."[3] Retreat into the greenwood and disappearance from the flow of ordinary life may not now seem a happy solution, but in the early days of the last century it was a courageous choice—perhaps the only option—and preferable to some to the closet's lies and deceptions and the unceasing fear of inadvertent exposure and ensuing censure.

Sex was rarely discussed openly by Victorians. Besides calling it "dirty," Forster's mother apparently never offered her young son a word of advice or any protection or factual information on the subject. Negative reactions by adults were plentiful but never became the reason for enlightening discussion. Like most children at the turn into the twentieth century, Forster unconsciously picked up impressions about sex from play with the garden boys, tussling with a tutor, the skewed and smutty talk of boys at public schools. In later years, looking back on his childhood experiences, Forster wrote in his "Locked Journal" about his early life at Rooksnest: "With Ansell I was intimate. I about 8–10, he older, 15 perhaps. We built a little house between a straw stack and hedge, and often lay in each other's arms, tickling and screaming. . . . Ansell was my first friend."[4] At eight or ten years of age, intimacy had a different meaning. The tutor tickled his ribs, "which I loved and hated, but loved most." At this time the boy learned that he could excite himself sexually by sliding up and down the trunk of a tree. And he had a dream about his tutor's genitalia that, he recognized when he recorded the memory twenty years later, had undoubtedly been embroidered by subsequent daydreams. As a child he believed his penis, which he called his "dirty," was "unique and a punishment."

Like many children, his childhood experience was an assorted mix of innocent early childish sexual stimulation plus misinformation picked up from equally uninformed boys. In his later years Forster acknowledged that he had grown up in a "haze" of elderly ladies. He certainly had no adequate male models. Uncle Willie Forster was apparently a detestable man of arrogant insensitivity, and the Whichelo uncles unsuitable examples, in spite of admirable qualities, because they had not attended university. Forster's situation was not unique; few families provided factual sexual information. His friends claimed that he was thirty years old before he knew where babies came from. Perhaps these several influences contributed to Forster's awkward combination of childish sexual stimulation and unassimilated clods of misinformation.

At boarding school Forster "learnt that there was queer stuff in [the] Bible." In all likelihood, as an eleven-year-old he understood only some parts of the biblical texts he was studying and further compounded imperfect understanding with misinterpretation of the vocabulary of the King James version: "Told my mother in the holidays that now I knew what com-

mitting adultery was. She looked worried, and said 'So you understand now how dreadful it would be to mention it, especially if a gentleman was there.'" She extinguished discussion
of the subject and afforded no clarification of his confused
ideas. Because Forster was easily bullied and humiliated by
other children, at school he was the butt of crude jokes and
pranks. But there he fell in love with an older boy, and as Forster later described it, it was "at least [a] first approach to what
can be called love, for the emotion was more definite than in
the cases of Ansell or McHarvey, and the sense of unrequited
affection came in." In dormitory horseplay some boys would
be made to crawl between the legs of others; Forster was
"nipped" between the legs of the boy he had a crush on, was
unable to move but "felt great joy."

A more significant and less innocent sexual encounter occurred at the age of twelve when the headmaster allowed him,
because of his supposed frail health, to take a solitary walk rather than watch the other boys in a sports contest. Rambling
on the downs, he came across a middle-aged man urinating in
full view, who then spoke to the boy and told him to play with
his penis and "pull it about." In innocent politeness the boy
acquiesced and was startled by the man's ejaculation. The man
did not touch the boy nor attempt to restrain him from leaving
but did offer him money, which the boy refused. The boy returned to school feeling increasingly uncomfortable and
wrote a confused letter to his mother. Horrified, she urged
him to go to the headmaster, enclosing a note she asked the
boy to convey. She herself delayed visiting her son at the
school until the end of the term, explaining "it was such a

dreadful thing that she could not speak to Mr. H. [Hutchinson, the headmaster] about it unless she were positively forced to."[5] She asked her son if he had "cured himself of his 'dirty trick' [masturbation]. I said I hadn't and she was so distressed and worried that I decided not to mention it to her again. Thus ended my last chance of a confidence. All this incident impressed me v. much, but as far [as] I can see, it had not any effect on my development. I connected it with no sensations of my own." The incident may have had no lasting sexual consequence, but the psychological cost was dear: At the age of twelve, Forster had learned that he could no longer confide in his mother or expect parental guidance or protection from her. Quite the contrary. From this tender age on, he would have to assume the adult role, providing his mother psychological cushioning from what she considered the repugnant aspects of life.

The boy did report the incident on the downs to the headmaster, who was in all likelihood a clergyman, as were most public-school headmasters of that era. The headmaster seemed more interested in protecting the man than defending the boy, for as headmaster and student walked together to the police station, he warned the boy against accusing supposedly innocent strangers and talked obscurely about the Bible and Adam and Eve and suggested mysteriously that "boys may do great harm to themselves," what harm he did not specify.[6] Years later Forster wrote that the headmaster had "lost a great opportunity of enlightening me, for I was full of curiosity and quite cheerful." Enlightenment was not in the headmaster's mind, however; he was undoubtedly more concerned about the harm that any possible scandal might do to the school's reputation. Fortunately the boy somehow avoided the common, if unconscious, shift of responsibility for such an episode from the adult to the child, thereby escaping a false sense of guilt and sin.

Forster the novelist later incorporated the hypocrisy and callousness of the headmaster—his insensitivity to a child's feelings in his spontaneous attempt to protect the offending adult—in a fictional scene in *Maurice*, his novel about homosexuality written in 1913. A teacher at a boarding school endeavors to tell a fifteen-year-old graduating student "the facts of life," using a stick to draw illustrations in the sand of the beach. Continuing their stroll along the beach, the man pontificates about sex and how one should never mention it, especially not to ladies, and expounds on the glory and nobility of womanhood and the responsibility men have to protect it. He speaks of the ideal man, "chaste with asceticism," and of "the great things—Love, Life."[7] All this monologue passes over the boy's head as the two wander slowly down the beach, until, looking behind him, the teacher discovers a party, including a lady, also strolling along the beach on a path that would take them directly to where the anatomical diagrams had been sketched in the sand. Frantic with fear, he starts to run back, hoping to erase the incriminating drawings, only to be halted by the boy's practical question, "Sir, won't it be all right? . . . The tide'll have covered them by now." Suddenly the lad, who has been, with polite bewilderment, attending to the man's pronouncements, sees him for what he is, and despises him and his explanations as false. "'Liar,' he thought. 'Liar, coward, he's told me nothing.'" (6) Whether the facts were true or not, the student didn't know or care; what mattered was his certainty that the teacher's socially acceptable adult morality about sex and men-and-women felt false and dishonest.

The graduating prep school student Maurice, now at King's College, is not introspective but recognizes the hypocrisy of his teacher's beliefs about sexuality. Like Forster himself—who wrote of his fellow students at boarding school that "if they were not son's [sic] of gentlemen they would not be so unkind, if only I was at the Grammar School!"[8]—Maurice, at boarding school, has suffered cruelty and bullying, his nature protectively coarsening. At university he discovers that grown men generally behave politely toward each other. He could cautiously try to make meaningful connections with his peers. But he continues to accept the traditional split between body and soul, between spirituality and carnality as preached from Victorian pulpits.

Maurice and Clive, who meet and fall in love at university, go through the same stages of love that Forster experienced in his own childhood. The first stage might be called innocence, a love that was friendly adoration and affection. While the two young men later privately acknowledge their mutual physical attraction, by wordless agreement they refrain from physical fulfillment, preferring a state similar to the ideal man's chaste asceticism expounded by the boarding-school teacher on the beach. In his "Notes on *Maurice*" at the end of the novel, Forster wrote that Clive "believed in platonic restraint and induced Maurice to acquiesce." (217) It is Clive's eventual open declaration of physical love that at first horrifies Maurice, then exhilarates him when he acknowledges his homosexuality, though he can't yet quite bring himself to use that word, preferring to say that he has "always been like the Greeks and didn't know." (50)

Clive even as a child had taken religion seriously; troubled by the imperative of the body, he felt himself tainted by Original Sin and struggled to suppress his erotic impulses. But while "he could control the body[,] it was the tainted soul that mocked his prayers." (55) Maurice's conventional horror at his friend's open declaration of love shatters Clive's carefully constructed Hellenistic philosophy of life, and the Christian sense of sin springs up again in the ruins. Still, Clive challenges Maurice's traditional religious beliefs, having in his teens been "obliged . . . to throw over Christianity. . . . He wished Christianity would compromise with him a little and searched the Scriptures for support. There was David and Jonathan, there was even the 'disciple that Jesus loved.' But the church's interpretation was against him; he could not find any rest for his soul in her without crippling it, and withdrew higher into the classics yearly." (56) Responding to Clive's challenges to his orthodox religious beliefs, Maurice can only bluster, "Religion means a lot to me. . . . Because I say so little you think I don't feel. I care a lot." (34) Under continuing pressure, Maurice intones the commonly accepted attitude of the British public: "No doubt I can't prove the thing—I mean the arrangement of Three Gods in One and One in Three. But it means a lot to millions of people, whatever you may say, and we aren't going to give it up. We feel about it very deeply. God is good. That is the

main point. Why go off on a side track?" (35) Yet, yielding step
by step—the Trinity, the Redemption—before Clive's probing,
Maurice finally "realized that he had no sense of Christ's existence or of his goodness, and should be positively sorry if
there was such a person. His dislike of Christianity grew and
became profound." (37) At home, confessing his atheism to his
mother, he finds no real argument: "No one took any notice,
for the suburbs no longer exact Christianity. . . . Did society,
while professing to be so moral and sensitive, really mind anything?" (40) Maurice's rejection of traditional Christian beliefs echoes Forster's personal experience.

Having read classics, Clive wishes to visit Greece on what
seems a quasi-religious pilgrimage to the home of the gods
with whom he had replaced the Christian deity. Maurice vigorously opposes the trip, not only for himself—classical Greece
is too intellectual for him—but because he intuitively senses
that Clive's definition of love has tended to emphasize the
head over the heart. Maurice wants both the soul and the
body. He did not know that in the Golden Age of Athens the
naked male body was a sign of a young man rigorously trained
in both physical prowess and civic participation to become a
full-fledged citizen of Athens. Love between two such men was
understood as a positive element of citizenship because "the
code of sexuality affirm[ed] equality, harmony, and mutual integrity."[9] Indeed, "in the gymnasium a boy learned how to use
his body so that he could desire and be desired honorably . . .
and [he] was meant to learn the way to make love actively ra-

ther than passively."[10] Yet strict rules regulated sexual contact between men in that time and place: Instead of penetration there was mutual massage with both men standing to emphasize equality and avoid any semblance of subordination or subjectivity. And later in life it was expected that these men would marry women and have sons whom they could, in similar fashion, raise to full citizenship, thus assuring Athens of future generations of well-trained soldiers and responsible civic leaders. Perhaps Clive could find no vestiges in modern Athens of the classical Greece he had come to love through his studies. If he hoped that Victorian England would accept anything like the strictly regulated homosexual relationships enjoyed in ancient Greece, that hope was vain. In the end Greece failed him; he had no choice: "He saw only dying light and a dead land. He uttered no prayer, believed in no deity, and knew that the past was devoid of meaning like the present, and a refuge for cowards." He wrote Maurice, "Against my will I have become normal. I cannot help it." (97)

Rejected by Clive, Maurice contemplates but rejects suicide. Experiencing deep loneliness, believing in nothing, he suffers degradation in a visit to his neighbor, the family physician and friend of the family. He turns in desperation to Dr. Barry to confess his homosexuality, only to be rejected again with exclamations of "rubbish, rubbish." Forster does not blame Dr. Barry, who had read nothing about homosexuality in his medical training, the only texts being in German. Dr. Barry "endorsed the verdict of society gladly; that is to say, his verdict was theological." (136) In faint hope of help, Maurice goes to a hypnotist, who suggests that he move to France or

Italy where homosexuality was no longer criminal. Becoming an expatriate wasn't an option—he had a profession in England. Both physician and hypnotist failed him. From the depths of his despair, Maurice sees salvation only in total immersion in his profession as stockbroker and in charitable good works, the immersion doubling as self-repression. "Fed neither by Heaven nor by Earth he was going forward, a lamp that would have blown out, were materialism true. He hadn't a God, he hadn't a lover—the two usual incentives to virtue. But on he struggled . . . because dignity demanded it." (122) Yet slowly, secretly, "the flesh [was] educating the spirit . . . developing the sluggish heart and the slack mind against their will." (128) Eventually Maurice gains a lover but not without overcoming fears of blackmail and a sharp internal battle—not inappropriate in 1913—over their difference in social class.

The institutional church enters the narrative directly only toward the end of the novel in the person of the Reverend Mr. Borenius, the new rector at Penge, Clive's family home, who, as a part of the retinue of Clive's wife—which included Alec Scudder, the gamekeeper—came with her when she married Clive. Mr. Borenius is so rigidly orthodox that he will vote for no one in the upcoming election who does not take communion regularly, not even for his patron, Clive, who is a candidate. As for the opposition candidate, a radical, he will not vote for him even though he *is* a communicating Christian. Maurice replies to Mr. Borenius's dogmatic assertions: "Bit particular, sir, if I may say so. Clive will do all the things you want done. You may be lucky he isn't an atheist." Surprisingly Mr. Bore-

nius declares dismissively that "the atheist is nearer the Kingdom of Heaven than the hellenist. 'Unless ye become as little
children—and what is the atheist but a child?'" (160–61)

Mr. Borenius's dogmatic reach touches the whole community, from Clive, once a classics scholar, now master of the
family estate, to a servant like the gamekeeper, Alec Scudder,
whom the rector wishes to see married—"settled with a helpmate"—before his fast-approaching date to emigrate to the
Argentine. Gratuitously, Mr. Borenius hints that marriage is
the desirable goal for "all young men." (161) To his horror, the
rector discovers that before he can marry off Alec, he will have
to confirm him and there isn't enough time "to prepare him
properly before he sails, even if the bishop could be prevailed
upon." (163) Maurice challenges Mr. Borenius, "How do you
know he'll communicate if he's confirmed? . . . I don't communicate." (163) Mr. Borenius retorts, "But you were given the
opportunity. The priest did what he could for you. He has not
done what he could for Scudder and consequently the Church
is to blame." Maurice replies, "I'm awfully stupid, but I think I
see: You want to make sure that he and not the Church shall
be to blame in the future. Well, sir, that may be your idea of
religion but it isn't mine and it wasn't Christ's." (163–64)

The final encounter between Maurice and Mr. Borenius
occurs as both wait for Alec to appear on shipboard. Maurice
fears the rector has guessed that he is in love with Alec for "he
knew now that there is no secret of humanity which, from a
wrong angle, orthodoxy has not viewed, that religion is far
more acute than science, and if it only added judgement to in-

sight would be the greatest thing in the world." (205) Mr. Borenius is more concerned with Alec's rejection of confirmation
and attributes it to his "sensuality," adding for emphasis,
"with women." (206) Brandishing the Anglican Church's conviction that spirituality is inexorably superior to the flesh, he
continues, "But when the nations went a whoring they invariably ended by denying God, I think, and until all sexual irreg-
ularities and not some of them are penal the Church will never
reconquer England." (206) Mr. Borenius is a close follower of
the traditional church that from its earliest time ordained the
split between the spirit and the body. He believes sex, even
heterosexual sex, is "dirty" and that the soul and the body
should forever be kept separate. Maurice, rejecting such a doctrine, is willing to pay whatever price church and society
might assess to punish his rebellion.

While Maurice slowly fights his way through the maze of
expectations of family and society to find the true center of his
being, Alec Scudder appears to have had no particular qualms
about his own nature. At first a little "cheeky" by Maurice's
standards in his role as gamekeeper, he seems to be the initia-
tor of "chance" meetings and brief conversations with Maurice and prepares the scene for their first sexual encounter by
placing a ladder near Maurice's window and discreetly remov-
ing it the next morning. Yet Alec, too, has an internal battle: It
is difficult for him to trust Maurice. Having had no felicitous
personal experience with anyone of a loftier social class, he
expects nothing long lasting from his one-night stands with
Maurice and finds it impossible to believe that Maurice truly
intends to relinquish his privileged social position for love of

a gamekeeper. He remains committed to emigration to the Argentine but without the helpmate that Mr. Borenius thinks he needs. The rector has come to the ship to bring Alec a letter of introduction to an Anglican priest in Buenos Aires "in the hope that he will get confirmed after landing," and he continues, "Absurd, is it not? But being neither a hellenist nor an atheist I hold that conduct is dependent on faith, and that if a man is a 'bit of a swine' the cause is to be found in some misapprehension of God. Where there is heresy, immorality will sooner or later ensue." (205) Hellenists and atheists have been linked earlier in Mr. Borenius's discourse. One might be pardoned for wondering if Mr. Borenius uses "hellenist" as a subtle synonym for homosexual (as well as indirectly referring to Clive) and whether "a bit of a swine" is intended to refer to Clive as well as Alec—and probably Maurice, too—none of whom matches his straitlaced requirements. In the end Alec does not appear on board before the ship sails. He has come to terms with his fear of trusting Maurice's commitment to love and companionship "for ever and ever" with him and accepts an equal personal risk by rejecting the socially acceptable future envisioned for him in the Argentine.

Defining Alec and himself as outlaws, Maurice gives up his work as a stockbroker, and they go together to live in the greenwood. Some critics have labeled this solution sentimental. But as Claude Summers says, "There is nothing sentimental in the notion of hard-won happiness earned through mutual trust and support."[11] This was as much of a victory as Forster could then imagine for men determined to live and love as homosexuals. It was a *happy* ending because no one committed suicide or was executed or was even sentenced to prison for two years at hard labor, according to the law at the time. As Forster phrased it, the only penalty society could exact was an exile that Maurice and Alec gladly embraced.[12] The novel remained unpublished for more than fifty years. After Forster's death the second Abinger edition of *Maurice* as edited by Phillip Gardner includes an epilogue written in 1914 as an alternate ending to the novel. In a few paragraphs the novelist delineates the grim reality of that era for all those touched by homosexuality—not only by the lovers but also by their families because of society's and the church's obduracy toward homosexuality. Fortunately Forster rejected this ending, which appears only as a tentative epilogue in the second edition of *Maurice.* Had Forster ended the narrative in 1913 with a suicide or prison sentence, it would have been seen as an acceptable morality story and therefore publishable. But Forster's personal integrity would not bow to such pressure; better that the novel should languish in a desk drawer for over half a century until religious and legal attitudes changed.[13]

"The Story of a Panic"

Though the Church is not specifically mentioned in Forster's earliest story, "The Story of a Panic,"[14] the theme is the struggle of the soul to find its true fulfillment in spite of the fetters of society's expectations. Because Forster considers the institutional church the underlying arbiter of such standards, he holds it responsible for the mind-set of its adherents. Set in

Italy and published in 1904, though written a year or two earlier, "The Story of a Panic" has as one of its symbols the Greek
god Pan, who, with his primal energy and natural spirituality,
is obviously preferred by the two young protagonists, Eustace,
the bored adolescent English visitor, and Gennaro, the unlettered Italian peasant who, like the god Pan, expresses his un-
fettered personality directly and forcefully. The Victorian
Christian values are exemplified by the English adults of the
touring group, who unquestioningly uphold the Sawstonite
code of conformity as defined by the tenets of the Victorian
church.

While the English tourists are enjoying a picnic lunch on a
beautiful wooded hillside, a sudden wind springs up, its force
frightening them into a panic. Fleeing in fear down the hill,
they do not notice Eustace's absence until they have reached
the safety of the hotel. A search party finds the lad still at the
picnic site, lying relaxed on the ground, oblivious to the fears
that consumed the rest of the foreign visitors. His experience
of the wind is that it has blown away all of the inhibitions of
his English upbringing, leaving him free to satisfy the direct
needs of his soul for freedom and self-expression. A struggle
follows between the staid adults trying to force the lad back
into the traditional mold and the two young friends who fight
to remain true to their natural instincts. Though the story begins realistically with overtones of primitive religious mysticism in the form of the god Pan, in the end realism gives way
to wishful imagination; Gennaro dies but Eustace escapes in a
kind of Peter Pan fantasy, forever free from the grip of traditional conformity. Summers suggests this kind of never-never

land is an early expression of the sanctuary to be found in the greenwood of *Maurice*.[15] Wilfred Stone adds a spiritual dimension when he sees the English lad "with the help of this pagan Christ [Pan] . . . creating a private religion out of the archetypes but not the substance of old orthodoxy."[16] The Church, ever vigilant about nonconformity, criticized "The Story of a Panic" just as it had criticized Charlotte Brontë's writings, but by the end of the nineteenth century, the language of the Church was milder; Forster's story was only called "hopelessly foolish."[17]

Homosexuality was not overtly in Forster's mind as he wrote this first short story, and he was much distressed to learn from a friend that another acquaintance was nearly salivating about the undertone of homosexuality in "The Story of a Panic." Forster, horrified, did not want to meet this person. But in later years he wrote in his "Notebook Journal" that "in a stupid and unprofitable way he [the acquaintance] was right and that this was the cause of my indignation. I knew, as their creator, that Eustace . . . and the waiter had none of the conjunctions he visualised. I had no thought of sex for them, no thought of sex was in my mind. All the same I had been [physically] [sic] excited as I wrote and the passages where S—— thought something was up had excited me most." Similarly Forster belatedly realized that he had been stirred by the fight scene in *Where Angels Fear to Tread* between Gino and Philip. "I neither knew nor wondered why, and even if I had heard of Masochism I should have denied the connection. . . . When Eustace escaped that night over the terrace—well, where did he go? Ladies have sometimes asked me. I don't know. But in my happier moments I can follow him and I have never to this day forgiven the author of 'Erotidia' [the acquaintance] because he thinks he knows and slips out after twilight in his strongest spectacles, year after year, for a peep of a nights [sic] lust."[18] To Forster, prurience and titillation had no more respectful confluence with a joyful, natural homosexuality than did the prohibition of the Church.

Mohammed el-Adl

In his own life Forster did not accept the chasm the Church discerned between the spiritual and the physical. He envisioned a unity of body and soul, each aspect potentially enriching and completing the other in an individual's life journey. He tried to uphold this unity in his own life and actions, but Forster himself was not exempt from the gamut of anxieties haunting the closeted homosexual, from thoughts of suicide to fear of exposure and blackmail. Forster was nearly forty years old when he experienced his first fully satisfying sexual relationship, with a tram conductor, Mohammed el-Adl, in Egypt during Forster's World War I Red Cross assignment there. Their affair lasted about eighteen months before Forster's duties were completed and he was sent back to England. While in Egypt, he would sometimes connect something that had just happened to him personally with a scene in the previously written but unpublished novel *Maurice*. Speaking of el-Adl, he wrote to his friend Florence Barger that "curiously like Maurice towards the end of the book, I have found it so hard to believe he was neither traitor or cad."[19] In another letter to Mrs. Barger, he wished that he "was writing the latter half of *Maurice.* I now know so much more. It is awful to think of the thousands who go through youth without ever knowing. I have known in a way before, but never like this. My luck has been amazing."[20] Forster personally had found with el-Adl not only sexual fulfillment but the true companionship of human souls that he felt was even more important in the long run. Together, with courage and persistence, the two men broke through the barriers of class and color to achieve "that 'athletic love,' or taking trouble over relationships, which he [Forster] had often preached."[21] It must be emphasized again that Forster wrote *Maurice* in 1913, more than five years before he himself ever experienced such a committed homosexual relationship. One can only remark on the amazing fertility of the novelist's imagination that in writing the novel he intuited so accurately the steps and missteps that Maurice and Alec took on their blind search for the path through the thickets of ignorance, fear and despair, painful loneliness and self-doubt—compounded by rejection and ostracism—to fulfillment in the novel's narrative.

Though the Christian church was not such a powerful presence in Egypt as in England, Forster and el-Adl had felt unspoken pressure from British functionaries, as well as from Egyptian social mores, to conform to society's standards. After some awkwardness in the early days of their friendship, they managed to surmount their educational, social, and financial

differences. Forster's "riches and Mohammed's poverty became a standing joke between them: Mohammed would take
hold of Forster's sleeve, which was grubby, saying, 'You know,
Forster, though I am poorer than you, I would never be seen
in such a coat. I am not blaming you. No, I praise you. But I
would never be seen so. And your hat has a hole, and your boot
has a hole, and your socks have a hole.' Forster would promise
improvement, but Mohammed would say, no, clothes were an
infectious disease, 'I had much better not care, and look like
you, and so perhaps I will—but not in Alexandria.'"[22]

Because the two men cared deeply for each other as human beings as well as sexual partners, they remained in touch
by letter, and on his 1921–22 trip to India, Forster stopped in
Egypt to see el-Adl, who was not in good health. On the return
voyage, he found him close to death from consumption and
stayed some time to help him and his family both financially
and emotionally. El-Adl died soon after Forster's return to
England. Forster grieved so deeply over the death of his friend
and lover that he fell into a depression, unable, of course, to
share with his mother the cause for his malaise. But he did find
encouragement and wisdom in talking with Leonard Woolf, a
longtime Bloomsbury friend and husband of Virginia Woolf,
who advised him to continue to work at his half-written Indian novel, no matter what. Woolf's sturdy support helped
Forster through this bad period.[23]

India

Though el-Adl was Forster's first sexual partner, his first infatuation was for Syed Ross Masood, the Indian student whom he
had met more than ten years before el-Adl. Infatuation quickly
developed into love for the handsome Muslim, and their
friendship ripened over the five years Masood was in England
(1906–11). They saw each other often and travelled together
at least twice to the continent. However, when Forster summoned the courage to declare his love in 1911, Masood was
noncommittal; he had written some affectionate letters that
Forster might eagerly have misinterpreted as suggesting more
love than Masood was prepared to offer. He was not repelled
by homosexual love, just not interested, and he never rejected
Forster as a friend. But he had provided Forster his first adult
lesson in unrequited love. Masood had opened India to Forster
and urged him to visit the subcontinent. When Forster made
his first visit there in 1912, Masood was a warm host at his
home in Aligarh. Forster was shocked at Masood's early death
in 1937.[24]

On his return to India in 1921–22 as secretary to the maharaja of Dewas Senior, Forster recalled having heard on his previous visit that Sir Tukoji censured homosexuality. In *The Hill
of Devi* Forster writes that he told himself, "The least I can do
is to cause no trouble,"[25] but in spite of his resolve, he became
involved in sexual tangles that caused him considerable embarrassment with his friend. In Egypt with el-Adl he had found
a relationship of equality and intimacy of the spirit as well as
the body, but in Dewas money and enhanced position were the

only appreciable goals of those whom he approached sexually, usually servants of the palace. The intense heat of the dry season in India stimulated him sexually ("provoked" is the word Forster used), and the afternoon siesta mandated by the temperature only exacerbated the stimulation because the heat was "too exhausting to read or reason." (311) In spite of Forster's injunctions, the young men boasted among their cohorts about money and of their supposedly increased influence because of being favored by the foreign gentleman who was close to the maharaja.

At the same time Forster felt he was being laughed at and joked about in a coarse, even humiliating, fashion by servants, and fearing that the gossip would eventually reach Sir Tukoji's ears, he confessed personally to his friend to try to contain any possible damage to relationships at the court. Sir Tukoji was kindness itself: Although acknowledging that he didn't "encourage those people," he understood that with Forster "it's entirely different" (315), presumably because Forster made it clear that for him homosexuality was not a matter of choice.

Sir Tukoji's generosity of spirit turned Forster's proffered resignation into greater confidence and understanding between the two men, Sir Tukoji even offering to find a "suitable" person. That person turned out to be the barber Kanaya. But though that relationship was fulfilled sexually and was somewhat longer lasting than earlier encounters with palace servants, it was not really satisfying to Forster: "I couldn't get from Kanaya the emotional response of an Egyptian, because he had the body and soul of a slave." (319) Though a weakly established relationship, its longer life span inevitably caused greater complications as suspicions and gossip reached higher and higher into the palace hierarchy until Sir Tukoji's own authority was in danger. Kanaya's foolish overreaching brought about his downfall when he assumed, as had earlier servants, that his personal social position had risen with this liaison and that he could lever it into some sort of position with the maharaja himself. Forster, angry with Kanaya, felt vengeful, an emotion that made him feel "bad" about himself and an emotion that he said he never again felt. When Forster finally left Dewas, he gave Kanaya money and received in return a complaint that it wasn't enough. Sir Tukoji's comment was that "it shows how utterly he has failed to appreciate the high position he had with you—and your goodness to him—of course he has no notion of that." (324) In retrospect, Forster wrote, "I caused so much trouble all around, and my intimacy with [Sir Tukoji], the only gain, would have been achieved anyway I think. I see myself disintegrated and inert. . . . I asked [Sir Tukoji] once whether I could dominate lust as he seemed to—for he visits his wife but rarely and her alone. He replied: 'Oh one can't teach those things. When you are dissatisfied with your present state of existence, you will enter another—that's all.'" (324) It is safe to consider that this advice could only have come straight from the Hindu heart.

"The Life to Come"

After returning from his tour as the maharaja's secretary, Forster found time, while finishing *A Passage to India,* to write in 1922 a short story entitled "The Life to Come."[26] The theme of the story is Love. It directly addresses the Christian dichotomy between the spirit and the flesh, which has for centuries led to a mirroring schism in the definition of Love between spiritual love and erotic love. Though Forster carefully abstains from identifying the location of the story, in all likelihood it is set in Africa. Because the core of the narrative is homosexual love and how the Church regarded it, "The Life to Come" lay in a drawer for half a century until published posthumously in 1972.

The story opens in the ecstatic afterglow—"Darkness and beauty, darkness and beauty" (221)—of a satisfying sexual encounter involving Paul Pinmay, a missionary, and Vithobai, the handsome young chief of the local tribe. (It is interesting to note that Forster always refers to the missionary as *Mr.* Pinmay, as if wishing to distance himself from this character—or possibly to emphasize the distance deliberately created by the white imperialists between themselves and the indigenous population.) Recently arrived in the village, the neophyte missionary goes straight to his proselytizing work at Vithobai's court, explaining why the chief and his people should quickly become Christians. The chief does not deign to answer but designates a courtier to present the case against conversion. The missionary persists, demolishing the arguments of the retinue of courtiers one by one, while the chief remains mute. At nightfall Vithobai dismisses the exhausted missionary, directing that he be shown to a crude hut built round the roots of a towering tree well outside the village stockade. Here he prepares to sleep but is interrupted by Vithobai's arrival: "I have come secretly. ... I wish to hear more about this god whose name is Love." (223) Eagerly Pinmay takes up his Bible, opening it to First Corinthians, chapter 13, which begins, "Though I speak with the tongues of men and of angels, and have not love . . . "

Vithobai is impressed with Pinmay's explanation of "the love of Christ and of our love for each other in Christ," saying, "This is the first time I have heard such words, I like them" (223) and draws closer to Pinmay. Inspired by what seems to him an eager response, the missionary "determining to win him there and then imprinted a kiss on his forehead and drew him to Abraham's bosom." (223) To the missionary the kiss was doubtless intended as the Christian "kiss of peace" and the embrace as that of brothers in the faith, both actions symbolic of the Christian *agape* love for all humankind equally. But the chief understands things quite differently and extinguishes the lamp. Later, rousing from the glow of his sexual fulfillment, the missionary catches sight of the discarded Bible on the floor, still open to First Corinthians, and in a fit of remorse, hurls it out of the hut into the adjacent stream where it is borne away by the current. Guilt following remorse leads him to think that the only response to the situation is suicide. But he cannot find the gun. Fear follows, then panic, then quick packing up to leave that place immediately. Unhinged by what he had been taught to regard as a sin, he prays to Nature in the form of the overarching trees "to keep his unspeakable secret, to conceal it even from God." (222) Pinmay's few moments of Edenic life, followed rapidly by shame and fear, echo the biblical Adam's impulse, after eating the forbidden fruit, to make aprons of fig leaves for himself and Eve and to hide from God among the trees in the garden of Eden.

Pinmay's immediate dilemma is how to account to the other missionaries for his sudden return to headquarters. He recounts the hostile nature of his reception in the village, skips over the rest and suggests that his native retinue, fearing an attack from the local tribesmen, convinced him to decamp immediately and return to the coast. He rationalizes the episode to himself until he has become the victim and Vithobai the evil seducer. Worse, wishing to explain away his involvement, Pinmay twists events to convince himself that by tempting him to sin Vithobai has willfully attacked Christianity itself through corrupting its minister. Having arrived at an explanation of his actions that soothes his mind, Pinmay feels able to pray. He confesses "his defilement (the very name of which cannot be mentioned among Christians)," and "having begun by recommending the boy [Vithobai] to mercy he ended by asking that he might be damned." (224) He has willed himself into forgetful hypocrisy to extricate himself from a situation he cannot truthfully divulge to his colleagues—or, seemingly, even to God. But just as he believes he has escaped with his reputation intact, the news comes that Vithobai and all his people have embraced Christianity.

The missionaries on the coast, in appreciation of his proselytizing prowess, reward Pinmay with a ten-year assignment back in the village. To Pinmay their approbation was a life sentence to penal servitude. He is nearly undone by his secret sense of guilt and sin; the responsibility for his undisclosed actions seems an unbearable burden. But bear it he must if he is to live up to the missionaries' spurious good opinion and the Church's moral and theological requirements for the bearer of the Christian message. Back at the village, Pinmay must somehow manage to control the other sharer of their secret. He becomes a petty dictator: "He who had been wont to lay such stress on the Gospel teaching, on love, kindness, and personal influence, he who had preached that the Kingdom of Heaven is intimacy and emotion, now reacted with violence and treated the new converts and even [Vithobai] himself with the gloomy severity of the Old Law." (225) He mistrusts the native people, attacks their beliefs, undermines their tribal organization and customs, even forces them into Western-style clothing, and prohibits dancing. He gains such control only through deceptions, hypocrisy, evasions, outright lies, and false promises, and the effects twist his previously openhearted soul into something terribly misshapen, almost dead.

Vithobai, too, is greatly affected, as are his people, but in their degradation Pinmay has help. The unholy triumvirate of Church, State, and Money has wreaked havoc on the unsophisticated natives and their natural surroundings. Church actions to substitute Christianity for native beliefs are given the implicit stamp of approval by the State, which, in its reach to establish an empire, reciprocally receives the tacit approval of the Church. Money enters the scene, with the approval of both State and Church, in the shape of entrepreneurial adventurers who manage to gain control of the chief's lands and vigorously exploit the natural resources of the region for their own gain. In writing of the subjugation of simple native peoples and the despoliation of their pristine lands, Forster may have been mindful of the brutal rape of the Congo under King Leopold of Belgium at the turn into the twentieth century. The bestial treatment of the native people and the despoliation of the land—its minerals and forests, resulting in erosion and floods, as well as loss of wild food supplies and arable land—is a dreadful account of man's inhumanity to man in pursuit of Mammon.[27] Why Forster waited until 1922 to write on the subject is not known, but he may have seen enough of a much milder exploitation in British India during his visits there to stimulate him to write in protest against any degree of exploitation wherever it might occur. But all this is secondary to the point of the story itself, which is Love.

When under Pinmay's control, Love is stamped down and nearly destroyed. And yet whenever Vithobai speaks with Pinmay—which by Pinmay's devising is as infrequently as possible—it is the tribal chief who utters the words of Love as he understands it:

> "Let us both be entirely reasonable, sir. God continues to order me to love you. It is my life, whatever else I seem to do. My body and the breath in it are still yours, though you wither them up with this waiting. Come into the last forest, before it is cut down, and I will be kind, and all may end well. But it is now five years since you first said Not yet."
>
> "It is, and now I say Never."

"This time you say Never?"

"I do." (231)

Vithobai is taken aback and doubly astonished—injured might be the better word—when Pinmay demands that he repent and take back his words. Vithobai refuses, and Pinmay replies, "Then you must be punished." Rather than being untrue to himself, without hope Vithobai suffers the crushing blow of Pinmay's rebuff: "Then as if to himself [Vithobai] said: 'First the grapes of my body are pressed. Then I am silenced. Now I am punished. Night, evening, and a day. What remains?'" (231)

The headings of the four sections of this short story in their order are "Night," "Evening," "Day," and "Morning." How to explain this pointed reversal of the natural passage of time? Possibly these subtitles mirror the third verse of the first chapter of Genesis in which God is separating light from darkness: "God called the light Day, and the darkness he called Night. And there was evening and there was morning, one day." After each biblical act of creation, the litany is repeated: "And there was evening and there was morning. . . ." Another metaphor also comes to mind: Night's darkness can be protective, while the light of day has its destructive side. Old paintings, antique fabrics, even furniture, we are told by antique dealers and museum curators, must be protected lest their colors be bleached away by too much light. Forster may be saying that the natural expression of homosexual love fades gradually into something unrecognizable when it comes under the unforgiving examining beam of Christian theology. As the stern, scrutinizing light of that disapproval becomes stronger and more intensely focused, homosexuality disappears. Or so the Church of that day undoubtedly hoped.

The role of the Christian missionary in the nineteenth century was daunting, to say the least. Charlotte Brontë in *Jane Eyre* draws a rigorous portrait of St. John Rivers, long-lost cousin of Jane Eyre, who is willing to endure any difficulty in order to be a "soldier of the Cross" and who relentlessly pressures her to marry him so that they might go out to India as missionary husband-and-wife. Willing to go as an equal but separate partner in the mission work, she refuses to marry him. Though he might carry out the physical obligations of marriage, Jane recognizes that the schism between body and soul would remain in full force in him—he doesn't have the heart of a husband—whereas she rejects such a rift.

In any case, in "The Life to Come," Forster is emphasizing the unnaturalness of reversing the natural order of things. Pinmay certainly has everything backwards. From the first he had striven to displace the blame solely onto Vithobai's shoulders; five years later he is still frozen in that interpretation, yet wondering, "Did God, in His mystery, demand from him that he should cleanse his brother's soul before his own could be accepted? The dark erotic perversion that the chief mistook for Christianity—who had implanted it?" (232)

Pinmay continues to stagger along under the burden of his original dishonesty until shortly before his final departure from the village at the end of his ten-year sentence, when he learns that Vithobai is dying. Morning has at last arrived, but Pinmay and Vithobai interpret its arrival differently. Pinmay sees it as a new day that will eradicate the sin that has lain so long upon his soul and permit him to escape into the future untainted by the guilty burden he has carried for a decade. His longed-for Morning is a clean slate. He thinks he can finally thank God "for permitting [Vithobai], since die we must, to pass away at this particular moment; he would not have liked to leave him behind, festering, equivocal, and perhaps acquiring some sinister power." (233) In an automatic pious reaction he grabs up the accoutrements of Holy Communion and hurries off to do his liturgical duty to "watch with him through this dark hour." (234) For his part Vithobai sees Morning at long last emerging into unsullied clarity from the shadowy gloom of nightfall and the mirage of dawn's shifting light. One man dreams of escaping reality, the other longs for complete illumination. Yet only the fresh light of Morning holds the promise of dispelling the miasmas of hypocrisy and deception that polluted the ten-year-long Night.

Pinmay finds Vithobai lying on the flat roof of his house, naked, without even a mattress because "it is not the custom of my ancestors to die in a bed." Always concerned about the proprieties, the missionary looks for something to cover the dying man. The only visible thing is a clutch of blue flowers wound around a knife. Fearing that Vithobai may be lapsing from Christianity and suspicious even of natural beauty, Pinmay exclaims, "You are not going back to your old false gods?" "Oh, no. . . . These flowers are only a custom, and they comfort me." Pinmay will not allow that: "'There is only one comforter . . .' He glanced around the roof, then fell upon his knees. He could save a soul without danger to himself at last. 'Come to

Christ,' he said, 'but not in the way that you suppose. The time has come for me to explain. You and I once sinned together, yes, you and your missionary whom you so reverence. You and I must now repent together, yes, such is God's law.'" But Vithobai will have none of it: "Why do you wait until I am ill and you old?" The missionary's reply parrots ten years of hypocrisy and pretense: "I waited until I could forgive you and ask your forgiveness. It is the hour of your atonement and mine. Put away all despair, forget those wicked flowers. Let us repent and leave the rest to God."

Vithobai's spontaneous little homily in reply may bring to the reader's mind echoes of Professor Godbole in *A Passage to India* and the Hindu philosophy he lived by. Says Vithobai, "I repent, I do not repent . . . I forgive you, I do not forgive, both are the same. I am good I am evil I am pure I am foul, I am this or that . . . What difference does it make now? It is my deeds that await me . . . I lie here empty, but you fill me up with thoughts, and then press me to speak them that you may have words to remember afterwards . . . But it is deeds, deeds that count, O my lost brother," and he recalls "that deed in the hut, which you say caused all, and which now you call joy, now sin. How can I remember which it was after all these years, and what difference if I could? It was a deed, it has gone before me with the others to be judged." Pinmay longs for "the holy salutation of Christ," a kiss of forgiveness and peace, but Vithobai will have none of such liturgical formalities. "My mouth is down here," he says. The missionary's urgent longing for Christian forgiveness and reconciliation leads him to lay his head on the dying man's chest. "Too late," whispers Vithobai, smiling a little. "'It is never too late,' said Mr. Pinmay, permitting a slow encircling movement of the body, the last it would ever accomplish. 'God's mercy is infinite . . . He will give us other opportunities. We have erred in this life but it will not be so in the life to come.'" And the two men talk from their hearts about love—but one is defining physical love, the other abstract spirituality. Vithobai sums it all up: "'Real and true love! Ah, that would be joyful . . . The life to come . . . Life, life, eternal life. Wait for me in it.' And he stabs the missionary through the heart."

Reverting to his old beliefs, he spreads the blue flowers over the missionary's body, exulting that he is the survivor. "For love had conquered at last and he was again a king, he had sent a messenger before him to announce his arrival in the life to come, as a great chief should. 'I served you for ten years,' he thought, 'and your yoke was hard, but mine will be harder and you shall serve me now forever and ever.'" (234–37) And leaving the dead Christian and his unopened Communion paraphernalia behind, "he swooped like a falcon from the parapet in pursuit of the terrified shade." (237)

Through exposing Pinmay's self-serving hypocrisy and the Church's unthinking repetition of its static theological beliefs as played out in liturgical practices, Forster probably achieved a personal catharsis. But because the story manuscript remained hidden for almost half a century, his readers were not able to share his hard-won wisdom, as they had in the works published in his lifetime. When the public was finally allowed to see "The Life to Come" in 1972, the institutional church was beginning to apply some of the actions of

Vatican II agreed upon in the preceding decade, and the concept of the wholeness of the human psyche was slowly starting to replace the old schizophrenic attitude about Love. By slow and faltering steps, society was beginning ever so tentatively to recognize homosexuality as a "given" and not a choice and concomitantly freed of the taint of sin. Judith Scherer Herz declares, "'The Life to Come' is a scriptural fiction."[28] The years since it was written have not diminished its power.

"The Machine Stops"

Other Forster short stories address the subject of the individual's search for his or her unique soul, a search so often crippled by postulates that impose adherence to standards elevating conformity above the individual's honest quest for truth. While theological dogma is the stultifying agent in "The Life to Come," in "The Machine Stops," published in 1909, early in Forster's writing life, it is Science—or rather, its derivative Technology that has sprung from human scientific discoveries—that cripples the human spirit.

"The Machine Stops" is a science-fiction allegory in which Forster's creative imagination is remarkably prescient. In the story Science replaces Religion, the Machine takes the place of God, and the book of rules and punishments for the inhabitants of this science-fiction world becomes the new holy writ. Written when Forster was only thirty years old, this tale may be seen as a template for his philosophy of life—and a dire prediction of what will happen to humanity if it does not actively nurture and protect its intrinsic spirit and creative ability. The underlying premise of the allegory can be couched in terms of Good and Evil, of spiritual life or death. Which will be paramount in the human soul is up to the individual.

The tale opens with Vashti, a middle-aged woman, sitting in her cell-like room, furnished with a rolling armchair and a reading desk. She need never get out of her chair, for whatever she requires, she has only to press a button. There are buttons for everything. Music will be heard, food and clothing will be provided, a bed will swing out of the wall, a bathtub full of hot water will rise from the floor, medical apparatus will drop from the ceiling, a communication system can be activated. This self-sufficient, isolated "civilization" exists far under the surface of the earth. Nature, to be found only on the surface, is abhorred and feared by inhabitants underground, and physical contact—even between family members—is to be avoided. Instead of face-to-face confrontation there is a disk that gradually assumes a bluish cast when activated, in which will appear a hazy picture of the person to whom she is talking. Always at her elbow is the Book of the Machine in which are instructions against every possible contingency: "If she was hot or cold or dyspeptic or at a loss for a word, she went to the book, and it told her which button to press. The Central Committee published it. In accordance with a growing habit it was richly bound."[29]

An electric bell rings in Vashti's room, signaling an incoming message, and the chair rolls her over to the communication center. Her son Kuno is on the phone; he wishes Vashti to come to visit him. Petulantly she reminds him that she can indeed see his image in the bluish disk and hear him. But virtual reality does not satisfy him; he wants direct contact, which is clearly displeasing to Vashti as she chides him, "You mustn't say anything against the Machine." (146) Kuno responds vehemently, "You talk as if a god had made the Machine. . . . I believe that you pray to it when you are unhappy. Men made it. . . . Great men, but men. The Machine is much, but it is not everything. I see something like you in this plate, but I do not see you. I hear something like you through this telephone, but I do not hear you. That is why I want you to come. . . . Pay me a visit, so that we can meet face to face, and talk about the hopes that are in my mind." (4) She relents, though getting to the airship launching station requires her to walk a bit. Or rather, to totter, for the mechanized life in the individual rooms so deep in the earth have robbed their inhabitants of their muscular strength. Indeed, with physical activity discouraged in this subterranean civilization, babies born with a strong musculature are destroyed. The airship with its passengers is ejected like a rocket from its underground station, and in due course Vashti arrives at Kuno's room, an exact replica of her own but far away beneath the other hemisphere of the outside world.

What Kuno did not want to confide to his mother through the agency of the Machine was that he has been threatened with the ultimate punishment of Homelessness—of expulsion from this cocooned and effortless existence, even death—because he was impelled to find a way to the surface of the outer world without permission from the Machine. To succeed in such an undertaking he has had to develop his body, to regain full use of his muscles. Then he discovered a narrow shaft that had been used long ago by earthly men employed to build the subterranean world. Slowly, painfully, he climbed an abandoned ladder until he was stopped by a slab covering the top of the shaft. Finding no fastenings and unable to reach across it, he was stymied until he seemed to hear a voice saying, "Jump. It is worth it. There may be a handle in the centre, and you may catch hold of it. . . . And if there is no handle, so that you may fall and are dashed to pieces—it is still worth it." (9–10) So Kuno jumped. There was a handle. His weight set something in motion, the handle revolved, and with the sudden release of air from below, he found himself blown out of the shaft and thrown to the ground in the outside world where he lay stunned, with the sun shining on his face. With the arrival of sunset he saw the changing color of the hills around him, hills that seemed alive, moving and rippling like muscles under the skin, and he saw the stars that configure the shape of a man in the constellation Orion. Kuno has learned much from this arduous journey of exploration—a sense of space, of the vitality of Nature and its connection with the past and hope of the future, of the power of human dreams, of the potency of intuition, of his willingness to take great risk, and suddenly he knew, "Man is the measure." (167) None of this could Vashti comprehend. She "was seized with the terrors of direct experience." (154) Vashti trembled at the consequences: "She knew that he was fated. . . . There was not room for such a person in the world." (172) But Kuno is seized by his newfound knowledge; striving to convince Vashti, he speaks passionately: "Cannot you see . . . that it is we who are dying, and that down here the only thing that really lives is the Machine? We created the Machine to do our will, but we cannot make it do our will now. . . . It has blurred every human relation and narrowed down love to a carnal act, it has paralyzed our bodies and our wills, and now it compels us to worship it." (176)

Though Kuno wants to escape, when he gains the surface, he is forced back into the underworld by an army of loathsome long white worms that entangle his legs and arms and drag him back into the shaft, but not before they kill a young earth woman who has tried to rescue him from their attack. This primeval battle of Good and Evil ends with Evil's victory. The final section of the tale describes the gradual deterioration of the Machine, trapping all the inhabitants of this strange world in a slow decline into death. Religion blooms again, but it is a primitive religion in the grip of superstition, trying by simplistic worship to propitiate fearsome, indefinable forces. Stronger demands for conformity coincide with baffling roadblocks in the Machine's administration; untended mechanical failures mount. There is nothing the inhabitants can do—the Machine simply ignores their complaints. The cause, Forster implies, lies within humanity, which, "in its desire for comfort, had overreached itself. It had exploited the riches of nature too far. Quietly and complacently, it was sinking into decadence." (186) Kuno knew what was happening and announced to Vashti, "The Machine stops." (187) She cannot believe him, but eventually after enduring gradually increasing dilapidation of the system, the inhabitants panic when the communication system breaks down, and there is only unendurable silence. Everyone, on enfeebled legs, tries to escape the silence and the complete breakdown of all the Technology that had made their lives so effortless. Because there had been no personal relations, there is no community; now everyone is fighting for individual advantage. But the violence does not last long—the foul air is being quickly exhausted. Vashti bursts into tears, and Kuno also. They weep for humanity:

> Ere silence was completed their hearts were opened, and they knew what had been important on the earth. Man, the flower of all flesh, the noblest of all creatures visible, man who had once made god in his image, and had mirrored his strength on the constellations, beautiful naked man was dying, strangled in the garments he had woven. Century after century had he toiled, and here was his reward. Truly the garment had seemed heavenly at first, shot with the colours of culture, sewn with the threads of self-denial. And heavenly it had been so long as it was a garment and no more, so long as man could shed it at will and live by the essence that is his soul, and the essence, equally divine, that is his body. The sin against the body—it was for that they wept in chief; the centuries of wrong against the muscles and nerves, and those five portals by which we can alone apprehend—glozing [sic] it over

with talk of evolution, until the body
was white pap, the home of ideas as col-
ourless, last sloshy stirrings of a spirit
that had grasped the stars. (196)

It is those tears that break down the artificial barriers between
son and mother; at last Kuno and Vashti could touch, could
talk directly, not through the Machine, could kiss. Kuno could
rejoice that though they would die, "We have come back to our
own ... We have recaptured life ... Humanity has learnt its
lesson." (197)

In this scene of devastation and death, Forster has emphasized a resurrection into real life again, an inner-directed life
of the spirit and the body, not the sterile life of automatic reactions to commands from some external power to be obeyed
without question. It is astonishing to realize that Forster, only
just turned thirty years old when "The Machine Stops" was
published, had developed such a richly faceted and prescient
philosophy, which served him through his long life. In this
early story lies the essential framework of Forster's philosophy of life—thinking for oneself no matter the consequences;
accepting the validity of that clarion cry, "... only connect"
(finally fully articulated in *Howards End*, published the next
year), including a vital connection with Nature; direct discourse, not spurious relationships experienced dimly through
a mechanical instrument; honestly knowing oneself and expressing one's emotions; belief in the holiness of the body and
its senses; the willingness to take a risk for freedom of spirit.
It takes no stretch of the imagination to realize that Kuno's

driven search for honest connection with Nature and with other people replicates Forster's own intuitive urgings. When Kuno finally struggles out of the spaceship into the real world, his sense of awe at finding the figure of a man in the night sky—Orion was Forster's favorite constellation—reflects in his character both Forster's sense of spiritual mystery and his humanistic values.

Some of Forster's cherished values are expressed negatively in "The Machine Stops," for instance, by the lack of community spirit and personal commitment in the subterranean world of the Machine; the vitiating effect of blind acceptance of dogma—whether of Religion or the State or Technology—on the human spirit; the fear of sin instilled by the institutionalized Machine through the threat of Homelessness as punishment for serious infractions. Given the trauma Forster experienced when he was forced to leave his beloved Rooksnest at the age of fourteen, only the ultimate punishment of Homelessness could adequately symbolize that greatest imaginable human loss to him. Also significant is Kuno's *independent* action; he does not attempt to organize dissent or lead a demonstration against the bureaucracy; he acts. In this, Kuno exactly reproduces Forster's own approach to social issues. The result of thinking for oneself leads to personal, if solitary, action; an individual can be responsible only for himself or herself. Group action could result in mindless following of someone else's agenda. Kuno's desperate attempt to escape to freedom outside, even at the risk of death, is replayed with Vashti as he tries valiantly to persuade her, in the face of the impending death of the Machine and its inhabitants, to accept the reality of a life enriched by direct, unfiltered communication with other human beings—a goal Forster was never to achieve in his own stultifying relationship with his mother. What must have seemed to the readers of his day nothing more than amusing science-fiction fantasy from Forster's imagination, now, nearly a century later, appears as uncanny prescience and a clear example of the abiding universality of his personal philosophy.

Mother

To suggest that Vashti directly represents Forster's mother is problematic. In many respects Lily was a remote mother like Vashti but not so remote as the fictional mother whose child, Kuno, was taken from her at birth to be raised in a communal nursery; for Vashti and Kuno there could be no shared home life. Forster and his mother had a house rooted in the land, and Lily did hire young boys not only to water the garden but to provide playmates for her son, and she did later exert herself to find a compatible prep school for her child. But Lily also exhibited the complacent social conservatism of the late Victorian period. Two years after he had written "The Machine Stops," Forster reported in his "Locked Journal," after an unsuccessful visit from Masood to the home that Forster shared with Lily, that "Mother has too little vigour and sympathy to care for youth."[30] Less than four months later Forster wrote, "Last night, alone, I had a Satanic fit of rage against mother for her grumbling and faultfinding and figured a scene in which I swept the mantlepiece with my arm and then rushed out of doors, or cut my throat. I was all red and trembling after. I write it down partly in the hope that I shall see its absurdity & so refuse it admittance again. More exercise is the cure—but I have had bad cold & cough.[31] On New Year's Eve, the night before his thirty-third birthday, he summed up the year 1911: "Terrible year on the whole. Have cheered mother a little, I think, but pleasure of home life has gone. Sorrow has altered her [Louisa Whichelo, her mother, was dying], and I have had to alter too, or leave . . . Am influenced very little now by her, for I cannot respect her as I used. (Hate writing this, for am in a tender mood: she has been sweet and herself again the last ten days . . . But all through the year, & in Nov. Dec. especially have felt as I write.) Am only happy away from home."[32] The next year was no better: "Mother freezes any depth in me. Alone, I can cling to beauty. I shall ever see life as a draggled mess of old people, surely."[33] The worst was yet to come. In May he recorded in his "Locked Journal": "Mother, speaking of my father later said 'He always put his foot down at the wrong time—like you—he wasn't a strong character.' She has never spoken against him before, nor so definitely to me. I feel ashamed of myself & disgusted. Shall I get through life without a fiasco? Can I do anything? To screw up the will power by discipline is not possible, but would I become spiritually more solid? It is an extra difficulty with mother too, now that I know she does not think highly of me. Whatever I do she is thinking 'Oh that's weak.'"[34] Not only had Forster, from an early age, been forced to assume the adult role, protecting his mother from the unpleasantnesses of life, but now, having written four successful novels, he had to learn that she failed to appreciate his intrinsic worth, finding him lacking in attributes important to her. Yet he did not walk out, and he did not abandon her. He stayed, not from weakness but from strength, the strength of character that may have come down to him from his Claphamite ancestors, a strength composed of family loyalty and a sense of personal responsibility, perhaps tinctured by his readings in Hindu philosophy, by a sense of responsibility for his surviving parent as she grew older and less able to manage things for herself. He did not need her nearly as much as she needed him; of this he was aware, and to this challenge he responded.

Plainly, the decade after he graduated from King's College, Cambridge, was a period of intense personal growth for Forster. By 1911 he was able to separate himself psychologically from his mother, moving into full adulthood with his first trip to India, followed later by war duty in Egypt, his first love affair, and a second trip to India, all within a ten-year period. In his mind he was no longer in a child-mother relationship; they were two adults, and he was psychologically the more mature. But she never seemed to realize that fact.

About the time that Forster was expressing his deep unhappiness with his mother's negative influence on his life, Roger Fry, painter and art critic, who organized the 1912 Post-Impressionist Exhibition in England, asked Forster to sit for a portrait to be included in Fry's own forthcoming show. The two men had met first at university, and their sporadic contacts continued personally and through the Bloomsbury group, of which both were considered by some to be members.

Fry undertook Forster's education in art history and particularly in Post-Impressionism, which over time Forster grasped even as he joked about it in describing his finished portrait in a letter to Florence Barger: "It is too like me at present, but he is confident he will be able to alter that. Post-Impressionism is at present confined to my lower lip ... and to my chin, on which soup has apparently dribbled. For the rest you have a bright healthy young man, without one hand it is true, and very queer legs, perhaps the result of an aeroplane accident, as he seems to have fallen from an immense height on to a sofa."[35] Though Forster's mother did not really like the portrait—probably because of the colors that Fry employed—Forster bought it and had it hung in the drawing-room of their house until a day when the local clergyman came to call on Lily. Having studied for some time the portrait with its green shadows on the face, he commented to Lily anxiously, "I hope your son isn't *queer*?"[36] As one more small piece of evidence of the baleful influence of mother and the church, the picture was banished forthwith far away to the care of Mrs. Barger.

In an undated, handwritten single page, probably written after her death in 1945 when he was sixty-six years old, Forster recorded some memories of his mother:

> Must clear up my relations with my mother, which though never hostile or tragic, did not go well after my grandmother's death, or even perhaps, after Cambridge. I recall a few radiant moments—one when I returned from India

in 1913, bringing presents for her, Ruth, & Agnes [servants], and arranging them with silks strewn and incense burning on the dining room at Weybridge. I remember her gasp of joy. Against her W. H. [West Hackhurst] period especially was her habit of saying that things— which usually belonged to me—were "too good for me" and she must have been in that sort of mood before my first prostate operation when though she knew I was dropping with weakness she insisted on my writing notes to *every* member of our family in order that no one might feel left out. She was always gracious to my friends, even when she resented them as she did Bob.[37]

The Buckinghams

After Forster returned from India in the early 1920s via Egypt, after Mohammed el-Adl's death, as he began to look about for another partner, he would from time to time bring home a friend for lunch or tea. While his mother was always polite to such visitors, after they had left, she invariably made some critical comment. To her horror, this one had appeared for lunch without a tie; that one couldn't manage the English language properly. A decade later, she considered Bob Buckingham ugly, his nose too large, although she did like May Hockey, his fiancée.

Already in his forties when he returned from his second time in India, Forster expressed "a great loss of sexual power—it was very violent 1921–22."[38] During the rest of that decade, he had several short affairs with men he met through a young Joseph Ackerley, a friendship that had roots in 1922 when Forster wrote a letter complimenting him on a recently published poem. The following year Forster recommended him for the post of secretary to the maharaja of Chhatarpur, a position Ackerley held in 1923–24. Their friendship continued, with many ups and downs, until Ackerley died only three years before Forster's own death.

Not until Forster was fifty-one years old (in 1930) did he finally establish a committed relationship. Perhaps "create" is a better word than "establish," for the new relationship was complicated. At one of Ackerley's parties Forster met Bob Buckingham, a twenty-eight-year-old police officer. Despite the difference in their ages, the men seemed to have some interests and attitudes in common. After several months of growing friendship, Forster felt certain enough to report to a friend that Bob had "fallen very violently in liking with him,"[39] and thought that possibly he, Forster, was falling in love. According to Furbank, it was not long before "the two, at this time, plighted some kind of troth."[40]

Furbank writes that Buckingham had, at the time he met Forster, just broken up with one young woman and in due

course found another—May Hockey—to whom he became engaged. Since Forster could not wish her away, they met, and
with his customary good manners and kindness toward others, he loaned Bob a key to his flat so that he and May could
meet there. This action did not suggest any renunciation on
Forster's part. For a considerable time Forster and May silently
contested for Bob, but Forster's railing against May was never
to her face and his jealous tantrums were never public. For her
part, May never argued with Forster or accused him of trying
to break up her marriage but quietly stood her ground. He was
a witness at their wedding but refused to stay for the celebration. Eventually the rivals found likeable qualities in each
other, and the heat of silent battle abated. Forster finally was
able to write in his "Commonplace Book" that he had achieved
happiness: "I have been happy for two years. It mayn't be over
yet, but I want to write it down before it gets spoiled by pain—
which is the chief thing pain can do in the inside life: spoil the
lovely things that had got in there first. Happiness can come
in one's natural growth and not queerly, as religious people
think. From 51 to 53 I have been happy, and would like to remind others that their turn can come too. It is the only message worth giving."[41]

The Buckingham's son, Robert, known all his life as Robin,
was given the middle name of Morgan, the name by which Forster was known among his friends, and Forster was chosen to
be the child's godfather. In that role he gave the nursery table
from Rooksnest to the Buckinghams for Robin. For Forster the
only role the Church could play in this triangular arrangement

was the formalistic one of bestowing on him the title of godfa-ther. Forster's relationship with May warmed gradually, and when, in the mid-1930s, she was forced to spend a year as a patient in a tuberculosis sanitarium, he visited her every week with books and flowers, writing letters between visits, per-sonal actions that exhibited more of Christian love and caring than churchly formalities could.

In this ménage à trois can be seen a new, more flexible form of the family, no longer consanguineous, but an ex-tended family based on shared interests and common affec-tion rather than legal documents. For Forster, strongly inter-ested though he was in sex, his ultimate goal was a companionship of spirit, and this he found over the years, though with the expectable ups and downs. May, who seemed to be aware of Forster's homosexuality from the beginning, ac-cepted it. Bob's attitude was more ambiguous; many years later, on what Forster supposed was his own deathbed, when he openly declared his love for Bob, Bob seemed surprised, claimed not to have known of Forster's homosexuality, and with evident rejection, distanced himself for some time from Forster. This in spite of the many trips they had made to-gether, frequent meetings through the years—though some-times with what seemed to Forster long periods of Bob's ab-sence—and a few oblique but obvious references in Forster's private diaries to sexual relations between them. Possibly Bob was afraid that open knowledge of his relationship with For-ster might affect him professionally. Although May was cogni-zant of Forster's homosexuality, that there might have been

sexual relations between the men had apparently not occurred to her. At the end it was she who saved Forster from
another rejection and the insurmountable pain—Homelessness—and kept alive the relationship built up over the years
among the three of them. She insisted that the Buckingham
house should continue to be his home and showed great compassion in continuing to care for Forster, eventually nursing
him in their home through his last illness. This was where he
wished to die and be buried.

Following the publication of his last novel, *A Passage to India*, in 1924, Forster's creativity was funneled into short stories
strongly homosexual in content, stories not published until after his death. In addition to these stories, written for his own
enjoyment—and others that he destroyed as unworthy of publication—Forster published biographies, essays, book reviews,
and articles solicited by the major English monthly magazines.
He also became quietly active in public causes dear to his
heart, homosexuality paramount among them.

Struggle for Legal Reform

Surprisingly, it was a committee of the Church of England that
was the original catalyst for the eventual repeal of the Labouchère Amendment which, since 1885, had mandated as
much as two years' imprisonment "with or without hard labour" for consenting adult men convicted of homosexual relations. In 1952, five years before any governmental action, the
Moral Welfare Council of the Anglican church, with clergy,

doctors, and lawyers among its members, began a study of homosexuality. Two years later the report of the Moral Welfare Council, "while not denying its [homosexuality's] 'sinfulness,' attempted to separate the ecclesiastical and legal aspects, and called for reform."[42] It is significant that in 1953, while this church study was in process, Forster and Kingsley Martin wrote tandem articles for *The New Statesman and Nation* under the heading of "Society and the Homosexual." In his piece, titled "The Abominable Crime," the heterosexual Martin, while repeating many of the myths—and a few of the facts—about homosexuality, wrote, "I think that Mr. E. M. Forster's article states the truth: it is a social evil, but its bad effects are greatly aggravated by our stupid, savage and out-of-date criminal law."[43] This is considerably stronger language than Forster used in his companion piece, "A Magistrate's Figures," but Forster draws the more powerful and realistic picture of the pall of terror under which the homosexual male then lived and enumerates some of society's suggestions for dealing with the problem, though without much conviction that "purity campaigns" or dubious medical treatment would "solve" the problem. Forster saw it as a problem of society, not of the individual. His desired solution, "if it could be achieved," would be "an immediate change in the law." Continuing, he depicts his dream even as he mirrors the stark reality of society's attitudes:

> If homosexuality between men ceased
> to be *per se* criminal—it is not criminal
> between women—and if homosexual

crimes were equated with heterosexual crimes and punished with equal but not with additional severity, much confusion and misery would be averted; there would be less public importuning and less blackmail. But it is unlikely that the law will be changed. Reformers are too optimistic here.... They do not consider the position of the average M.P., through whom the reform must take place. An M.P. may be sympathetic personally, but he has to face his constituency and justify his vote, and experience has shown how hostile an electorate can be to anything it considers sexually unusual. ... Change in the law is unlikely until there is a change in public opinion; and this must happen very slowly, for the great majority of people are naturally repelled by the subject and do not want to have to think about it. ... Less social stigma under the existing law— that is all that can be hoped for at present; and there are some grounds for hope. ... There is more discussion, less emotion, fewer preconceptions. More laymen read modern psychology, which even when it does not satisfy raises salutary doubts. The stigma attaching to

the homosexual is becoming more pro-
portioned to the particular facts of each
case.[44]

Early public pressure for change had been stimulated by
the trial of Oscar Wilde and kept alive by Havelock Ellis and
Edward Carpenter and a few others who publicly acknowledged their homosexuality. Over the decades various groups
were established to further the study of homosexuality, and
for a time Forster may have been a member of at least one of
these educational groups. Self-understanding and public education was the goal, carried out through open lectures, dissemination of pamphlets aimed at the general public, and publication of research, including some studies conducted by
foreign groups involved in the same learning process. The
British Society for the Study of Sex Psychology published foreign research on homosexuality, such as the writings of Magnus Hirschfeld, a major figure in the struggle for homosexual
reform in Germany. Forster's comments in *Maurice* on the ignorance of English doctors about German studies of homosexuality may well have sprung from the Fourteenth International Medical Congress, which met in London in 1913, the
year in which Forster was writing *Maurice*. A scheduled pro-
gram on homosexuality was apparently a revelation to the ordinary medical man attending the congress. Over the decades
the effort at public education continued, sometimes in abey-
ance because of war, sometimes struggling to overcome political opposition, occasionally buttressed by foreign research,
occasionally slowed by governmental concerns about national

security. The publication in England in the 1950s of the American Kinsey Report dramatically raised the level of public involvement in discussion. Several years after the Moral Welfare Committee of the Church of England had published its recommendations, the government, goaded by widespread public clamor, established a departmental inquiry in the Home Office with Sir John Wolfenden as chairman. State and Church each had its own goal in mind in responding to public calls for decriminalization of homosexual relations between consenting adults. While the Church was obviously interested in continuing to brand homosexuality at least as a religious sin, the government itself felt compelled to uphold public "moral purity" and refurbish its role as protector of the youth of the nation from "corruption." In drafting the Sexual Offences Act, which finally passed in 1967, the government's problem, in the light of "moral purity" and its responsibility for protecting young people from exploitation, was defining "the age of consent." Sixteen, eighteen, and twenty-one years were all suggested and debated. Forster agreed with medical men who said that by sixteen adult sexual development was fixed. Since young men of eighteen frequently entered the work force or military service, to set twenty-one as the age on which they could be said to achieve sufficient adult maturity to decide sexual questions for themselves seemed to many to be hypocritical.

The Report of the Wolfenden Committee on Homosexual Offences and Prostitution was finally presented to Parliament in 1957 after lengthy research, closed-door debate, public clamor, and political obstruction, but opposition to decriminalization continued strong. With the advent of a more liberal

Labour Government after 1964, the Sexual Offences Act of 1967 was arduously pushed through Parliament more than half a century after public agitation arose and a decade after the decriminalization of homosexual relations between consulting adults had been publicly recommended by an official government committee. While the 1967 act accomplished decriminalization, it did not legalize homosexuality and was considered more restrictive than the Wolfenden Committee's report. It is significant to note that the act "was not brought about by homosexuals campaigning for their own rights. Nevertheless it represented a fissure in the walls. Through it the more radical forces that appeared after 1968 could begin to force their way."[45] Discrimination did not vanish, nor police harassment. Efforts toward more complete liberation and equality for homosexuals continued.

One may wonder why Forster remained closeted when some of his homosexual friends, such as Edward Carpenter, were willing to engage in battle with Church and State and to struggle to overcome the inertia of public ignorance and disinterest. To suggest that Forster's main concern was protection of his reputation as one of England's foremost novelists seems unworthy, for in his brief tenure as a political activist, mainly in the 1930s, he had staunchly taken some unpopular public positions. Very possibly his motivation was protection of his mother. Her inability to surmount what she considered unpleasant circumstances was well documented, as was her social conservatism. But even after her death in 1945, he did not submit the manuscript of *Maurice* to a publisher. Yet he was troubled about his decision. In a 1948 letter to Christopher

Isherwood, Forster wrote, "I am ashamed at shirking publication but the objections are formidable."[46] Perhaps Forster did not want to be narrowly identified in the public mind as "the homosexual author." Perhaps he preferred to be accepted as a writer who could with authoritative insight describe the restricting boundaries forced on the homosexual person—if the homosexual wanted to function in society—and with equal authority describe the distortion of the heterosexual individual by his or her family in the effort to create a socialized human being acceptable to society. In either scenario what mattered was *not* the pain and hypocrisy engendered by ignoring the individual's unique gifts but molding a person by society's template. In Forster's novels the heroic characters are those who follow their inner light, not the demands of society for conformity.

What other objections might intrude after his mother's death are left unexplained. Forster was a very private person, naturally reticent, and not disposed to call attention to himself. With a deep-seated aversion to group action, probably dating from his King's College experience, he tended to take an individual stand—preferably in written form. Forster wrote in 1960, "Since *Maurice* was written there has been a change in the public attitude here [regarding homosexuality]: the change from ignorance and terror to familiarity and contempt. . . . I . . . had supposed that knowledge would bring understanding. . . . What the public really loathes in homosexuality is not the thing itself but having to think about it. If it could be slipped into our midst unnoticed, legalized overnight by a decree in small print, there would be few protests. Unfortunately it can only be legalized by Parliament. . . . Consequently the Wolfenden recommendations will be indefinitely rejected."[47] In this prognostication Forster was eventually proven too pessimistic. Four years later—still three years short of the 1967 passage of the Sexual Offences Act—he confided to his diary, "How *annoyed* I am with Society for wasting my time by making homosexuality criminal. The subterfuge, the self-consciousness that might have been avoided."[48] By the time Parliament finally acted, Forster was eighty-eight. His lifelong sense of personal privacy and unwillingness to actually mount the public stage, combined with the peace and quiet craved by most people of such advanced age, perhaps caused him to question what good would result from his coming out at the end of his life and what distressing sensationalism might arise if he did. One can never know for certain. Three years later he died. The following year *Maurice* was published, and the "Terminal Note" appeared.

Examining the pervasive influence of homosexuality in Forster's life, Summers writes,

> Forster's homosexuality is a crucial aspect of his personality and his art. It gave him that feeling of standing "at a slight angle to the universe" . . . and it fueled his anger at social and political injustice, making him contemptuous of the conventions that separate individu-

als and impede instinct. His acute consciousness of the homophobia that poi-
soned the dominant culture of his day—
as most graphically illustrated by the
persecution of Oscar Wilde, which occurred during Forster's late adolescence
and early manhood—haunted his imagination throughout his life. ... Significantly, however, Forster never felt
guilty for his sexuality, and, accepting
homosexuality as part of the wholeness
of his personality, he never wished to be
heterosexual. When Leonard Woolf
asked him whether he would like to be
"converted" to heterosexuality, he an-
swered without hesitation, "No."[49]

Church and State cherished their insistence that homosexuality was sinful, wrong, and unnatural. It was a blight to be
extirpated if possible or, at the least, its adherents to be penal-
ized for insisting on being true to their nature. Forster's anger
at the end of his life toward both Church and State was as
strong as it had been when he achieved adulthood. As early as
1906, when he was twenty-seven, he had commented in his
"Notebook Journal" on "the poison of *organized* religion" and
continued that "the church cannot purify herself from within
but only by the action of agnosticism. Why has the attempt to
reach God made man so horrible? I think because they have

mistaken the obstacle which is not the animal but the mechanical."[50] While Forster does not define "animal" and "mechanical" in this Journal entry, it is not too wild a conjecture to suggest that "animal" refers to human intuition and "mechanical" to unthinking repetition of religious dogma and social and political conventions. This definition was an early phrasing of what Forster always considered the destructive influence of imposed codes of conduct on the individual's instinctive reactions. "Agnosticism" is a philosophical stance acknowledging that certain religious assumptions cannot be proven, of questioning, and of scrutinizing the theological pronouncements of the religious hierarchy, referred to in Forster's comment as "they" who mistook the obstacle. By extension, Forster seems to suggest the possibility that a sufficient mass of individual active doubters, practicing "that most precious gift of thinking for oneself," could urge the institutional church into a more pure expression of Christian beliefs.

Writing within a year of Forster's death, Norman Pittenger, a don at King's College, argued in the *Christian Century*, an American religious monthly, a more modern understanding of sin, a definition that Forster would undoubtedly have found congenial: Sin "is the willful breaking of, or the refusal to enter upon, relationships in love and of love. God is the 'cosmic Lover' and man is the child of his love; sin is a violation of the relationship between them whether directly or through rejection and refusal of love in human contacts. . . . Sin is the willed decision against love, with all its tragic consequences." Pittenger is appealing to the Christian church for a *"more* Christian moral attitude"—an acceptance of homosexuals as equal children of God and inclusion as equal members in any congregation. He concludes, "I venture to say that had this good, humble and loving man felt such welcome and acceptance, he might have taken a different attitude toward organized Christianity and the faith it professes."[51] But Forster himself never revised his belief that "Christianity remains untrue, and harmful as a guide in private—particularly sexual—conduct." This statement was scratched out on a piece of West Hackhurst stationery, probably in the 1930s under the menacing shadow of Hitler. Forster went on to conclude, "But it has more guts in it than culture, and so can stand up to the State. Religion will be man's only defence against Totalitarianism."[52]

Chapter Eight
Public Life, Political Actions

Forster could accept with equanimity the unexpected appearance of chance in his life. He was not afraid of it, he knew he could not control events.[1] His friendship with Syed Ross Masood was pure happenstance; they were close neighbors for a brief time before the young Indian went up to Oxford. Without this impetus, India might never have become a persistent theme throughout Forster's long life. Within three years of meeting Masood, Forster wrote that "public affairs interest me more, especially when they touch Italy, Germany, or India."[2] Germany also entered Forster's life experience by chance; he spent five months there in 1905 as tutor for the children of Countess von Arnim, the English wife of a German count. Forster's interest in German Romanticism and nineteenth-century German culture would later surface in *Howards End* in the Schlegel sisters and their memories of their German father.

Other aspects of Forster's life were more foreordained than opportunistic. He fortunately grew up in a democracy that, in spite of its flaws, usually considered individual freedom of thought a given. His cultural heritage provided a fertile ground for Forster's lifelong concern with freedom of conscience, British democracy, India, the Empire, classless equality, roots, and relationships. Such themes were woven together in his writings and through private and public actions embellished the tapestry of his life.

India

Forster wrote miscellaneous short essays on India that were published in the years just before World War I, products not of Cambridge but of his self-education. Not until after that conflict was over and his second trip to India in 1921 did his intense interest in the subcontinent and his broad exposure to India and its peoples come to fruition in *A Passage to India*, with its profound understanding of the complex relationships between English people and Indians. His growing reputation as a knowledgeable commentator on things Indian increased his public exposure.[3]

In 1922 *The Nation & the Athenaeum*, a London periodical, published three articles under the heading "By Our Indian Correspondent." That Forster is the author of all three can be assumed from his inclusion of them in the scrapbook of his pieces published over the years in assorted magazines. The first essay described the rising tide of Indian nationalism. The long-held British assumption of cultural—and racial—superiority, accompanied often by rudeness and incivility to Indians, was being replaced by greater Indian self-assurance and less tolerance of inequality and officially mandated English courtesy and superficial equality. But the damage had been done:

"The decent Anglo-Indian [English civil servant in India] of to-day," Forster wrote, "realizes that the great blunder of the past is neither political nor economic nor educational, but social." The article ended with the flat statement that "never in history did ill-breeding contribute so much towards the dissolution of an Empire."[4] A week later Forster commented in "The Prince's Progress" on a royal visit against the best advice of the provincial governors (English government-appointed bureaucrats), who cited hostile public opinion. But with the viceroy and some of his Indian advisers and the government back in Whitehall in favor, the prince came anyway and was greeted with studied indifference in the form of many empty streets. In Calcutta a meticulously planned riot was deliberately scheduled to occur before his announced arrival so he skipped Calcutta altogether. The riot went on as scheduled, and because of it hundreds of young Indian men were imprisoned. If the English of all ranks in India, Forster wrote, had "taken their stand upon a common humanity instead of the pedestal of race—then the foundation of a democratic Empire might have been well and truly laid."[5] Forster predicted a darkening future for British-Indian relations.

Eight months later, in an article with the by-line "From Our Correspondent Lately in India," Forster wrote of India's reaction to the dismemberment of the Ottoman Empire, the political punishment meted out to Turkey by the Western powers for taking the side of the Germans in World War I. Forster reported that Indians, both Hindu and Muslim, sided with the Turks against the greater power of the European nations, who sought to thwart Kemal Ataturk's efforts to create in Turkey a modern secular state. But the British did not heed the Indian protests, even while acknowledging that many units of Indian troops served loyally in the British army against the Germans. In his two earlier articles the heart of the problem in British-Indian relations was race; this time it was religion that Forster described—Pan-Islamism and religious discrimination.[6]

In 1924 *A Passage to India* was published, the recurring threads of race, religion, cultural superiority, ethnicity, economics, and politics all woven into the novel that became the most famous of his works. The timing of publication was fortuitous; interest in India had been recently heightened by a case of libel, widely reported in the press, brought by an English civil servant against an Indian official. Commentary and personal expressions—pro and con—were plentiful, Forster's empathy towards Indians and distaste for English administrators of the colonial government arousing vigorous reactions. Sales of *A Passage to India* were strong; in the United States 30,000 copies were sold in the first month. Over the years Forster's novel was credited with alerting generations of English readers to the central dilemma of the ensuing struggle for Indian independence, not to be achieved until 1947, another world war and a quarter century later.

Forster made many lifelong Indian friends, visiting in their homes in India, encouraging them at Cambridge University, and easing family visits to England. He broadcast to India for the BBC during World War II and in 1945 was invited by the All-India PEN Club to come back to India for a three-day PEN conference in Jaipur, after which he spent three months traveling and visiting friends, lionized everywhere he went. He had not been in India since the early 1920s, and he felt his soul revitalized by his immersion in India once again. He included a vivid report of that trip, under the title "India Again," in the 1951 collection of his essays, *Two Cheers for Democracy*.

After the publication of *A Passage to India*, Forster wrote a number of short erotic stories, mainly for his private amusement, and continued to publish book reviews and increasingly frequent political essays on current affairs in monthly periodicals. These essays often openly reflected his personal philosophy, including occasional biblical phrases or allusions to Christian teachings. In Forster's public writing the name of God appears as naturally as mention of Dante and Virginia Woolf, or freedom of speech, art and culture, and totalitarianism. Unlike writers who locate politics solely in the secular domain, Forster wove religious motifs into his political essays, yet never used the public arena for proselytizing. Considering his grateful discovery in India that the spiritual and the secular could be united in daily life, his use of that unifying principle was entirely natural.

Forster's public image gradually enlarged after the success of *A Passage to India*. Never a political firebrand, he was nonetheless avidly interested in various political issues, and simply writing about such questions began to seem inadequate. From time to time he abandoned his preference for avoiding the limelight to take part in overt political action. Though circumspect about homosexuality, on questions of freedom of expression and government censorship, the British Empire in India, democracy at home, and the equality of all people, he was prepared to act publicly, whatever the personal consequences might be. In action on the political battlefield, Forster sometimes temporarily abandoned his usual individual posture, acknowledging reluctantly the importance of mass dissent to confront the immense power of government. Forster once asked himself, "What can the individual do except protest, stop [stay] away, give his reasons, and hope that others will stop away? What notice will be taken . . . what publicity will be given . . . the alternative is violence—shouting and brawling. . . . Violence certainly wins publicity. My objection to it is . . . that it would only work for a very short time and then be repressed by the more efficient violence which is always at the command of the modern state."[7] Individual protest was preferable, he believed, indeed necessary as an example of moral behavior, but the public influence of a single voice was likely to be modest and easily ignored. Forster was concerned that group action, though intended to be nonviolent, could easily degenerate into shouting and brawling and worse, provoking official suppression. Yet the possibility that group action might be required could not be denied.

Censorship

A well-known outcry against government censorship, in which Forster was a prominent participant, arose in 1920 over the lesbian novel, *The Well of Loneliness*, by Radclyffe Hall. It quickly ran into public opposition and even objections from the home secretary on grounds of threatening the nation's morals. At the same time Forster's own novel about homosexuality, *Maurice*, languished in a desk drawer, unseen except by a few trusted friends. Forster's temperamentally retiring nature made him reluctant to step into the limelight. His predilection for the margins over center stage was strengthened by a deep antipathy toward charismatic individuals who rallied worshipful disciples to increasing allegiance to some private agenda of the leader. Yet he felt morally impelled to protest the suppression of Hall's novel. He drafted a letter questioning the legality of the government order to withdraw it from public sale and, having rounded up a number of noteworthy literary signatories for the letter, approached the author herself. But the letter did not please her: It failed to state explicitly that the book was a masterpiece. Hers was an opinion Forster could not support.[8] Nevertheless he objected unreservedly to official censorship. The government's suppression of the book incited protest in the press—including an anonymous article by Forster entitled "The New Censorship" and a subsequent letter that he and Virginia Woolf signed.[9] The police brought a prosecution against the book, and a date for hearing the case was set. Forster had gathered a number of well-known authors as witnesses to attack the government's action, but the magistrate in charge, taking matters into his own hands, bypassed the witnesses and "pronounced the book obscene on his own authority."[10] An anonymous official stated the government's objection: Hall "had not stigmatised this [lesbian] relationship as being in any way blameworthy."[11] Unlike Maurice and Alec

in Forster's *Maurice*, the characters in *The Well of Loneliness*
did not live "happily ever after," but its unhappy ending was
insufficiently abject to satisfy the government's moral objections.

Shortly after the decision supporting the government's
suppression of *The Well of Loneliness*, Forster wrote the Society of Authors, politely refusing their invitation to become a
member because the society prohibited any form of discussion
of Hall's book. It was a cowardly stance he could not accept.[12]
In the spring of 1929, Forster wrote a short article, "The 'Censorship' of Books," broaching the subject of homosexuality
and stating his position that nonpornographic books—which
he defined as concerned with literary intent, not "physical
provocativeness"—"like *The Well of Loneliness*, ought not to
be suppressed, and this not merely for the convenience of the
authors concerned, but from the point of view of the public,
which has a right to information even if the information when
received should prove uninteresting."[13] Forster was saying
politely that people ought to be educated even if they disliked
the subject.

National Council for Civil Liberties

Forster had felt useful in the struggle over *The Well of Loneliness* and energized by his effort to quash censorship. In 1934
he became involved with the newly formed National Council
for Civil Liberties, a group orchestrating public responses to
governmental actions—or inactions—infringing on individual
liberty. The council had its genesis in objections to the use of

police agents provocateurs to break up the hunger marches of jobless and hungry protesters at the peak of the Great Depression. The original intention of the council was to recruit observers who, from the sidelines, would scrutinize the behavior of the police and report instances of police infractions. The council's polite and indirect approach suited Forster's own temperament and, at the same time, complemented his concern for individual liberty and freedom from censorship. He agreed to be one of the observers and quickly became the council's first president. But the council and Forster soon found themselves organizing and leading direct action in widespread public protest against a new censorship measure entitled the Incitement to Disaffection Bill, popularly known as the Sedition Bill.[14]

The government's motivation for the Sedition Bill was the distribution of communist tracts among the military ranks. It proposed to prohibit the dissemination—and even the possession—of writings that might "seduce soldiers or sailors from their duty or allegiance."[15] The government attempted to reintroduce the General Search Warrant, condemned by the Lord Chief Justice almost two centuries before, in 1765, as "subversive of all human comfort."[16] The historical case involved John Wilkes, an eighteenth-century political reformer. The very wide net that the proposed Sedition Bill would cast seemed to the Council for Civil Liberties a threat to civil liberties and freedom of speech that went far beyond the immediate cause. The council quickly circulated to every member of the House of Commons its analysis of the bill's implicit threat to individual freedom and organized protest meetings, first of its own members, then larger public protests to which it invited representatives of political parties, churches, and pacifist groups. In the early days of the council in the spring of 1934, it had invited the Communist Party to provide observers, and probably about the same time, a secret police report asserted that "the activities of the N.C.C.L. were directed ... from Communist Party headquarters." Participants intimately acquainted with the history of the National Council for Civil Liberties vehemently protested this description when—but only years later—the police report came to light.[17]

The Sedition Bill struggle intensified in October of 1934 with a public meeting sponsored by the council, with H. G. Wells as the principal speaker. Though the subject of the protest was the bill, Wells, just back from a trip to Russia, was so outraged by the suppression of speech he had witnessed in several totalitarian countries that, never mentioning the bill itself, he inveighed exclusively against censorship under totalitarian rule. He was loudly heckled by Communists in the audience, and in the press the following day the protest within the protest meeting was headlined as a communist demonstration. Several weeks earlier Forster had been invited by *Time and Tide,* an independent, nonparty weekly news magazine, to write a column under his own name. Indignant over the biased reporting of the previous day's protest, Forster wrote a signed editorial (today it would probably be called an op-ed piece) entitled "Still the Sedition Bill!" to give a factual account of the protest. With his usual tact, he did not directly

attack the press, instead reminding readers of the historic importance of providing citizens with an accurate and objective
account of public affairs. He pointed out facts that had not
been included in the press accounts—that the protest had
drawn three thousand people, that the first speaker had given
a clear exposition of the dangers of the Sedition Bill, and other
speakers included the Bishop of Birmingham; J. B. Priestley;
the writer Hannen Swaffer; and, of course, H. G. Wells, all of
whom, except for a perfunctory sentence about the bishop,
had gone unmentioned in press reports. Forster attempted to
stimulate countervailing actions; he urged readers to speak
out "politely but . . . continuously" until the bill came to a final
vote five days later and to lobby their MPs. Forster ended his
editorial by asking why Ramsay MacDonald, the Prime Minister in 1934, who in 1925 had strongly condemned the General
Search Warrant, was now, less than a decade later, proposing
to "fasten" it on the people.[18] Forster did not mention that he,
too, had addressed the crowd at the time of Wells's remarks.
But Stephen Spender, writing to Christopher Isherwood
shortly after the event, said that "Morgan made much the best
speech of the evening. He was beautifully eloquent, and at the
same time personal, so that he had a separate hold on each
member of the audience."[19] Considerably watered down, the
bill passed, but the council and Forster remained vigilant
against recurring efforts at censorship.

The vexing question of communist involvement continued to hound the National Council for Civil Liberties through-

out the decade of the 1930s and into World War II and the postwar years. At one time Forster felt the council was being attacked from both sides simultaneously, on the one hand for
being pro-communist, and on the other by the Communists
for not being sufficiently aggressive in efforts to regain freedom of the press for their newspaper, *The Daily Worker*,
closed earlier by government action. In June and July of 1941,
Time and Tide printed serious allegations of communist control of the council, as well as an accusation that "a number of
its recent activities have been calculated to hinder rather than
to help the war effort." Officers of the organization quickly replied, refuting such accusations and insisting that the National
Council for Civil Liberties "has opposed and will continue to
oppose all attempts to use the war situation for enforcing laws
and regulations which prevent proper criticism of the authorities ... such as imprisonment without a charge being preferred and without any kind of judicial trial." They insisted
also that "to do these things is not to hinder the war effort, but
to fight for the maintenance in wartime of fundamental constitutional principles without which our law would closely approximate to Nazi law."[20] The personal probity of Forster and
his fellow officers of the council was never questioned, though
some observers claimed to see a damaging naïveté, while others suggested possible co-option by the Communists, a charge
vehemently denied by the council and Forster. Without any
practical political experience and lacking the instinct for political in-fighting, Forster was clearly at a disadvantage against
more skilled political practitioners for whom co-option was an
easy gambit. For its part the council and Forster struggled to

keep focused on protesting perceived governmental infringe-
ment on civil liberties and continued their surveillance to protect freedom of expression for individuals, the press, writers
and artists, and those who opposed blatant government censorship.

"Notes on the Way"

Over the years the magazine *Time and Tide* invited public figures to write the column "Notes on the Way" for just a few
weeks on subjects of their choice before relinquishing the
space to another contributor. Forster accepted this short assignment several times. Commenting in his column of June 16,
1934, on a recent rally of the Blackshirts, an organization of
English fascists, Forster excoriated the attitude and actions of
Sir Oswald Mosley, the Blackshirt leader. Forster's column was
satire, but he was deadly serious about Mosley's virulent
threat to freedom of thought and expression. Members of the
audience who came to hear Mosley speak at an open meeting
were alarmed when fighting broke out. Violence became brutality directed at the Blackshirts' principal enemies, the
avowed communist protesters, present in some numbers at
the meeting. Sir Oswald afterwards complained, according to
Forster's account, that "the police . . . should either have kept
order . . . or should have allowed him to keep it. He had given
his instructions to the Commissioner of Police several days beforehand . . . : no Communists were to approach [the meeting
place]. His instructions had been ignored and rioting had re-

sulted, for which he was not responsible."[21] To Forster, Mosley's arrogance was breathtaking. With his "private army"
Mosley maintained that he could control the streets better
than the police. This "army," according to Forster, was made
up of people bored by their role in life, "young bank clerks and
little typists who don't know how to enliven life." Mosley
"gives them uniforms, grades and a cause and foe, and sends
them forth as Samurai and Amazons to slosh the Reds."[22] Such
bank clerks and typists presupposed Leonard Bast in *Howards
End*, Forster's novel of nearly a quarter-century earlier, who,
in a similar dead-end position, tried to give meaning to his life
through books and music, struggling by blind instinct to keep
alive the rooted values of his noble-peasant grandfather.[23] A
generation further from their roots, the ill-paid workers about
whom Forster wrote in *Time and Tide*, similarly stuck in menial, repetitive jobs, seemed to have lost connection with a
sense of place. They seemed to have lost their ability to think
for themselves, becoming easy targets for the charismatic
Mosley, Forster believed.

Forster saw three possible paths ahead: "Fascism is infinitely the worst. Firstly, there is the present order, which I
prefer. . . . I like Parliament and democracy. . . . In the second
place, there is Communism, an alternative which will destroy
all I care for and could only be reached through violence, yet
it might mean a new order where younger people could be
happy and the head and the heart have a chance to grow. . . .
If my own world smashes, Communism is what I would like in
its place. . . . And, thirdly, there is Fascism, leading only into

the blackness which it has chosen as its symbol, into smart-
ness and yapping out of orders, and self-righteous brutality,
into social as well as international war. It means change without hope. Our immediate duty . . . is to stop it, and perhaps we
can best do that by convincing Sir Oswald's backers that it will
not pay. . . . He tells us, and no doubt correctly, that there is
Russian money behind Communism. What secret money lies
behind him, and what view does it take of his offer to super-
sede the police?"[24] Forster's ambivalence about Communism
is evident. His rational mind reflected the abundant evidence
of communist violence and suppression of thought and speech
while his spirit clung to the faint hope that the equality of ide-
alized communism (as distinct from the version then practiced by Stalinist Russia)—if his own world succumbed—might
become the reality, bringing happiness and the possibility of
personal growth to oncoming generations. The similarity between the idealistic communist slogan—"from each according
to his ability, to each according to his need"—and the historical actions of the earliest Christian communities—"and all
who believed were together and had all things in common;
and they sold their possessions and goods and distributed
them to all, as any had need" (Acts 2:44–45)—has been widely
acknowledged. Forster carried a very faint hope for the rebirth of "pure" communism, none at all for fascism, which he
said he would have fought against had he not been too old for
service. Democracy was, above all, what he preferred. His battle with Hitler and Mussolini was waged in print for freedom
of mind and spirit and speech.

Official Secrets Act

In 1938 Forster and the National Council for Civil Liberties became involved in another censorship fracas, this time about the Official Secrets Act of 1920, which required citizens to supply any information they had about others who might be *suspected* of breaking the law governing official secrets.[25] Though the Official Secrets Act was supposedly intended to punish spies, the 1938 incident involved a journalist. About the same time, the government refused to allow the House of Commons to hear a question it considered prying into national security secrets. In the following year the resulting outcry led to an amendment that restricted application of the act to espionage only.

This attack by the government on freedom of speech led Forster to lash out in uncharacteristically barbed language against official censorship that would set one citizen against another, destroying the threads of connection and the common trust "where two or three are gathered together," in the words of Forster's biblical reference. In this essay, "They Hold Their Tongues,"[26] a number of such biblical references appear, intimately connecting freedom of speech with freedom of the human spirit and emphatically including the freedom to think for oneself. The gist of the essay clearly springs from Forster's personal feeling about the connection between God and humankind. Using the opening verses of the Gospel of John to introduce his own thoughts, Forster segues to the modern instance: "The light shineth in the darkness, and the light comprehendeth not the darkness. It was the true light, which

lighteth every man that cometh into the world, but it has had
to be put out. There is no place in a modern war for spontane-
ity, and never before has the spirit of man been so menaced
and insulted."[27] The word "freedom" is "the light" for which
Forster is mourning. (In the Gospel of John "the light" is a metaphor for Jesus, but it is unlikely that Forster was suggesting
Jesus as a preferred example. For Forster, "light" is a metaphor
for illumination, leading to understanding.) Forster's essay is
a furious funeral sermon over the corpse of freedom of expression and links "the darkness" with censorship and the threat
of bureaucratic punishment. The requirement to report anything *seemingly* suspicious is, he believes, destructive of the
warp and weft of community that weaves individuals together
through trust and mutual acceptance. To Forster, the governmental demand that individuals report suspicions of irregu-
larity would destroy the fiber of community, setting individual against individual.

Forster remained involved with the National Council for
Civil Liberties until well after the end of the war, finally resign-
ing in 1948. Eternal vigilance against governmental attempts
to impose censorship of any kind remained a primary focus,
and even as late as 1960, when he was more than eighty years
old, he testified against the government's attempt to impose
the Obscene Publications Act, passed in 1959, to ban the unex-
purgated version of D. H. Lawrence's *Lady Chatterley's Lover*
from dissemination in England on grounds of obscenity.[28] Unlike his private criticism of *The Well of Loneliness,* Forster had
no doubts about the literary merits of Lawrence's novel. With

the verdict this time in favor of freedom of expression, Forster rejoiced at being on the winning side of a legal battle.

"What I Believe"

The passionate feelings that Forster expresses in the essay, "They Hold Their Tongues," had already been touched on in his personal creed, which he was framing at least as early as January 1938, the month of his fifty-ninth birthday. This declaration of personal values was published that year in New York as the first of a series entitled "Living Philosophies" in the *Nation*, and in London as "Credo" in the *London Mercury and Bookman*.[29] In *Two Cheers for Democracy*, a collection of his essays published in 1951, this essay bears the more evocative title, "What I Believe." Following on this upbeat title, the first sentence of the essay is an equally passionate—but negative—statement: "I do not believe in Belief," followed quickly by his exhortation to the reader "to formulate a creed of one's own." The first paragraph closes: "My motto is: 'Lord, I disbelieve—help thou my unbelief.'"[30] This variation of the biblical verse, "I believe, Lord, help thou my unbelief," emphasizes Forster's delicate differentiation between "disbelief" as a denial of belief and "unbelief" as an absence of belief, possibly only temporary. As has been previously mentioned, Professor Godbole declares in *A Passage to India* that "absence is not non-existence." While not denying the possibility of a personal creed, Forster stands firm against a formalized system of belief with a capital *B*.

What Forster does believe in is personal relationships. His allegiance to the person rather than the institution is informed by his belief that "the individual is closer to the Infinite than is bureaucracy." Though he is cognizant always of the possibility that people can be unreliable and changeable, he risks being fond of individuals and trusting them. "What is good in people—and consequently in the world—is their insistence on creation, their belief in friendship and loyalty for their own sakes." Personal relationships are, after all, "a matter for the heart, which signs no documents." Despite possible fickleness, Forster states that "one can . . . show one's own little light here, one's own poor little trembling flame, with the knowledge that it is not the only light that is shining in the darkness, and not the only one which the darkness does not comprehend."[31] Forster takes his own stand regardless of what others do:

> Personal relations are despised today. They are regarded as bourgeois luxuries, as products of a time of fair weather which is now past, and we are urged to get rid of them, and to dedicate ourselves to some movement or cause instead. I hate the idea of causes, and if I had to choose between betraying my country and betraying my friend, I hope I should have the guts to betray my country. ... There lies at the back of every creed something terrible and hard

for which the worshipper may one day
be required to suffer, and there is even a
terror and a hardness in this creed of
personal relationships, urbane and mild
though it sounds. Love and loyalty to an
individual can run counter to the claims
of the State. When they do—down with
the State, say I, which means that the
State would down me.[32]

The famous and dramatic snippet, "if I had to choose between betraying my country and betraying my friend, I hope I should have the guts to betray my country," is the essence of Forster's personal creed, which, when quoted apart from its context, may appear more like bravado than a tacit acknowledgment of the heavy price such a courageous individual stand may incur. By "betrayal" of his country, Forster does not condone spying on the government and transmitting national secrets to the enemy. Instead he implies that failure to support a friend who may be feeling the disfavor of the government for, as a theoretical example, refusing to accept suppression of speech or bureaucratic censorship, would be tantamount to betraying that friend. Forster himself disagreed with his government about World War I, feeling it was unnecessary, but he served with the Red Cross in Egypt. His feelings about World War II were quite different: He felt passionately that Hitler and the Nazis must be defeated. Forster praises Democracy—when it operates under normal circumstances—as "less hateful" than other forms of government because it does acknowledge the importance of the individual, inclusivity, equality of opportunity, and freedom to express one's innate creativity and even to criticize governmental actions. The press and Parliament come in for both praise and criticism, the press for its investigative reporting and efforts to educate the public on important issues, and Parliament for its willingness to debate those issues openly. So Forster gives "Two Cheers for Democracy: one because it admits variety and two because it permits criticism. Two cheers are quite enough: there is no occasion to give three."[33]

BBC Activities

From his struggles with the National Council for Civil Liberties in the 1930s, it was not a big leap for Forster to keep a critical eye on the BBC. He had been invited in 1928 to give a talk for the BBC; his connection with the organization expanded in 1931 with a series of book reviews.[34] By the late 1930s he had several friends on the staff, but he believed that the BBC was so concentrated on the war that the voice of literary creativity was overridden. Eventually his concern reached the upper levels of the BBC. Forster challenged the paucity of programs on literature, which he considered a valuable national asset—less than an hour a day out of perhaps fifteen or sixteen hours of daily broadcasts. The BBC finally held an open discussion, resulting in the more frequent reappearance of literature in broadcast schedules.[35] During the war Forster regularly broadcast to India so that part of the Empire, so distant yet so

vital to the British war effort, would continue to feel connected with London. At the same time Forster did not shrink
from criticizing both the government and the BBC for black-
listing certain artists because of their political activities. In a
reprise of the demonstration against the Sedition Act in the
early 1930s, Forster and supporters and the National Council
for Civil Liberties, staged a large public protest meeting
against the government's efforts, through manipulation of the
BBC board of directors, to control the speech of well-known
occasional BBC commentators. Speaking at the mass meeting,
Forster emphasized the smothering effect of such censorship
on ordinary citizens, who, out of fear, would feel impelled to
"hold their tongues." Within a few days of the rally, the government and the BBC backed down.[36]

At the end of the war, Forster did not lower his guard about
censorship and, in 1956, confronted the BBC unsuccessfully
over its handling of religious themes. In his private papers
Forster called that controversy "Non-Religious Broadcasts—
Mrs Knight Affair."[37] It is clear from his handwritten notes
that by "non-religious" Forster meant non-Christian, that is,
not holding to the orthodox Christian doctrine. According to
Forster's account, Mrs. Knight, invited to speak, had expressed
some thoughts with which the BBC disagreed. Unwilling to allow her comments to stand on their own, the BBC chose an
orthodox Christian speaker to refute her arguments. Forster
objected. Talks by "non-Christians . . . should *not* be rounded
off by a Christian, who would tell the Listening Public where
the non-Christian went wrong. . . . I did not want him to tack

on to the series and to have the insidious advantage of the Last Word." Forster proposed to the BBC that "Mrs. Knight should be asked to speak again—she or someone who shared her outlook. This suggestion was not turned down as much as shelved." Later Forster proposed a series of debates by non-Christians uncensored by the Christian "Last Word." The BBC did not oblige. But Forster did make clear his point of view: "I'm not so much interested in the rightness or wrongness of opinions as I am in gathering all opinions fairly expressed. To put it another way, I would not oppose religious broadcasting, and I think it not only unwise to do so but definitely wrong. All I am out for is to get non-religious stuff some of the freedom on the air that is accorded with religious stuff— and in particular not to have it hamstrung by that Last Word." In a comparable context on another occasion, Forster condemned "a fairmindedness which is not really fair and which has little to do with the mind."[38]

International Politics

In 1935 Forster was invited to head the English delegation to an International Congress of Writers, to be held in Paris, organized by André Malraux, then identifying himself as a Communist. The putative subject was "Defence of Culture," but the conference was intended as a stage for the Soviet Union, which would send a roster of officially approved Soviet writers to stake its claim on the international literary scene. Malraux attempted to dictate what Forster should and should not say in his speech.[39] That the event was being staged according to a hidden agenda did not escape Forster, and perhaps for this very reason he tried to persuade a roster of English writers to accompany him. Believing it was important, in typical Forster fashion he spoke his mind, a lonely voice in a hall full of people who would "endure no concrete accusation" of communist suppression of free expression or of censorship of writing that did not meet Stalinist standards.[40] In his speech, which he entitled "Liberty in England," he acknowledged that race and class were determining factors inhibiting true liberty. Nevertheless, he chose to "defend culture" by pointing out the insidious encroachment of censorship. For Great Britain, Forster said, the real danger (except war) lay in Fabio-fascism: "Fabio-fascism was the dictator-spirit 'working quietly away behind the facade of constitutional forms, passing a little law (like the Sedition Act) here, endorsing a departmental tyranny there, emphasizing the national need of secrecy everywhere, and whispering and cooing the so-called "news" every evening over the wireless, until opposition is tamed and gulled.'"[41] Though treated rather rudely both by Malraux and André Gide, Forster nonetheless agreed to join a committee of the Permanent Bureau. He considered it important that a dissenting voice should be heard for liberty, but the committee was essentially moribund.

Two years later Forster was invited to attend a "Conversation" of thirty men of letters sponsored by the League of Nations' Committee for Intellectual Co-operation. Discussion of the "Immediate Future of Letters" caused Forster more distress: "There was plenty of frank honest speaking, but no attempt to translate speech into action, nor any machinery for doing so. . . . The 'Conversation' liked questions to be asked and opinions stated, but it was not in favour of answers or arguments or of any general rise in the forensic temperature. . . . The question of the position of literature in the modern non-democratic State . . . was never properly grappled with. Courtesy and charm were maintained, but at the expense of reality." The only action taken was formation of a subcommittee, "that abortive child of parents already dead."[42]

Impending War—and the War Years

Deeply concerned about national and international politics in the decade of the 1930s, Forster struggled to counter his government's attempts to censor or control public speech and stifle communication, as Mussolini and Hitler loomed ever larger on the international scene. He was pessimistic about the chance of avoiding the spiritual and physical devastation of another world war. He clung to the hope that humanity, in the urgent pursuit of victory over the powers of evil, would not forsake its vigilance for the life-giving values he prized. In the early 1930s, Oxford University students, followed by students at Cambridge University and other English universities, had declared their antiwar sentiments, and in the ensuing national reaction to the students' declaration, Forster praised their courage in speaking out. He predicted that the war to come would inflict universal destruction: "Bacterial bombs as well as poison gas will fall from the sky, the distinction between combatants and non-combatants will disappear, women and children will be as suitable a target as men, and it is not this or that king and country which will go down in the general catastrophe but all kings and all countries. War has moved from chivalry to chemicals, and unless we can get this into our heads we are doomed, kings included." While Forster gave credit for this prognostication to his mentor and friend Goldsworthy Lowes Dickinson, whose biography he was then writing, he shared the feelings of his longtime friend, who had died the year before. He wrote that "the teaching of the Sermon on the Mount, which once he [Lowes Dickinson] had found paradoxical, seemed to him in the light of the modern developments of warfare to be the merest common sense. The peace makers are not only blessed, but they have become in the course of events the children of this world also. Unless peace can be made and maintained there will be nothing for anyone to inherit."[43] Forster's picture of the likely horrors of war proved to be a remarkably prescient view of the general devastation of the world war that came, and of subsequent wars.

In the decade of the 1930s, Forster published numerous articles in national journals against war and extolling pacifism. In a time when the traditional expressions of patriotism were becoming more strident and rigid, while trying to convince his readers, he recognized that

> some people will say that my scruples
> are groundless, others that they are fu-

tile. Others—and they will be the majority who read these notes—will blame me
for not acting before. In no case am I in
a position to preach. But I do think that
another little thing the private individual can do against war is to look through
his investment list and make sure he
isn't financing it [war] *directly*. ... I
don't want to poison foreign women and
babies. And I don't believe that, by doing
so, or threatening to do so, I can stop foreigners from poisoning me.[44]

Forster's comments on the war went well beyond his willingness to be a lonely voice; he displayed an uncommon courtesy toward those readers who might not agree with him, and
he never lost his magnanimous spirit about the traditional culture of the enemy. While many self-described patriots were
excoriating everything German, Forster carefully distinguished between the beneficent historical influence of German culture and Hitler's malevolent leadership and manipulative exploitation of that cultural heritage. When war came,
with the life of Britain at stake, in a three-part anti-Nazi series
broadcast over the BBC in 1940, Forster praised the German
national culture that, through the centuries, had slowly developed from the inner core outward, expressing how a people
viewed the world and life. Such an indigenous national culture, he said, has the potential of rising to the level of "super-
national" in times of challenge, thereby "contributing to the

general good of humanity." His example of such a culture was, of course, England. In contrast, Hitler's "culture" was governmental "culture" that would warp a truly national culture into something harsh and rigidly defined, imposed from the outside on the core of the indigenous national culture, to support the ambitions of the tyrant. By this means, Forster said, Hitler brutally manipulated the honorable history of German culture as a prelude to his goal of forcing all of Europe to accept his domination. But before attacking the rest of Europe, Hitler had to subvert the fertile German seedbed of free thought to create a template of controlled thought and expression based on his notion of the innate superiority of "Aryan" Germans. Hitler had to crush the historical German national culture. He staged many huge book burnings and blacklisted scholars in arenas as disparate as sculpture and theology. Many artists and intellectuals fled Germany. Hitler then embarked on the deliberate extermination of the Jews, and also of homosexuals and gypsies.

In the last broadcast of the series, Forster addressed the question, "What Would Germany Do to Us?" He knew that many English people understood that, in defeat, German peace terms would be appalling, but they could not imagine that English culture itself would be destroyed in the process. Warning that English culture would not be exempt from destruction, Forster reminded his readers of Hitler's treatment of Czechoslovakia and Poland, where Hitler-inspired institutions and beliefs were substituted for Czech and Polish music and art, history and education and language. Many professors and teachers were summarily dismissed, many seized and dispatched to concentration camps. Forster declared the war must be waged and Hitler defeated. Individual creativity and freedom were the core of culture, the heart of civilization, and had to be protected, he concluded. In the face of the uncertain prospects of 1940, he clung to the hope that "in this difficult day when so many of us are afraid . . . it is a comfort to remember that violence has so far never worked. Even when it seems to conquer, it fails in the long run. This failure may be due to the Divine Will. It can also be ascribed to the strange nature of Man, who refuses to live by bread alone, and is the only animal who has attempted to understand his surroundings."[45]

It has been said that Forster's name was on Hitler's personal list of English people to be exterminated after England was defeated. Whether Forster was aware of that at the time he was broadcasting is not known, but it is doubtful the knowledge would have deterred him. It probably would have had the opposite effect. In any case, his anti-Nazi broadcasts must have earned Hitler's censure, guaranteeing a prominent place on Hitler's list.

A few days after the almost miraculous rescue of 300,000 British and French troops from the beach at Dunkerque and a month before the beginning of the desperate Battle for Britain in the summer of 1940, Forster was one of forty-five signatories of a letter from the International PEN Club of London to writers around the world. Their "Appeal to the Conscience of the World" underscored again the danger to freedom of conscience, not only for the people of the British Isles but for all the world: "We ask you to make it clear to people in your country that we with our Allies are not fighting only for ourselves, but for the belief we share with every man, of any race and religion, who holds that men should respect each other and minds should be free. . . . We are fighting for the consciences of our children" and "for the people of every nation, without exception." The hopes of these English writers was for "a lasting peace . . . based only on justice," and excluding revenge.[46]

The next year Forster's essay "Tolerance" was published. In it he stated baldly, "'Except the Lord build the house, they labour in vain who build it.' Beneath the poetic imagery of these words lies a hard scientific truth, namely, unless you have a sound attitude of mind, a right psychology, you cannot construct or reconstruct anything that will endure. The text is true, not only for religious people, but for workers whatever their outlook. . . . Surely the only sound foundation for a civilisation is a sound state of mind."[47] As usual, Forster did not explain precisely what he meant; he expected the reader to tease out the meaning of the metaphor. But it should be clear from his opening sentences that he did not think mere tinkering with the old order would be adequate to the requirements of international relationships in the postwar era. His use of the phrase "except the Lord build it" quite possibly refers to that mysterious conduit to the Creative Spirit that, Forster believed, each individual possessed, the connection that Forster often called intuition. When intuition is encouraged to develop naturally, Forster believed, it can become that "sound attitude of mind," a strong connection with the divine, and a firm foundation for an improved civilization.

Attempting to define the "proper spirit," Forster did not cite Love, which, though of paramount importance in private life, he considered useless in public life because it could be vague and sentimental and incapable of universal application. His solution was tolerance, which he saw as having a certain practicality. After the British had endured months of nightly bombing raids, "tolerance" may have been the only acceptable word to describe an intentional change of attitude toward enemies that so many British citizens had long been condemning in hostile phrases. In an imaginary postwar meeting with a German soldier, Forster personalized the dilemma of the "proper spirit." Attempting to love the person who had been trying to kill him would be impossible, said Forster, but with effort tolerance could lead to equal respect for all humanity. His refusal to dehumanize the enemy in the name of patriotism reminded his readers of the need to respect the individual, all individuals, no matter the temptations and justification for hatred. Forster did not look on tolerance as "a great eternally-established divine principle" but saw it rather as "necessary for the salvation of this crowded, jostling modern world."[48] Putting oneself "in someone else's place," he wrote, is "a desirable spiritual exercise."[49] Forster warned that tolerance should never be confused with weakness. Tolerance requires, in Forster's view, more spiritual muscle than the word superficially implies.

While Forster was subscribing to the highest moral principles, he was also sparring with "patriots" who had condemned
the few English writers and intellectuals who years earlier had
left England to work in the United States. His friends W. H. Auden and Christopher Isherwood were two of these. Forster regarded the attack on them as a distraction from the real enemy; people like Auden and Isherwood were not undermining
their homeland. Forster thought it better to pay attention to
the English quislings working behind the scenes in London for
Hitler's victory; they should be ferreted out and exposed. At
the same time Forster's old concerns continued. He strongly
supported individuals jailed by the government for undisclosed reasons; they must, he declared, receive the protection
of a fair and public hearing.

While presenting a public face of hope in those perilous
days—tenuous hope, but hope still alive—Forster was not exempt in his private life from the fears and anxieties of a population suffering saturation bombing and urgent calls by the
government for more servicemen and home-defense personnel. Night after night from his London flat, Forster watched
the city burning. After the home of Florence Barger was destroyed by bombs, Forster invited her to stay at the West
Hackhurst house in Abinger, Surrey, where his mother lived
and where he stayed part-time. When at West Hackhurst, Forster volunteered for war work, for even Abinger suffered
bombing and deprivation. Florence Barger was one of a pro-
cession of family and friends given shelter there during the
war. Some left after only a few months, plagued by Lily Forster's personality, which had become more quarrelsome with

age. In addition to his aging mother, Forster's personal anxieties included Bob Buckingham, the love of his life, a police officer who had been a pacifist but gradually turned toward direct involvement. Though by government order police officers were frozen in their positions in order to preserve social order in the turmoil and devastation of war, eventually police personnel were allowed to volunteer for the air force. Forster, terrified at the thought of losing Bob in the war, was relieved when he was rejected because of poor eyesight. The war weighed on Forster's spirits, as on everyone's. He continued to publish literary essays, occasionally lectured publicly, attended a PEN conference in 1945 on the tercentenary of Milton's "Areopagitica," and worried about his friends on the continent from whom he had not heard in years.

The clearing horizon after Germany's surrender brought relief but also some new challenges to Forster. His mother's death shortly before the end of the European war was a mixed blessing; while Forster experienced some relief from her critical presence, he felt so intensely bereft that many friends and relatives had to rally round in support. And in a repetition of the abrupt loss of Rooksnest when he was fourteen years old, the specter of homelessness arose again when the owners of the land on which the West Hackhurst house stood made known their wish to regain control of their property. The renewed anxiety of potential homelessness ended happily and by chance. About this time King's College at Cambridge invited Forster to become an Honorary Fellow, and a comment in his letter of acceptance led to an invitation also to take rooms in the college itself. He lived there contentedly almost a quarter of a century in the last years of his long life. Counterbalancing new traumas in the immediate postwar period were the invitation to visit India again and the prospect of a trip to the United States, as well as renewed contacts with friends in Europe. Perhaps most gratifying was the expectation of more frequent contact with Bob Buckingham. Gradually relinquishing his political roles, Forster returned to speaking out as a respected individual voice in book reviews and essays on subjects close to his heart and eventually wrote the biography of his great-aunt Marianne Thornton and the era in which she lived. The current of his life, like the life of his country, was no longer dammed up by war.

Part Five

Billy Budd :
Humanism and Spirituality
United

Chapter Nine

"Unquenchable Lights" and
"The Far-Shining Sail"

Bits of Forster's philosophy of life lie scattered in his writings like shards of sea glass found on the beach when the tide recedes. Like pale sea glass these philosophical fragments do not loudly proclaim themselves, but their meaning and value are discernible in Forster's lucid prose and in the way he lived. Scarred by his childhood exposure to dogmatic Victorian Christianity, with its insistence on doctrine and liturgy, and repelled further by his King's College experience at Cambridge of the rigid didactics of those convinced of their own rectitude and the errors of others, Forster remained deeply fearful of the power both of institutions and of charismatic personalities to manipulate the thoughts and actions of docile audiences. His own faith lay in the humanity of innumerable individuals, not in the manipulation of a crowd. Yet Forster's personal response to life was never insulated from spiritual yearnings. To him, the human and the divine were indivisible.

Individualism itself suggests a lonely stance, a singular isolation. Forster was not afraid to stand alone; he cherished his
right to think for himself and felt that somewhere, among chaotic humanity, are persons of similar persuasion. In spite of
what he experienced or observed, he believed that, at heart,
people were radically good and that such goodness shone in
the menacing darkness like little flickering lights symbolizing
the power of one, as it has been called. Contrasted with the
piercing concentration of a Great Leader's searchlight or a bureaucratic institution's massive power, the wattage of those
little flickering lights was scattered throughout society like
the haphazard pattern of sea glass on the sand. As a single light
each one may have seemed puny, but when many were focused together, their concentrated brilliance demanded attention.

Radically good people, Forster believed, risked loving and
living to the fullest; they did not barricade themselves against
the possibility of failure or rejection by society. They lived "as
if" it were the best of times, knowing full well it was not. By
living "as if," they were not crushed by the vagaries of life but
in their courageous outlook kept open "a few breathing holes
for the human spirit" as a personal affirmation and as a signal
of fraternity with others, known and unknown, of a similar
disposition wherever they might be found.

Nothing in Forster's beliefs or actions suggests that such
individualism was time-limited. Nor did individualism pre-
clude a number of persons from coalescing into a group sharing common interests. Indeed, he urged people to make meaningful connections with others. To him, "only connect" was

more than a clever epigraph; it epitomized his philosophy, a never-ending effort to connect—whether with Nature or one's own intuitive and creative gifts or with individuals' hidden being, or with humanity as a whole, or with a mysterious Creator. It gave strength, stability, and depth to his life and writings. When Forster set out to create connection, that connection usually put down deep roots, gradually nurturing and sustaining the relationship. This hidden foundation was expressed instinctively by Forster's feelings and actions and only occasionally articulated in public words.

Forster was reticent in his personal life. He lived up to the nickname *le taupe* (the mole) bestowed by friends in King's College days. He was also humble, neither pompous nor pretentious, eschewing as much as possible the public stage. Though a radical thinker, he never carried a banner in a protest march, apparently believing that such attention seeking would have less lasting influence than a calm presentation of well-reasoned ideas in a personal discussion or in a magazine article or review or a letter to the editor. With his special gift of language, Forster could couch his beliefs in such a graceful way that his readers scarcely recognized them as radical. Even the rapier thrust of language that demolished another's argument could seem almost painless in Forster's hands. His respect for other people, even those with whom he did not agree, usually prevented him from leaving bodies on the philosophical battlefield. Abjuring leadership—his or another's—because of its potential for a grave misuse of power, he was nonetheless a courageous actor. His philosophy found its way into his novels and other published works, usually through his

characters and the complications of their behavior, but sometimes in the direct authorial voice.

Personal relationships were of paramount importance to
Forster even as he acknowledged that they could change over
time. While reliability—one's own as well as others'—was the
goal, Forster noted that a relationship "is a matter for the
heart, which signs no documents." Whatever others may do or
fail to do, "one can ... show one's own little light here, one's
own poor little trembling flame, with the knowledge that it is
not the only light that is shining in the darkness, and not the
only one which the darkness does not comprehend."[1] Love
and loyalty are needed, and sometimes also great courage.

Forster's experiences at King's College led him to connections with a number of individuals in what may be called his
extended family. Some of these relationships developed
through the Apostles, a long-standing literary/philosophical
society to which Forster was elected. He retained a strong connection all his life with many of the Apostles. To other groups
such as Bloomsbury, he gave a more limited commitment.
Gradually Forster's "little twinkling lights" expanded into a
web of relationships that transcended national boundaries
and reached as far afield as India.

Forster never denies the existence of force and violence.
In "What I Believe," his personal credo, he faults equally those
who depend on force and violence and mystics who "declare
that force does not exist." (70) He acknowledges that force and
violence are "the ultimate reality." (71) At the same time he
urges individuals not to be overwhelmed by them but to cultivate kindly human relations and express their own natural

creativity. He defines such kindness and creative spirit as civilization, "the chief justification for the human experiment" (71). "What is good in people—and consequently in the world—is their insistence on creation, their belief in friendship and loyalty for their own sakes; and though Violence remains and is, indeed, the major partner in this muddled establishment . . . creativeness remains too, and will always assume direction when violence sleeps." (72)

Forster's "good" people are sensitive, affectionate, tolerant, and hopeful. He calls such people his "aristocracy," aristocrats not of birth, position, or possessions but of spirit. They "are to be found in all nations and classes, and all through the ages. . . . They represent the true human tradition, the one permanent victory of our queer race over cruelty and chaos." Although most people live and die in obscurity, yet their little lights are unquenchable, and their temple "is the Holiness of the Heart's Affection, and their kingdom, though they never possess it, is the wide-open world." Throughout history they have been beacons of hope—"unquenchable lights of my aristocracy! Signals of the invincible army!" (73–75)

Though Forster was a mild-mannered and retiring man, he never wavered in his basic beliefs. His philosophy was individual, neither weak nor vacillating, but it had, and still has, universal vision. Stephen Spender describes it thus: "I should add to those whom I praise [Virginia Woolf, T. S. Eliot, Cyril Connolly, Christopher Isherwood, W. H. Auden] the name of E. M. Forster, the best English novelist of this century, and one of the most acute of its moralists. But Forster's strange mixture

of qualities—his self-effacingness combined with a positive assertion of his views, his whimsicality combined with a great
precision, his almost pagan amorality combined with his mi-
nute preoccupation with moral issues, his love of freedom
combined with an impressive self-discipline, would make it
wrong to describe him in connection with a group, even of his
friends. He is one of the most comforting of modern writers,
and at the same time one of the most uncomfortable."[2]

Although Forster's insistence on individual action and responsibility may seem contradicted by his equal emphasis on
human connection, he never pretends that disparities do not
exist. He believes that contradictions must be accepted, not
submerged or compromised away. He does not pretend to
have all the answers, nor claim to have *the* answer. But, re-
peatedly, he teases apart the disorder and chaos of human actions to uncover eternal values, such as beauty, spirit, creativity, respect, kindliness. It did not matter to Forster that his
philosophy might not coincide with popular ideas. In his own
credo he is passing on the torch, the unquenchable light of his
deepest values in an offer of "mutual improvement" to any
reader who wishes to accept the gift.

While praising democracy moderately, Forster adminis-
ters a sharp slap to the Christianity he had rejected at Cambridge when he writes in "What I Believe" that "no form of
Christianity and no alternative to Christianity will bring peace
to the world or integrity to the individual; no 'change of heart'
will occur." (71) He declares his hope for the future: "The Saviour of the future—if ever he comes—will not preach a new

Gospel. He will merely utilise my aristocracy, he will make effective the good will and the good temper which are already existing. . . . I cannot believe that Christianity will ever cope with the present world-wide mess." (75) He credits its influence to the money supporting it, rather than to its spiritual appeal. Forster believes that the indwelling spirit would probably have to be recast "in a non-Christian form." (76) His credo, "What I Believe," which opens with the ringing statement, "I do not believe in Belief," concludes with a declaration of Forster's continuing faith in the decency of ordinary human beings, who in spite of the most strenuous efforts of dictators will continue to express an individual spirit.

Forster's antipathy toward the then-current expression of Christian values never included rejection of intuitive spirituality. His libretto for Benjamin Britten's opera *Billy Budd,* first performed in 1951, just short of Forster's seventy-third birthday, is an unequivocal statement of both his humanism and his transcendent beliefs. The love of humanity and a natural acceptance of the inscrutable mystery of life are united in the character of Billy Budd. Though Eric Crozier, who had already worked with Britten, was named co-librettist, acknowledging the theatrical experience Forster himself lacked, the enlarged, and significantly reshaped, Billy Budd of the opera was mainly Forster's interpretation. Forster also altered somewhat the characters of other personae of Herman Melville's story. Whereas Melville emphasized Captain Vere's dilemma in dispensing discipline, Forster shifted the focus of the opera to the human and spiritual implications of Billy's life. In such shifts of emphasis, Benjamin Britten concurred.

Melville's original story was set in 1797 against the backdrop of the French Revolution and in the midst of open conflict between England and France, when the British government feared that the cataclysm of the French Revolution might be exported to England. Indeed, a brief uprising among the sailors at Spithead had been put down, followed by a more significant rebellion at the Nore so potentially dangerous to political stability that the British government dubbed it the "Great Mutiny." Ranking naval personnel were warned of the possibility of mutiny among their crews. Into this situation came Billy Budd, taken by impressment from the merchant ship *Rights-of-Man* on which he was returning to port after an extended voyage. The outward-bound man-of-war *Bellipotent,* lacking its full complement of able seamen, had the right to stop merchant shipping and take some of their crew to fill out the requirements of the naval vessel. That Billy was a foundling, knowing nothing of his parentage, made it easier for him to accept impressment than for others who were expecting to return to family and the warmth of the cottage hearth. The captain of the *Rights-of-Man* was loath nevertheless to surrender Billy to the *Bellipotent,* calling him the "jewel" of his crew and recounting how Billy's presence created peace among his fractious seamen. But he had no choice in the matter.

In Melville's hands Billy seemed to be what Forster in *Aspects of the Novel* called a two-dimensional "flat" character. As a foundling, he was left in a silk-lined basket on the doorstep of a substantial house in Bristol. Growing up as best he could in eighteenth-century England, he was illiterate and in his innocence seemed almost simple-minded; Melville described him as a "child-man." Melville's adult Billy lacked inner reflection and had no discernible gift of leadership but was eager to perform his duties well. By his nature and his exuberant singing, he spread joy and camaraderie, unwittingly playing the role of peacemaker. A single blemish—an occasional stutter when heartfelt emotion was blocked from quick articulation—reminded the reader of Billy's mortal fallibility, but he could defend himself physically, if not verbally, against bullies.

Melville's attention in this story was focused on Captain Vere's dilemma in adhering strictly to the naval code of that turbulent time, which demanded of all aboard the ship absolute obedience to its rules and regulations. Though principally a means of controlling a motley crew, that code required strict adherence also by officers, including the captain, particularly to punishments ordained for various infractions. John Claggart, the master-at-arms, was charged with enforcing obedience by the crew, a crucial duty in that time of uncertain loyalty. Like Billy, Claggart's own history was mysterious but, in contrast to Billy's background, empty of known facts. Claggart's background was deliberately hidden. He had joined the navy as an ordinary seaman when an adult, suggesting expediency rather than free choice. Because of his age and experience, he quickly became a petty officer and soon was appointed master-at-arms, a position corresponding to chief of police ashore. Melville suggested that when the happy-go-lucky Billy so summarily joined the crew, Claggart felt a sudden virulent envy toward him, an emotion he carefully kept hidden. Soon Claggart felt threatened by Billy's quick popularity among the below-decks crew. Melville also hinted ever so delicately at homoeroticism on Claggart's part, a trait that suffered the greatest opprobrium and was sufficient reason for secrecy. Whatever Claggart's motivation for inventing his tale of Billy's insurrectionary plottings—whether envy of Billy's easy popularity or an imagined threat to his leadership—Claggart created a tissue of assumptions embroidered with lies and accused Billy of treason. In a confrontation with Claggart before the captain, Billy was shocked to hear himself accused of such trumped-up charges. Struck dumb by the sudden rush of strong feelings and unable to express his anger in words, Billy lashed out with a blow to Claggart's head, and Claggart fell down dead. Although Vere's instinct told him that Billy was defending his innocence against Claggart's slander, Billy had struck an officer and caused his death; for either infraction there was only one punishment—death. Under the military code, Billy, the innocent victim of slander, instantly became the offender, and the slanderer, the victim. Captain Vere exclaimed, "Struck dead by an angel of God! Yet the angel must hang!"[3] The captain believed in the sailor's innocence and integrity, but the law of the sea allowed him no discretion. When Captain Vere informed Billy that he was to be hanged, Melville imagined what might have occurred in the private interview between captain and seaman. He pictured Vere as the biblical Abraham, in anguish, embracing his son Isaac before preparing to sacrifice him at God's command. For Billy Budd, the rigid law of the sea was the altar.

Forster's Billy is a more complex, rounded character than Melville's, thoughtful and capable of growth. Forster endows his Billy with introspection and an intuitive spiritual element almost completely lacking in the Melville story. Composer and librettist consulted, and Britten agreed with Forster that Billy Budd's spiritual nature was critical. Forster, reflecting his life-long antipathy to the traditional beliefs of the established church, wrote in a letter to Britten in the early days of planning the opera: "I have thought a good deal of our conversation about Christianity and some time we must talk again. I love the tenderness and pity and love, but they have a tendency to become interfering and weepy, which repels me and is, I think, bad."[4] In a subsequent letter Forster wrote to Britten that "Melville, I believe, was often trying to do what I've tried to do. It is a difficult attempt, and even he has failed; the ordinary loveable (and hateable) human beings connected with immensities through the trick of art. Billy *is* our Saviour, yet he is Billy, not Christ."[5] It recalls Forster's earlier wish for a Christ of unpretentious human dimensions: "Christ not as an evangelical shop walker [supervisor] but as the young carpenter who would smoke a pipe with me in his off time and be most frightfully kind."

While, in Melville's story, Claggart invented his case against Billy on his personal interpretation of the eyewitness report by the sole officer in charge of impressing Billy from the merchant ship *Rights-of-Man*, in the opera libretto the young sailor sings out his fond farewell to his former ship from the deck of his new ship—in the opera named *Indomitable*—

before an audience of his new shipmates as the vessel pulls away from the merchant ship. Apprehensive of the powerful influence of the French Revolution, several officers of the *Indomitable* conflate the merchant ship's name, *Rights-of-Man,* with the potent political slogan of that era.

"Beauty, handsomeness, goodness" is a phrase several officers use in praising Billy; only Master-at-arms Claggart employs it in jealousy. Feeling threatened, he describes Billy as "the light [that] shines in the darkness, and the darkness comprehends it and suffers,"[6] identifying himself with darkness and inverting the ending of the biblical reference, John 1:5. This verse appears more than once in Forster's writings, perhaps because in it light is the symbol of goodness and deep intuitive understanding.[7] Forster's equivalent secular metaphor is his "unquenchable lights" of the human spirit. Claggart's operatic monologue recounting his visceral reaction to Billy's heroic goodness and innocence graphically expresses his intention to destroy the young man's happy spirit and bring about his death. Speaking of Billy as his secret adversary, Claggart sings that "if love still lives and grows strong where I cannot enter, what hope is there in my own dark world for me? ... That were torment too keen. ... I will destroy you." (Libretto, 33)

Though warned of Claggart's perfidy by Dansker, an older crewman, open-hearted Billy cannot comprehend that beneath the master-at-arms's pleasantries and seeming kindnesses lies an obsessive drive to destroy him. If Billy is *like* Christ, then Claggart is *like* Judas—only perhaps worse, since

Judas's betrayal was one-on-one, a direct personal action involving just Jesus and Judas, whereas Claggart's wish to see Billy dead could be accomplished only by deliberate deceit through ruthless manipulation of frightened accomplices and by fabrication of false evidence. Judas killed himself in remorse; Claggart felt no remorse and simply intended to protect his own position and power while causing Billy's death. In shaping Claggart's character, Forster "took a hint"[8] from William Plomer's preface to the 1946 London edition of Melville's novel, suggesting a difference between evil of deliberate choice and "natural depravity," an inherent state that Melville linked to the unconscious,[9] a state that Claggart recognizes in the opera: "Would that I lived in my own world always, in that depravity to which I was born." (32) In 1946 "natural depravity" was a euphemism for homosexuality as an inherent state.

Three operatic monologues delineate the characters of Claggart and Billy Budd. In the third scene of the first act, Claggart sings of his desperate need to rid himself of the threat he perceives in Billy. Forster's dissatisfaction with the music for this soliloquy caused serious friction with the composer, and in a letter in early December 1950 to Britten, Forster distinguished between his words and Britten's music:

> Very glad of what you say about the monologue. It is *my* most important piece of writing and I did not, at my first hearings, feel it sufficiently important musically. The extensions and changes you suggest in the last lap may

> make the difference for me, besides be-
> ing excellent in themselves.
>   With the exception of it, all de-
> lighted me. Most wonderful.

Then, more directly expressing his disappointment with the music, Forster continued:

> I want *passion*—love constricted, per-
> verted, poisoned, but nevertheless *flow-*
> *ing* down its agonizing channel; a sexual
> discharge gone evil. Not soggy depres-
> sion or growling remorse. I seemed
> turning from one musical discomfort to
> another, and was dissatisfied. I looked
> for an aria perhaps, for a more recog-
> nisable form. I liked the last section best,
> and if it is extended so that it dominates,
> my vague objections may vanish. "A
> longer line, a firmer melody"—exactly.

The intensity of his own feelings undoubtedly blinded Forster to Britten's sensitivity. Britten could not compose with any-one looking over his shoulder, and Eric Crozier, the co-librettist, had to soothe the ruffled composer and contrive to keep Forster from visiting Britten at his Aldeburgh home till tempers cooled. By December 12 Crozier wrote that "Britten was busy rewriting."[10]

The sexual metaphor suggests that Forster, through the libretto, is expressing his adamant opposition to the assertion of State and Church that homosexuality is a crime to be punished by the full power of the law. It seems evident that Forster is declaring that "a sexual discharge gone evil," a perversion of inherent physical love, was forced on men by the criminalization of homosexuality.

Billy Budd's two operatic monologues occur as, in chains, he awaits his execution. In the first, a poem complete with rhythm and rhyme, Billy outlines the ritual steps of his execution, his realism overlaid by a dreamy haze. "Billy himself caused much less trouble than I expected," Forster wrote to Lionel Trilling in April 1949. "*He* has a monologue at the end—or rather two: first the dreamy 'Billy in the Darbies,' followed by old Dansker bringing in not too obtrusively the eucharist of grog and biscuits . . .—and then a heroic one about Fate; the black sea where he has caught sight of the far-gleaming sail that is not Fate."[11]

The military ritual of death under sentence required the ministrations of a chaplain, and, in Melville's version of the story, the chaplain, though adhering to traditional forms, recognized that Billy's natural innocence was a surer spiritual guide than the formalities of confession and salvation when facing divine judgment. In the opera libretto the chaplain himself does not appear, but Billy tells of his visit and reports that he liked the story the chaplain told of the "good boy hung and gone to glory, hung for the likes of me." (60) But of more significance to Billy—and also to Forster—is Dansker's surreptitious arrival bearing communion in the form of grog and biscuits. Billy recognizes that his old shipmate is risking being caught and punished. Melville's story, however, includes no such scene; one can only surmise that this intimate scene, with its spiritual symbolism, was created by Forster as a concrete example of his own challenging credo: "If I had to choose between betraying my country and betraying my friend, I hope I should have the guts to betray my country." Dansker has the courage Forster admires. That Dansker's action also epitomizes the spiritual dimension of Forster's libretto is made doubly clear in Forster's letter to Lionel Trilling, in which he gives this staged meal its religious name of eucharist.

The second monologue amplifies the spiritual motif in the libretto. It is fate, Billy sings, that has decided the happenings and the outcome; it was fate that caused him to strike Claggart with his fist since his tongue was tied by his powerful emotions. It is fate, too, in the form of the naval code, that forces Captain Vere to sentence Billy to death. In the courage and largeness of his spirit, Billy blesses the captain, mourning that he will not be around to assist his captain in the future and admonishing the crew to help him since he cannot.

As for himself, though sad to be parting from his shipmates and sorrowing that he will never again look down at the deck from his foretop position high in the rigging, Billy sees, in his mind's eye, "a sail in the storm, the far-shining sail that's not Fate, and I'm contented. I've seen where she's bound for. She has a land of her own where she'll anchor for ever. Oh, I'm contented. Don't matter now being hanged, or being forgotten. ... Don't matter now. I'm strong, and I know it, and I'll stay strong, and that's all, and that's enough." (61) From early in the opera, the endless sea symbolizes life in all its portentous uncertainty—"We're all of us lost, lost for ever on the endless sea" (19)—a stark contrast to the safe harbor, the home port and reunion with family that most sailors long for. Even in his own bleak predicament, shackled and awaiting death, Billy has found contentment and courage within his unshackled soul, a faint sign of hope represented by the far-shining ship in its eternal safe anchorage beyond time. As he prepares to die, Billy calls out a blessing upon Captain Vere, inspiring a reciprocal response from the shocked and incredulous crew who have been mustered up on deck to witness his hanging.

Billy Budd was enthusiastically received at its premiere at Covent Garden in December 1951, inspiring Forster to write soon after to Benjamin Britten, "You and I have both put into it something which lies deeper than artistic creation, and which we both understand. It could never have got there but for both of us. I hope to live and write on it in the future, but this opera is my Nunc Dimittis, in that it dismisses me peacefully, and convinces me I have achieved."[12]

Some of the bits of philosophical sea glass scattered through the portrayal of Billy emphasize values important to Forster. Even in the absence of a direct authorial voice, the reader of the libretto or the listener at the opera may discern in the words and the scenes vivid expressions of Forster's personal beliefs. The whole *Indomitable* crew, including the officers and especially the captain, disbelieved the charge of mutiny that the master-at-arms had raised against Billy, but his shipmates of whatever rank found themselves trapped, like Billy himself, in a system of blinkered justice that had no al-

lowance for mercy. Yet death itself could not end Billy's beneficent influence. In Melville's story, though not in the opera libretto, the spar from which Billy was hung became a potent
talisman for the lowly sailors, a chip from it like "a piece of the
Cross"[13] to them.

Forster's treatment of Billy's death is more deeply spiritual
than Melville's own rendering. In *Billy Budd*, through the art—
and artifice—of opera, Forster brings together humanism and
spirituality through Billy, an ordinary seaman, one of Forster's
"good people," one of his "aristocrats." Captain Vere has been
given two powerful lines defining humanism as personified by
Billy, the first when he must inform the young seaman he is to
be hanged. Loath to pronounce sentence because he believes
in Billy's natural innocence, and wondering how Billy can par-
don him, he beholds in Billy "the mystery of goodness." (58)
Billy feels no anger toward the captain and has no need to forgive him; he understands instinctively that Captain Vere is
caught between his belief in Billy's innocence and the inflexi-
ble naval regulations. The captain senses that he has been
saved by Billy's magnanimous spirit; "the love that passes understanding has come to me." (63)

In the epilogue of the opera, set many years after Billy's
hanging, the captain, as an old man, remembers Billy and his
own responsibility for Billy's death. He sings that Billy "has
saved me, and blessed me, and the love that passes understanding has come to me. I was lost on the infinite sea, but I've
sighted a sail in the storm, the far-shining sail, and I'm content. I've seen where she's bound for. There's a land where
she'll anchor for ever." (63) He is content, having also caught

sight intuitively of the far-shining sail that Billy saw in his imagination the night before his execution. Like Billy, but years later, the captain expresses the hope of an eternal safe harbor. The idea of a far-shining sail had come independently to the captain.

Through the medium of opera, Forster has portrayed a character who loves humanity and encompasses a vigorous intuitive spirituality. Billy Budd is a man of faith—belief in himself, faith in the decency of other people, and with a sense of hope in the mystery of something yet to be experienced.

Notes

Chapter One

[1] This chapter is a revision of my article, "The 'Noble Peasant' in E. M. Forster's Fiction," *Studies in the Novel* 20, no. 4 (Winter 1988): 389–403, published by the University of North Texas, Denton, Texas.

[2] E. M. Forster, "A Presidential Address to the Cambridge Humanists," Summer 1959, E. M. Forster Archives, in the Modern Archives of King's College Library, Cambridge University, Cambridge, England, Vo 8/22 at fo 135, no pagination. All quotations left unnumbered in this chapter are from this typescript in the E. M. Forster Archives. The Presidential Address was subsequently published in the *Bulletin of the University Humanist Federation*, no. 11 (Cambridge Number) (Spring 1963), by the University Humanist Federation, 13, Prince of Wales Terrace, London, W8, 2–8. Only very recently has this speech, under the title "How I Lost My Faith," become available in book form in Forster, *The Prince's Tale and Other Uncollected Writings*, Abinger edition, vol. 17, ed. P. N. Furbank (London: André Deutsch, 1998), 310–19, thus making this hitherto elusive article available to a wider readership.

[3] Forster, *The Longest Journey*, Abinger edition, vol. 2, ed. Elizabeth Heine (London: Edward Arnold, 1984), 183.

[4] Forster, "Credo," *The London Mercury and Bookman* 38, no. 227 (September 1938): 404. This essay is included in Forster, *Two Cheers for Democracy,* Abinger edition, vol. 11, ed. Oliver Stallybrass (London: Edward Arnold, 1972) as "What I Believe," 65–73.

[5] Forster, "Notebook Journal 1903–1909," Vo 3/9, entry of September 17, 1907, Cambridge Univ., England, King's College Modern Archives, Forster Archives. Italics added.

[6] Ibid., entry of April 18, 1908.

[7] See J. B. Beer, *The Achievement of E. M. Forster* (London: Chatto and Windus, 1962); John Colmer, *E. M. Forster: The Personal Voice* (London: Routledge and Kegan Paul, 1975); Frederick C. Crews, *E.*

M. Forster: The Perils of Humanism (Princeton, NJ: Princeton Univ. Press, 1962); K. W. Grandsden, *E. M. Forster* (New York: Grove Press, 1962); James McConkey, *The Novels of E. M. Forster* (Ithaca, NY: Cornell Univ. Press, 1957); Wilfred Stone, *The Cave and the Mountain* (Stanford, CA: Stanford Univ. Press, 1966); Alan Wilde, *Art and Order: A Study of E. M. Forster* (New York: New York Univ. Press, 1964), among others, for comments on the moral dimension of Forster's writings. See also Alexandra Yarrow's perceptive article, "Sympathy in the Novels of E. M. Forster," *Aspects of E. M. Forster*, ed. Heiko Zimmermann, April 21, 2002, http://emforster.de/pdf/yarrow.pdf. This is only a small taste of Forster criticism available and a small selection of the criticism I have consulted.

[8] P. N. Furbank, *E. M. Forster: A Life*, vol. 1, *The Growth of the Novelist (1879-1914)* (New York: Harcourt Brace Jovanovich, 1978), 133.

[9] Ibid., 81.

[10] Forster, *Where Angels Fear to Tread*, Abinger edition, vol. 1, ed. Oliver Stallybrass (London: Edward Arnold, 1975), 108.

[11] Furbank, *A Life*, 1: 117; Forster's italics.

[12] Ibid., 40.

[13] Frances Partridge, *Everything to Lose, Diaries 1945-1960* (Boston: Little, Brown, 1985), 228-29.

[14] Forster, *Two Cheers*, "Cambridge," 346. See note 4 for bibliographical data.

[15] Forster, *Abinger Harvest and England's Pleasant Land,* Abinger edition, vol. 10, ed. Elizabeth Heine (London: André Deutsch, 1996), "Notes on the English Character," 13.

[16] Furbank, *A Life*, vol. 1, Mrs. Failing, 64; Charlotte Bartlett, 65; Mrs. Honeychurch, 2.

[17] P. N. Furbank and F.J.H. Haskell, "E. M. Forster," interview of June 20, 1952, in Malcolm Cowley, ed., *Paris Review, Writers at Work* (New York: Viking Press, 1958), 32.

[18] Forster, *Howards End*, Abinger edition, vol. 4, ed. Oliver Stallybrass (London: Edward Arnold, 1973), 191.

[19] George H. Thomson, *The Fiction of E. M. Forster* (Detroit, MI: Wayne State Univ. Press, 1967), 80–81.

[20] Forster, *A Room With a View*, Abinger edition, vol. 3, ed. Oliver Stallybrass (London: Edward Arnold, 1977), 110.

[21] Furbank, *A Life*, 1: 119.

[22] In an interview with Angus Wilson in 1957, Forster denied that Mrs. Munt, the Schlegels' aunt, might have been capable of such a momentary vision, but "Stephen, of course, had something of the sort." Angus Wilson, "A Conversation with E. M. Forster," *Encounter* no. 5 (November 1957): 54.

[23] Forster, *The Machine Stops and Other Stories,* Abinger edition, vol. 7, ed. Rod Mengham (London: André Deutsch, 1997), "The Eternal Moment," 182.

[24] Alfred Kazin, "Howards End Revisited," *Partisan Review* 59, no. 1 (Winter 1992): 29–43; reprinted in *Twentieth Century Literary Criticism* 125 (2003), 114–20.

[25] Thomson, *Fiction of E. M. Forster*, 185.

[26] Ibid., 26.

[27] Forster, *Two Cheers,* "The *Raison d'Etre* of Criticism in the Arts," 115.

[28] Forster, *A Passage to India*, Abinger edition, vol. 6, ed. Oliver Stallybrass (New York: Holmes and Meier, 1979), 245.

[29] Michael Orange, "Language and Silence in *A Passage to India*," in G. K. Das and John Beer, eds., *E. M. Forster: A Human Exploration* (New York: New York Univ. Press, 1979): 154.

[30] Wilson, "A Conversation," 54; Forster's italics.

[31] Forster, *Two Cheers*, "What I Believe," 70–71.

Chapter Two

[1] This chapter was originally published as Jeane N. Olson, "E. M. Forster's Prophetic Vision of the Modern Family in *Howards End*," in *Texas Studies in Literature and Language* 35, no. 3 (Fall 1993): 347–62. This article was reprinted in *Twentieth-Century Literary Criticism* 125 (2003), 120–28.

[2] Lawrence Stone, *The Family, Sex and Marriage in England, 1500–1800* (New York: Harper and Row, 1979), 22.

[3] Ibid.

[4] Peter Gay, *The Tender Passion* (New York: Oxford Univ. Press, 1986), 4.

[5] Ibid., 106.

[6] Ibid.

[7] Ibid., 107. For further insight into the nineteenth-century English middle-class family, see also F.M.L. Thompson, *The Rise of Respectable Society* (Cambridge, MA: Harvard Univ. Press, 1988). For contemporary personal accounts of parent-child relations, see Linda Pollock, *A Lasting Relationship: Parents and Children over Three Centuries* (Hanover, NH: Univ. Press of New England, 1987). For an understanding of the buffering role of servants in isolating children from parents, see Theresa M. McBride, *The Domestic Revolution* (New York: Holmes and Meier, 1976).

[8] Forster, *Where Angels Fear to Tread*, 69.

[9] Quoted in Leonore Davidoff, "Mastered for Life: Servant and Wife in Victorian and Edwardian England," *Journal of Social History* 7 (Summer 1974): 406.

[10] For a discussion of the entry of clerks into the lower middle class, see F.M.L. Thompson, *Rise of Respectable Society,* 68-69. For bibliographical data, see chapter 1, note 7.

[11] Furbank and Haskell, "E. M. Forster," 23–25.

[12] Forster, *Howards End,* 58.

[13] From a 1910 letter to Goldsworthy Lowes Dickinson, quoted in Furbank, *A Life,* 1: 191.

[14] Forster, *Commonplace Book,* ed. Philip Gardner (Stanford: Stanford Univ. Press, 1985), 91.

[15] Furbank, *A Life,* 1: 24–25.

[16] P. N. Furbank, "The Personality of E. M. Forster," *Encounter* 35, no. 5, (November 1970): 61–68; see especially 65.

[17] Ibid., 64.

[18] Furbank, *E. M. Forster, A Life*, vol. 2, *Polycrates Ring (1914–1970)*, 40.

[19] Colmer, *Personal Voice*, 3. For bibliographical data, see chapter 1, note 7.

[20] Quoted in ibid.

[21] Forster, *Marianne Thornton, A Domestic Biography, 1797–1887*, Abinger ed., vol. 15, ed. Evelyne Hanquart-Turner (London: André Deutsch, 2000), 48. See also Forster, *Marianne Thornton, A Domestic Biography, 1797–1887* (New York: Harcourt, Brace, 1956), 41.

[22] See Judith Scherer Herz, "Forster's Three Experiments in Autobiographical Biography," *Studies in the Literary Imagination* 13 (Spring 1980): 64.

[23] Quoted in Peter Parker, *Ackerley: A Life of J. R. Ackerley* (New York: Farrar Strauss Giroux, 1989), 157.

[24] For contemporaneous reviews, see Philip Gardner, *E. M. Forster, the Critical Heritage* (London: Routledge and Kegan Paul, 1973). See also Frederick P. W. McDowell, *E. M. Forster, an Annotated Bibliography of Writings about Him* (De Kalb: Northern Illinois Univ. Press, 1976), and Helmut E. Gerber, "E. M. Forster: An Annotated Checklist of Writings about Him," *English Fiction in Transition* 2 (Spring 1959): 4–27, bound in *English Literature in Transition,* vols. 1–3 (1957–60). Also see McDowell's articles in *English Literature in Transition,* especially "E. M. Forster: Recent Extended Studies," 9 (Fall 1966): 156–68; "Bibliography, News, and Notes: E. M. Forster," 10 (Spring 1967): 47–64; and "Recent Books on Forster and on Bloomsbury," 12 (Fall 1969): 135–50. Present-day scholars provide subtle insights into specific personal relationships, but no one seems to address the *family* as a major theme. However, Don Austin, in "The Problem of Continuity in Three Novels of E. M. Forster," *Modern Fiction Studies* 7 (Autumn 1961): 219, recognizes the possibility of spiritual, as well as genetic, children.

[25] I. A. Richards, "A Passage to Forster: Reflections on a Novelist," *Forum* 78 (December 1927): 918.

[26] Lionel Trilling, *E. M. Forster* (New York: Harcourt Brace Jovanovich, 1963): 33–34. Trilling designates Mrs. Wilcox, Mrs. Eliott, and Mrs. Moore as his "heroines."

²⁷ Ibid.

²⁸ See ibid., 87.

²⁹ James Hall, *The Tragic Comedians, Seven Modern British Novelists* (Bloomington: Indiana Univ. Press, 1963), chap. 2, "Family Reunions."

³⁰ George H. Thomson, *Fiction of E. M. Forster,* 185.

³¹ Ibid.

³² Gardner, *Critical Heritage,* 167, citing a review by George B. Dutton in the *Springfield Sunday Republican* (Springfield, MA), Jan. 1, 1922. Dutton was a professor of English at Williams College.

³³ I am grateful to the reader of an earlier version of this article for this felicitous phrase, with which I wholeheartedly agree.

³⁴ See Hall, *Tragic Comedians,* 23–24.

³⁵ Ibid., 11.

³⁶ Ibid., 22–23.

³⁷ See ibid., 18. Notice also Hall's somewhat different interpretation of Mrs. Wilcox as a mother figure.

³⁸ Ibid., 23.

³⁹ Forster, *Albergo Empedocle and Other Writings of E. M. Forster,* ed. George H. Thomson (New York: Liveright, 1971), "Pessimism in Literature," 137–38; emphasis added.

⁴⁰ Forster, *Arctic Summer and Other Fiction,* Abinger edition, vol. 9, ed. Elizabeth Heine and Oliver Stallybrass (London: Edward Arnold, 1980), 122.

⁴¹ Forster, *Albergo Empedocle,* 140.

Chapter Three

¹ For a lengthy bibliography regarding Forster's Presidential Address to the Cambridge Humanists, 1959, see chapter 1, note 2. All phrases in quotation marks, except where specifically footnoted, are from this document.

² Forster, *Marianne Thornton,* Abinger ed., 162–63; Harcourt, Brace, 175–76.

[3] *Encyclopaedia Britannica,* vol. 8 (Chicago: Encyclopaedia Britannica, 1946), 896, s.v. "evangelicalism." For a succinct description of modern evangelicalism, see "Is God Still the Center?" by Mark Noll, an eminent American historian of religion, in Abernethy and Bole, *The Life of Meaning: Reflections on Faith, Doubt, and Repairing the World* (New York: Seven Stories Press, 2000), 229–35.

[4] Forster, *Marianne Thornton,* Abinger ed., 34–35; Harcourt, Brace, 26.

[5] Ibid., Abinger ed., 28; Harcourt, Brace, 19.

[6] See comment on a sermon by Mr. Venn, *Marianne Thornton,* Abinger ed., 65; also see Henry Thornton's letter to his wife in Harcourt, Brace, 61.

[7] Ibid., Abinger ed., 40; Harcourt, Brace, 32.

[8] Forster, *Two Cheers,* "Henry Thornton," 186.

[9] Ibid., 188.

[10] Forster, *Abinger Harvest,* "Battersea Rise," 239.

[11] Forster, *Two Cheers,* "Henry Thornton," 187–88.

[12] Forster, *Marianne Thornton,* Harcourt, Brace, 248–49. See also Abinger ed., 54, re Mrs. Hannah More. See also Abinger ed., 224, and Harcourt, Brace, 248–49, re Marianne Thornton's efforts to educate tradesmen's daughters. Also see Abinger ed., 135, re hopes of helping to educate neighbors' children. See Forster, *Abinger Harvest and England's Pleasant Land,* Abinger ed., 234. Each volume of *Marianne Thornton* has a chapter on "Education," Abinger ed., 224; Harcourt, Brace, 248.

[13] Ibid., 54.

[14] "Locked Journal," Vo 4/4, entry of April 5, 1912, Forster Archives.

[15] Forster, *Prince's Tale,* 325.

[16] Forster, *Abinger Harvest,* "Battersea Rise," 239.

[17] "Notebook Journal, 1903–1909," Vo 3/9, entry of December 31, 1903, Forster Archives. This date is the eve of Forster's twenty-fifth birthday.

[18] Forster, *Howards End,* 192–93.

[19] Furbank, *A Life,* 1: 25.

[20] Quoted in Judith Scherer Herz and Robert K. Martin, eds., *E. M. Forster: Centenary Revaluations* (Toronto: Univ. of Toronto Press, 1982), 298–99.

[21] Gillian Naylor, *Bloomsbury: Its Artists, Authors and Designers* (Boston: Little, Brown, 1990), 8.

[22] Ibid., quoting from Mill's "Utilitarianism," first printed in 1861 in *Fraser's Magazine,* published in book form in 1863.

[23] See Noel Annan, *Leslie Stephen, The Godless Victorian* (New York: Random House, 1984), 195, quoting M. Carré, *Phases of Thought in England* (1949), 312, who was quoting D. Masson, *Recent British Philosophy* (1867), 8.

[24] For a detailed description of the effects of Evangelicalism and Utilitarianism in nineteenth-century India, see Percival Spear, *A History of India,* vol. 2 (London: Penguin Books, repr., 1990), chap. 10, "The New Policy."

[25] See ibid., 169–70, re the Ilbert bill and its consequences.

[26] Annan, *Leslie Stephen,* 288–89.

[27] See Benjamin Farrington, *What Darwin Really Said* (New York: Schocken Books, 1966). I am grateful to Professor Farrington and to Stephen Jay Gould, who wrote the foreword to Professor Farrington's book, for my layman's understanding of the theory of evolution. Any errors in understanding or interpretation are my own.

[28] Arguing on purely religious grounds, Gregory of Nazianus and Augustine, two early Christian thinkers, maintained that "it would have been impossible to hold representatives of all species in a single vessel such as Noah's ark; hence some . . . must have come into existence only after the Noachian flood." To them it was obvious that some species "had developed in historical times from God's creations." In the Middle Ages Albertus Magnus and his student Thomas Aquinas entertained seriously the possibility that organisms might change by some natural process. See *The New Encyclopaedia Britannica (Macropaedia—Knowledge in Depth),* 15th ed. (Chicago: Encyclopaedia Britannica, Inc., 1995), 18:855–56, s.v. "The Theory of Evolution."

[29] Farrington, *What Darwin Really Said*, 91.

[30] *Encyclopaedia Britannica*, 18:859.

[31] I am indebted for this insight to Professor James C. Livingston, Department of Religion, College of William and Mary, Williamsburg, Virginia, who, when I heard him speak some years ago at the Woodrow Wilson Center in Washington, D. C., was studying British religious thought. Subsequently his work has been published as *Religious Thought in the Victorian Age: Challenges and Reconceptions* (London: Continuum), 2007.

[32] For a lucid discussion of the changes in the late nineteenth and early twentieth centuries resulting from the development of "modernism," see William P. Everdell, *The First Moderns: Profiles in the Origins of Twentieth-Century Thought* (Chicago: Univ. of Chicago Press, 1997).

[33] Forster, *Room With a View*, 27.

[34] Reynolds Price, *Three Gospels* (New York: Scribner, 1996), 239.

[35] "Notebook Journal 1903–1909," Vo 3/9, entry of May 2, 1908, Forster Archives.

[36] Ibid., 1905, opposite p. 68, Forster Archives. See also *Longest Journey,* Abinger edition, vol. 2, appendix B, "Memoirs," "Uncle Willie," 298.

[37] P. N. Furbank, "Personality of E. M. Forster," 61–68.

[38] George H. Thomson, *Fiction of E. M. Forster,* 54, quoting from Elizabeth Bowen, *Collected Impressions* (New York: Knopf, 1950), 123.

[39] "Notebook Journal 1903–1909," Vo 3/9, undated entry of June 1905, Forster Archives.

[40] Forster, *Albergo Empedocle*, "Dante," 146.

[41] "Locked Journal," Vo 4/4, entry of June 16, 1911, Forster Archives.

[42] Forster, *Albergo Empedocle,* "The Beauty of Life," 171, first published in *The Working Men's College Journal,* 1911.

[43] Ibid., 175.

[44] Quoted in Furbank, *A Life,* 2: 45–46.

[45] On a single sheet of West Hackhurst stationery, found in xiii/11A, Forster Archives. Probable date 1930s.

[46] Forster, *Two Cheers,* "Henry Thornton," 187.

[47] Forster, "Credo," see chapter 1, note 4. This personal statement of belief and disbelief, called "Credo" when first published, Forster later re-named "What I Believe." The two titles have identical texts.

[48] See Kathleen Norris, *Amazing Grace* (New York: Penguin Putnam, 1998), 20.

[49] Forster, *Commonplace Book*, 55.

[50] The phrase belongs to Angelica Garnett. See her memoir of Bloomsbury and family life at Charleston, *The Eternal Moment* (Orono, ME: Puckerbrush Press, 1998), 117. Her title is the same as one of Forster's short stories.

[51] Shusaku Endo, *A Life of Jesus,* trans. Richard A. Schuchert (New York: Paulist Press, 1973), 33–34. See Matthew, chaps. 3 and 4. Endo is freely expanding the biblical quotation of Jesus' words, which are "Repent, for the kingdom of heaven is at hand." See also Luke 3:7, in which John labels his audience as a "generation of vipers."

Chapter Four

[1] Forster, *Where Angels Fear to Tread.*

[2] Forster, *Selected Letters of E. M. Forster,* vol. 1, *1879–1920,* ed. Mary Lago and P. N. Furbank (Cambridge, MA: The Belknap Press of Harvard Univ. Press, 1983), letter 60, Forster to R. C. Trevelyan, October 28, 1905, 83–84. Also found in *Where Angels Fear to Tread,* Abinger edition, vol. 1, appendix A, "An Exchange between Forster and R. C. Trevelyan."

[3] Forster, *Longest Journey.*

[4] Forster, *Room With a View.*

[5] This episode echoes the Thornton family dispute known as "The Aylward Incident," in which a beloved widowed cousin considers marrying a respected and older citizen who drops his "aitches." Only Forster's mother supported the widowed cousin. Other family

members reluctantly agreed. The marriage was reputed to be a happy one though the widowed cousin's position in local society was degraded because her husband was in Trade. He owned a music shop. See Forster, *Marianne Thornton,* Abinger ed., 276–80; Harcourt, Brace, 308–14, for Forster's account.

[6] Forster, *Howards End.*

[7] Forster, *Howards End,* intro. Benjamin DeMott (London: Penguin Books, repr. Signet, 1992), vii. DeMott describes Forster's technique as "author-and-audience collaboration." "Reader and writer are together in diffident bewilderment, confusion, mixed response, sentimentality, true belief."

[8] Peter Burra, "Peter Burra's Introduction to the Everyman Edition," in Forster, *Passage to India,* Abinger edition, vol. 6, appendix B, 316–17. Burra's article was originally published in its entirety as "The Novels of E. M. Forster," in *The Nineteenth Century and After,* no. 693 (November 1934): 581–94.

[9] Olson, "The 'Noble Peasant,'" 389–403.

[10] Immanuel Kant, *Critique of Judgment* (1790), trans. Werner S. Pluhar (Indianapolis, IN: Hackett, 1987), 335.

[11] Angus Wilson, "A Conversation," 55.

[12] K. W. Gransden, "E. M. Forster at Eighty," *Encounter* 12, no. 1 (January 1959): 81.

[13] Forster, *Albergo Empedocle,* "The Beauty of Life," 175.

[14] G. Lowes Dickinson, *The Greek View of Life* (New York: Macmillan, 1967), 92.

[15] Ibid., 98.

[16] Ibid., 25.

[17] Forster, *Abinger Harvest,* "Cnidus," 168.

[18] "Notebook Journal 1903–1909," Vo 3/9, entry of July 15, 1903, Forster Archives.

[19] Forster, *Abinger Harvest,* "Notes on the English Character," 4–5.

[20] The phrase is used in Furbank, *A Life,* 2: 40; athletic love was the product of courage and persistence, "of taking trouble over relationships, which he had often preached."

Chapter Five

[1] "Locked Journal," Vo 4/4, entry of July 19, 1912, Forster Archives.

[2] Forster, *Abinger Harvest and England's Pleasant Land*, Abinger ed., vol. 1, "Hymn before Action," 330. See also *Abinger Harvest* (New York: Harcourt, Brace, 1936), "Hymn before Action," 343.

[3] "Locked Journal," Vo 4/4, entry of April 8, 1911, Forster Archives, reporting on conversation during two previous days in London with Masood and his Indian friend. Forster's italics and spelling.

[4] Ibid., entry of June 16, 1911.

[5] Furbank, *A Life*, 1: 222.

[6] Forster, *The Hill of Devi*, Abinger edition, vol. 14, ed. Elizabeth Heine (London: Edward Arnold, 1983), "The Individual and his God," a broadcast by Forster on the Eastern Service of the BBC on November 22, 1940, 240.

[7] Ibid., 239.

[8] Ibid., 13. Forster's italics.

[9] Elaine Pagels, *The Gnostic Gospels* (New York: Random House, 1979), xxxv. Also see Pagels, *Beyond Belief, The Sacred Gospel of Thomas* (New York: Random House, 2003).

[10] Forster, *Hill of Devi*, 13–14.

[11] Ibid., 14.

[12] Forster, "The Golden Peak," a review, *Athenaeum* (May 14, 1920): 631–32.

[13] See Elton Trueblood, *The Humor of Christ* (New York: Harper and Row, 1964), 25 ff. Since this slim volume is probably hard to find, it may be helpful to repeat some of Trueblood's enumeration of writers who recognized Jesus' humor: Ernest Renan, Tennyson, and Harry Emerson Fosdick, in general; T. R. Glover, *The Jesus of History* (New York: Association Press, 1917); G. K. Chesterton, *Heretics* (New York: Dodd, Mead, 1927), also Chesterton's *Orthodoxy;* Gary Webster, *Laughter in the Bible* (St. Louis, MO: Bethany Press, 1960), chapter entitled "Jesus' Use of Humor;" Dudley Zuver, *Salvation by Laughter* (New York: Harper and Brothers, 1933); D. N. Morison, *The Humour of Christ* (London: 1931); also Buttrick, *The*

Interpreter's Dictionary of the Bible, vol. 2. Trueblood especially calls attention to the article by L. M. Hussey, "The Wit of the Carpenter," *American Mercury* 5, no. 19 (July 1925).

My own additions include more recent authors on the subject, such as William Beaven Abernethy and Philip Joseph Mayher, *Scripture and Imagination: The Empowering of Faith* (New York: Pilgrim Press, 1988), 38; Reynolds Price, *Three Gospels,* 141; see also Karl Rahner's comments on laughter in Norris, *Amazing Grace*, 357.

[14] Trueblood, *Humor of Christ,* 15.

[15] Robert McAfee Brown, ed., *The Essential Reinhold Niebuhr* (New Haven, CT: Yale Univ. Press, 1986), 49.

[16] Trueblood, *Humor of Christ,* 48. Trueblood's italics.

[17] Ibid., 52.

[18] L. M. Hussey, "Wit of the Carpenter," 330. For bibliography, see note 13 above.

[19] Forster, *Hill of Devi,* 238–39. This misconception about Khajuraho brings to mind Forster's comment as a sixteen-year-old schoolboy in an essay he wrote on the churches of Normandy. Crediting rugged northern builders for the successful completion of the churches, Forster used enthusiastic phrases such as "fantastic forms and grotesque shapes." To the adolescent Forster they were extravagantly admirable, "not the creation of a diseased mind, like the gods of India." Quoted in Furbank, *A Life,* 1: 48.

[20] Ibid., 27, 28. Forster invokes the acropolis comparison earlier, 7. Later he describes Devi as wearing "a cap of rock like a military bandsman's," 170.

[21] For understanding the role of the goddess Devi in her multiple manifestations, see the excellent catalog *Devi, The Great Goddess* (Washington, DC: Smithsonian Institution, Arthur M. Sackler Gallery, 1990), in connection with the exhibition of the same name, having chapters by a dozen scholars, as well as many illustrations of Devi in her various manifestations.

[22] During his first visit to Dewas Senior in Christmas week of 1912, Forster and the Darlings lunched out of doors with Sir Tukoji who

cautioned, "But not too near those red stones, Malcolm, I had rather not." *Hill of Devi,* 11. Later Forster wrote that for Sir Tukoji, "Red paint on a stone could evoke it [the unseen]," 70.

[23] Forster, *Hill of Devi,* 64.

[24] Ibid., 78.

[25] G. K. Das, *E. M. Forster's India* (Totowa, NJ: Rowman and Littlefield, 1977), 99. Other Indian scholars of Forster have contributed greatly to the Westerner's understanding of India, Hinduism, and Forster himself as seen through Indian eyes. Among them are V. A. Shahane, ed., *Focus on Forster's "A Passage to India"* (Bombay: Orient Longman, 1975), with a distinguished roster of contributors. Shahane is the author of a significant article, "Symbolism in E. M. Forster's *A Passage to India:* 'Temple,'" *English Studies* 44, no. 6 (December 1963). M. M. Masood and Nirad G. Chaudhri have also added to our understanding of Forster's reaction to India in articles published in *Encounter.* See Chaudhri, "Passage To and From India," *Encounter* 2, no. 6 (June 1954): 15–24. Masood's article, "Amritsar to Chandrapore, E. M. Forster and the Massacre," *Encounter* 41, no. 3 (September 1973): 26–29, is particularly important. A very useful compendium is Rukun Advani, *E. M. Forster as Critic* (London: Croom Helm, 1984), especially chapter 3, "Forster's View of Religion." Also of value is the *Aligarh Journal of English Studies* 5, no. 1 (1980), published by Aligarh Muslim University; this issue is devoted entirely to Forster with articles by both Western and Eastern Forster scholars.

For an expansive overview of the history of the Indian subcontinent from prehistoric times until the arrival of the Mughal emperors, see A. L. Basham, *The Wonder That Was India,* first published in 1954, later reprinted in a hefty paperback by Grove Press of New York, 1959. Subsequent scholarship has added details and expanded the knowledge available to Basham, but his volume is still an invaluable source—especially, for purposes of this chapter, his section on "Religion: Cults, Doctrines and Metaphysics," which is book length in itself.

[26] K. M. Sen, *Hinduism* (1961; repr. New York: Penguin Books, 1991), 14. Sen's italics.

[27] Ibid., 17.

[28] Das, *Forster's India*, 108.

[29] Ibid., 98.

[30] Ibid., 5, quoting from Forster, "The Mission of Hinduism," *Daily News and Leader* (April 30, 1915): 7.

[31] Mahood, "Amritsar to Chandrapore," 26–29.

[32] Forster, *Hill of Devi*, 298. A typescript of this lecture entitled "Three Countries" can be found in *E.M. Forster, Essays, Lectures &c.,* Series II, vol. 1 in bound volume Vo 8/22 . Forster read it in Milan and Rome, November 1959.

[33] Regarding Persian influence on Indian life, see Spear, *History of India,* vol. 2.

[34] Forster, *Passage to India*, 14.

[35] V.A. Shahane, "*Passage to India*: 'Temple,'" 425–26, especially footnote 11.

[36] Forster, *Hill of Devi*, 64.

[37] My interpretation of Mrs. Moore is obviously influenced by my Western—and American—philosophical upbringing. For a finely nuanced discussion of Mrs. Moore from an Indian critic's point of view, see Chaman L. Sahni's essay, "The Marabar Caves in the Light of Indian Thought," in Shahane, ed., *Forster's "Passage to India."*

[38] Forster, *Passage to India*, 24.

[39] Mahood, "Amritsar to Chandrapore," 29.

Chapter Six

[1] Forster, *Passage to India,* 167.

[2] T. G. Vaidyanathan makes this point in his insightful chapter, "In Defence of Professor Godbole," in Shahane, ed., *Forster's "Passage to India,"* 49.

[3] Forster, *Hill of Devi*, 222. Also to be found in *Encounter* 18, no. 1 (January 1962), "Indian Entries," 25.

[4] Quoted in Wilfred Stone, *Cave and Mountain*, 333.

[5] Rajeev Sethi, ed., *Aditi: The Living Arts of India* (Washington, DC: Smithsonian Institution Press, 1985), 173.

[6] Vaidyanathan's chapter in Shahane, ed., *Forster's "Passage to India,"* 42–62, is a masterful analysis for anyone who wishes to understand the character of Professor Godbole through Hindu—i.e., non-Western—explication of the religious concepts emphasized in Forster's depiction of this important character. Vaidyanathan's quotation of Tukaram's poem is to be found on p. 55; the division of the poetry into lines is my choice.

[7] Forster, *Hill of Devi,* 73.

[8] Forster, "The Blue Boy," a review of W. G. Archer, *The Loves of Krishna* (London: Allen and Unwin), in *Listener* 57, no. 145 (March 14, 1957), 444.

[9] Quoted in ibid.

[10] Das, *Forster's India,* appendix B, "Call Me a Non-Believer: Interview with E. M. Forster," 118.

[11] James McConkey, *Novels of E. M. Forster,* 11–12.

[12] Quoted in Elizabeth Cleghorn Gaskell, *The Life of Charlotte Brontë* (London: Dent, 1966), 128, 139. See also Gaskell's description of several clergymen of the early nineteenth century, 72–75; also Charlotte Brontë's reaction to some clergy visitors to her home, 193.

[13] Quoted in Rebecca Fraser, *The Brontës—Charlotte Brontë and Her Family* (New York: Fawcett Columbine, 1988), quotes selected from 320 and 321.

[14] Quoted in ibid., 282.

[15] Quoted in ibid., 344. See also 356 for praise by another cleric.

[16] See Anne Brontë, *Agnes Grey* (London: Dent, 1959), chap. 11, "The Cottagers."

[17] C. W. Hatfield, ed., *The Complete Poems of Emily Jane Brontë* (New York: Columbia Univ. Press, 1941), poem 146, 163.

[18] Quoted in Fraser, *The Brontës,* 283. Brontë's italics.

[19] George Eliot to Harriet Beecher Stowe, November 11, 1874, quoted in Eliot, *Middlemarch, An Authoritative Text, Backgrounds, Reviews and Criticism,* ed. Bert G. Hornback (New York: W. W. Norton, 1977), 600.

[20] Ibid., 671, from the essay by Bert G. Hornback, "The Moral Imagination of George Eliot," quoting F.W.H. Myers, *Essays—Modern* (London, 1883), 268–69. Myers's italics.

[21] Ibid., 602, George Eliot's Journal, January 1, 1873, quoted from J. W. Cross, *George Eliot's Life as Related in Her Letters and Journals* (New York: Harper and Bros., 1885), 3: 191–92.

[22] George Eliot, *Adam Bede*, ed. and intro. John Paterson (Boston: Houghton Mifflin, 1968), 9.

[23] Ibid., 156.

[24] See N. John Hall, *Trollope, A Biography* (Oxford: Clarendon Press, 1991), 293. Trollope's *Clergymen of the Church of England*, which was published in 1866 by Chapman and Hall, was a collection of sketches printed previously in the *Pall Mall Gazette.*

[25] For a discussion of "status professionalism" versus "occupational professionalism"—or the "gentleman theory" versus the "pastoral ministry theory"—see Joseph H. O'Mealy, "Scenes of Professional Life: Mrs. Oliphant and the New Victorian Clergyman," *Studies in the Novel* 23, no. 2 (Summer 1992): 245–61.

[26] Quoted in Fraser, *The Brontës,* 299.

[27] This and subsequent quotations are all from a typescript of Forster, "Letter to *The Twentieth Century*," dated January 1955; see vo 5/4, Forster Archives. Forster's italics and capitalization.

[28] Quoted in Das, *Forster's India,* appendix B, "Call Me a Non-Believer," 119.

[29] Xavier Rynne, *Letters from Vatican City*, Vatican Council II (First Session): Background and Debates (New York: Farrar Strauss, 1963), 9.

[30] See Garry Wills, *Why I Am a Catholic* (Boston: Houghton Mifflin, 2002), especially chap. 18, "The Great Rebirth."

[31] See Eduard Schillebeecks, *The Real Achievement of Vatican II*, trans. H.J.J. Vaughan (New York: Herder and Herder, 1967); also Louis M. Savary, S. J. and Thomas J. O'Connor, eds., *The Heart Has Its Seasons: Reflections on the Human Condition* (New York: Regina Press, 1970). See also Wills, *Why I Am a Catholic,* note 30.

[32] Hans Küng, *On Being a Christian*, trans. Edward Quinn (New York: Doubleday, 1984), 177. Küng's italics. This book was first published in German in 1974 and in English in 1976.

[33] Ibid., 198.

[34] Ibid., 200.

[35] Ibid., 31.

[36] Robert W. Funk, Roy W. Hoover, and the Jesus Seminar, *The Five Gospels: The Search for the Authentic Words of Jesus, New Translation and Commentary* (New York: Macmillan, 1993). Quotations are from the dedication and p. 5.

[37] See Marcus J. Borg, *Meeting Jesus Again for the First Time* (San Francisco: HarperSanFrancisco, 1994). Another challenging and insightful volume for the modern reader is Patrick Henry, *The Ironic Christian's Companion: Finding the Marks of God's Grace in the World* (New York: Riverhead Books, 1999).

[38] Forster, *Two Cheers*, Part 2, "What I Believe," 71. My italics.

[39] Claude J. Summers, *E. M. Forster* (New York: Ungar, 1983), 20, quoting Christopher Isherwood, *Down There on a Visit* (New York: Simon and Schuster, 1962), 162. Isherwood's italics.

[40] Forster, "Letter to *The Twentieth Century*."

[41] Wilde, *Art and Order*, 157.

[42] See Stone, *Cave and Mountain*, 296, quoting from Forster, *Alexandria, A History and a Guide,* first published in Alexandria, Egypt, by Whitehead Morris Ltd., 1922. Second edition, Alexandria, 1938. First American edition, New York, 1961, with introduction by Forster, which is also included in Durrell's edition. See also Forster, *Alexandria, A History and a Guide,* introduction by Lawrence Durrell, notes and afterword by Michael Haag (New York: Oxford University Press, 1986), 80–81. My references to *Alexandria* are to the Durrell edition of 1986.

[43] Forster to Mrs. Florence Barger, Vo 34/1–2, xviii Barger, F/EMF.

[44] See Advani, *Forster as Critic,* "Forster's View of Religion." Advani presents an analytical précis of Forster's many comments on religion, listing articles, comments, and broadcasts by Forster over

his long lifetime. However, Advani does not include religious references in Forster's fictional works.

[45] R. N. Parkinson, "The Inheritors," in Das and Beer, *Human Exploration,* 68.

[46] Stone, *Cave and Mountain,* 7. Stone's italics.

[47] Ibid., 20, quoting from Forster, *Two Cheers,* "Does Culture Matter?," 104.

[48] Ibid., quoting from Forster, *Two Cheers,* "Our Second Greatest Novel?," 219.

[49] Ibid.

[50] Ibid., 260.

[51] Ibid., 108, quoting from Forster, *Two Cheers,* "Anonymity," 82–83.

[52] Ibid., 339.

[53] Ibid., 303–4, quoting from Forster, "The Gods of India," *The New Weekly,* May 30, 1914, "The Gods of India," 338.

[54] A paraphrase of a comment in a sermon by the Reverend Kenneth D. Fuller, then pastor, Cleveland Park Congregational United Church of Christ, Washington, DC, November 9, 2003.

[55] Furbank, *A Life,* 2: 227, footnote, from a letter from W. H. Auden to Christopher Isherwood, quoting from Christopher Isherwood, *Christopher and His Kind, 1929–1949* (New York: Farrar Straus Giroux, 1976), 306.

[56] Humphrey Carpenter, *W. H. Auden, A Biography* (Boston: Houghton Mifflin, 1981), 226, quoting a 1934 review by Auden.

[57] Ibid., 226.

[58] Forster to Christopher Isherwood, February 28, 1944, *Selected Letters,* vol. 2, letter 367, 206. Forster's italics.

[59] See note 55.

[60] Forster, *Marianne Thornton,* Abinger ed., 59; Harcourt, Brace, 54.

[61] Ibid., Abinger ed., 66; Harcourt, Brace, 62.

Chapter Seven

[1] Nicola Beauman, *Morgan: A Biography of E. M. Forster* (London: Hodder and Stoughton, 1993), 120, quoting Jeffrey Weeks, *Coming Out: Homosexual Politics in Britain* (London: Quartet Books, 1977), 14. See also Jeffrey Weeks, *Coming Out: Homosexual Politics in Britain from the Nineteenth Century to the Present*, rev. ed. (London: Quartet Books, 1990).

[2] *Maurice* was printed in two editions. The first was published by the Trustees of the late E. M. Forster (New York: W. W. Norton, 1971), 60. The second edition is the Abinger edition, vol. 5, ed., intro., and notes by Philip Gardner (London: André Deutsch, 2nd ed., 1999), 45.

[3] *Maurice*, Norton ed., 250. In other versions "Notes on *Maurice*," is sometimes called "Terminal Note." Under either title the text is identical.

[4] "Locked Journal," 1910, xii/8, Forster Archives. Other quotations in this section, unless specifically footnoted, are from this source.

[5] Furbank, *A Life,* 1: 37.

[6] The quotation is found in both the "Locked Journal" and Furbank, *A Life,* 1: 38.

[7] Forster, *Maurice*, Norton ed., 14. Quotations from the text of *Maurice* in this section are from the Norton edition.

[8] "Locked Journal," 1910.

[9] Richard Sennett, *Flesh and Stone: The Body and the City in Western Civilization* (New York: W. W. Norton, 1994), 66.

[10] Ibid., 46 and 47.

[11] Summers, *E. M. Forster,* 147. Summers's chapter on *Maurice* is brilliant. In my opinion, this volume cannot be recommended too highly for the depth and subtlety of Summers's insights into Forster as a novelist and a human being.

[12] See Forster, *Maurice*, Norton ed., "Terminal Note," 250.

[13] In addition to Philip Gardner's introduction to *Maurice,* critics who have written frankly about the effects of Forster's homosexu-

ality—some sympathetically, some not—include Claude J. Summers; Wilfred Stone; P. N. Furbank; Nicola Beauman; and Robert K. Martin and George Piggford, eds., *Queer Forster* (Chicago: Univ. of Chicago Press, 1997), especially chap. 2, Gregory W. Bredbeck's "'Queer Superstitions': Forster, Carpenter, and the Illusion of (Sexual) Identity." Also see Wilfred Stone, "'Overleaping Class': Forster's Problems in Connection," *Modern Language Quarterly* 39, no. 4 (December 1978): 386–404.

For a broad and deep understanding of Forster's homosexual development, see Wendy Moffat, *A Great Unrecorded History, A New Life of E. M. Forster* (New York: Farrar, Straus and Giroux, 2010). In a tour de force, Moffat sets Forster's homosexual experiences in their place in the larger picture of homosexuality in England from Oscar Wilde through two world wars to Forster's death.

[14] Included in Forster, *The Machine Stops and Other Stories*, Abinger ed., vol. 7, ed. Rod Mengham (London: André Deutsch, 1997).

[15] See Summers, *Forster,* 242.

[16] Stone, *Cave and Mountain*, 136.

[17] Quoted in Furbank, *A Life*, 1: 113.

[18] "Notebook Journal 1903–1909," Vo 3/9, opposite page 70, Forster Archives. Forster had written the word "physically" and then crossed it out in the "Journal." See also Furbank, *A Life*, 1: 113–14.

[19] Furbank, *A Life*, 2: 39.

[20] Ibid., 2: 40.

[21] Ibid.

[22] Ibid., 2: 39.

[23] For a detailed account of the development of Forster's relationship with el-Adl, see Furbank, *A Life,* vol. 2.

[24] For a detailed account of Forster's relationship with Masood, see Furbank, *A Life,* vols. 1 and 2.

[25] Forster, *Hill of Devi*, appendix D, "Kanaya," 310.

[26] See Forster, *The Life to Come and Other Stories*, Abinger edition, vol. 8, ed. Oliver Stallybrass (London: Edward Arnold, 1972).

[27] For a readable popular account highlighting the efforts of some American missionaries and an English businessman-turned-reformer to make known the ravages of King Leopold's administration of the Congo, see Pagan Kennedy, *Black Livingstone* (New York: Viking, 2002), especially 131–44, 147ff., 155–64, 167–75, and 180–86. Kennedy's account, which focuses mainly on the actions of one American missionary, quotes first-person accounts of atrocities and newspaper reports of speeches and other actions aiming to expose the savagery practiced under King Leopold's imprimatur. For a more broad-gauged historical study of this vicious exploitation of the Congo, see Adam Hochschild, *King Leopold's Ghost* (Boston: Houghton Mifflin, 1998).

[28] Quoted in Summers, *Forster,* 276.

[29] Forster, *The Machine Stops,* "The Machine Stops," 91.

[30] "Locked Journal," July 17, 1911, xii/8, Forster Archives.

[31] Ibid., November 1, 1911.

[32] Ibid., December 31, 1911. Also quoted in Furbank, *A Life,* 1: 204.

[33] "Locked Journal," March 5, 1912, xii/8, Forster Archives.

[34] Ibid., May 14, 1912.

[35] Furbank, *A Life,* 1: 206.

[36] See ibid., 206–7. Presumably Forster's italics.

[37] "Locked Journal," xi/11, Forster Archives.

[38] Quoted in Furbank, *A Life,* 2: 135.

[39] Ibid., 2: 167.

[40] Ibid.

[41] Ibid., 2: 169.

[42] Weeks, *Coming Out,* 1990 rev. ed., 164. The 1977 edition was quoted in footnote 1. See also *The Wolfenden Report,* Report of the Committee on Homosexual Offenses and Prostitution, authorized American edition, intro. Karl Menninger, M.D. (New York: Stein and Day, 1963). The report is dated August 12, 1957.

[43] *The New Statesman and Nation* (October 31, 1953): 508–9.

[44] Ibid., 509.

[45] Weeks, *Coming Out,* 1990 rev. ed., 156.

[46] Forster to Christopher Isherwood, June 25, 1948, in *Selected Letters*, vol. 2, letter 384, 231.

[47] Forster, *Maurice*, "Terminal Note," Norton ed., 255.

[48] Forster, *Arctic Summer*, quoted in "Editor's Introduction," p. xxx. Forster's italics.

[49] Summers, *Forster*, 5.

[50] "Notebook Journal 1903–1909," Vo 3/9, entry of September 17, 1906. Forster Archives.

[51] Norman Pittenger, "E. M. Forster, Homosexuality and Christian Morality," *Christian Century* 88 (December 15, 1971): 168–71. Pittenger's italics.

[52] On a single sheet of West Hackhurst stationary, found in xiii/11A, [1930s?]. Forster Archives. The 1930s date is the considered assumption of Michael Halls, the curator of the Forster Archives at the time the "Handlist of the Papers of E. M. Forster, Honorary Fellow" was compiled for the King's College Modern Archives, Cambridge University.

Chapter Eight

[1] This chapter makes no attempt to cover the whole gamut of Forster's political actions, which are well documented in Furbank's authorized biography. Episodes have been selected to illustrate main threads of Forster's personal philosophy.

[2] "Notebook Journal 1903–1909," Vo 3/9, December 31, 1909.

[3] Forster's first appearance as a political commentator and critic may have been in 1919. His subject was not India but Egypt, where he had been posted to the Red Cross during World War I. Forster explicated and supported the Egyptian position. See Furbank, *A Life*, 2: 57ff.

[4] Forster, "Reflections in India—Too Late!," *Nation and Athenaeum* (January 21, 1922): 614.

[5] Ibid., "Reflections in India—The Prince's Progress" (January 28, 1922): 644.

[6] Ibid., "India and the Turk" (September 30, 1922): 844.

[7] Forster, "Notes on the Way," *Time and Tide* (June 2, 1934): 694–96.

[8] For details of the contretemps between Forster and Hall, see Furbank, *A Life,* 2: 153–54.

[9] Ibid., 2: 154, originally published in *Nation and Athenaeum*, September 1, 1928.

[10] See Furbank, *A Life,* 2: 153–55.

[11] Judge Sir Chartres Biron found against the novel because, he said, Hall had not characterized the relationship between the two women as sufficiently "blameworthy"; the unhappy ending was not abject enough to be seen as a moral lesson. Judge Chartres Biron is quoted in Weeks, *Coming Out,* 1990 rev. ed., 109. In turn Weeks is quoting from Vera Brittain, *Radclyffe Hall: A Case of Obscenity?* (London, 1930), 154, quoting Norman Birkett.

[12] See Forster's letter to Mr. Thring, president of the Society of Authors, in *Selected Letters of E. M. Forster*, vol. 2, letter 287, 85–86; also in Forster archives, King's College Library Modern Archives, xviii.

[13] Forster, "The 'Censorship' of Books," *The Nineteenth Century and After*, no. 626 (April 1929): 444–45.

[14] While this chapter spotlights selected examples of Forster's political actions, Furbank's *A Life*, vol. 2, presents an admirably clear and detailed outline of the broad and complicated scope of Forster's activities from *The Well of Loneliness* through the 1930s and World War II. His detailed account of Forster's actions through these troubled political times is invaluable.

[15] For a more detailed account of the NCCL, and also of the matter of the Sedition Bill, see Furbank, *A Life*, 2: 186ff.

[16] Forster, "Still the Sedition Bill!" *Time and Tide* 15, no. 43 (October 27, 1934). Though Forster's comments in this period originate in various sources, *Time and Tide*, a non-party news weekly (now defunct) found the NCCL a subject worthy of follow-up.

[17] See Furbank, *A Life*, vol. 2, "Notes," 333, re text p. 187.

[18] Forster, "Still the Sedition Bill!"

[19] Stephen Spender, *Letters to Christopher Isherwood*, ed. Lee Bartlett (Santa Barbara, CA: Black Sparrow Press, 1980), letter 20, dated October 21, 1934, 68.

[20] See "Diary," *Time and Tide* (21 June 1941): "a number of its recent activities have been calculated to hinder rather than to help the war effort." Also see ibid., June 28, 1941, "Letters to the Editor," "has opposed and will continue to oppose all attempts . . . without any kind of judicial trial," and "to do these things is not to hinder the war effort . . . closely approximate to Nazi law," 539. See also ibid., June 28, 1941, "The National Council for Civil Liberties," 536–37, for more details of the accusations against the Council.

[21] Ibid., Forster, "Notes on the Way" (June 16, 1934): 765.

[22] Ibid., 766.

[23] Re the "noble peasant," see chapter l.

[24] Forster, "Notes on the Way," *Time and Tide* (June 16, 1934): 766.

[25] See Furbank, *A Life,* 2: 231ff.

[26] "They Hold Their Tongues" was originally published September 30, 1938, in the *New Statesman and Nation*, reprinted in *Two Cheers for Democracy*, Abinger ed., vol. 11, 1972, 28–30.

[27] Ibid.

[28] For a fuller discussion, see Furbank, *A Life,* 2: 311–12.

[29] *London Mercury and Bookman* 38, no. 227 (September 1938), "Credo," 397–404; also published the same year in New York in the *Nation* as the first of a series entitled "Living Philosophies"; later included in *Two Cheers for Democracy,* 1972, Abinger edition, vol. 11, 65–73.

[30] Though the essay may be called "Credo" or "What I Believe," the body of the essay is identical in the three sources cited in note 29.

[31] Forster, *Two Cheers,* 66.

[32] Ibid.

[33] Ibid., 67.

[34] For an overview of Forster's relations with the BBC, see Furbank, *A Life,* 2: 170–73.

[35] Ibid., 2: 240.

---

[36] Ibid., 2: 241–42.

[37] Quotations in this paragraph are from the Forster Archives, vi/22-A, 1956, Summer? Date added at a later time by a curator. Forster's italics.

[38] Forster, "The University and the Universe," *Spectator* (March 17, 1933): 368.

[39] Furbank, *A Life,* 2: 192. For a fuller account of the Congress of Writers, see ibid., 192–96.

[40] Forster, "International Congress of Writers," *New Statesman and Nation* (July 6, 1935): 9.

[41] Furbank, *A Life,* 2: 193.

[42] *Spectator* (August 13, 1937): 269 and 270.

[43] Forster, "The University and the Universe," 369.

[44] Forster, "Notes on the Way," *Time and Tide* (June 2, 1934): 696. Forster's italics.

[45] Forster, *Two Cheers*, "Three Anti-Nazi Broadcasts," 31–42. The first broadcast is called "Culture and Freedom"; the second, "What Has Germany Done to the Germans?"; and the third, "What Would Germany Do to Us?"

[46] *Time and Tide* (June 22, 1940).

[47] Forster, *Two Cheers*, "Tolerance," 43.

[48] Ibid., 46.

[49] Ibid., 45.

Chapter Nine

[1] Quotations in the first few pages of this chapter can be found in earlier chapters and are largely drawn from Forster, "What I Believe" in *Two Cheers.* The reference to "the darkness that does not comprehend" is from John 1:5.

[2] Stephen Spender, *World Within World: The Autobiography of Stephen Spender* (Berkeley: Univ. of California Press, 1966), 167.

[3] Herman Melville, *Billy Budd, Sailor: An Inside Narrative* (Chicago: Univ. of Chicago Press, 1962), 101. Forster employed this quotation in the libretto of the opera.

[4] Forster to Benjamin Britten, September 30, 1948, *Selected Letters*, vol. 2, letter 385, 233.

[5] Ibid., to Benjamin Britten, December 20, 1948, letter 387, 235. Forster's italics.

[6] *Billy Budd*, Opera in Two Acts, revised version 1961, music by Benjamin Britten, libretto by E. M. Forster and Eric Crozier, adapted from the story by Herman Melville (London: Boosey and Hawkes), act 1, scene 3, 33.

[7] The biblical text reads, "The light shines in the darkness, and the darkness has not overcome it." *Revised Standard Version of the Bible*, New York: Thomas Nelson and Sons, 1952.

[8] Furbank, *A Life,* 2: 284. See also 1946 John Lehmann edition of Melville's *Billy Budd*, which has the William Plomer introduction.

[9] Melville, *Billy Budd,* intro. by William Plomer (London: John Lehmann, 1946), 9.

[10] Forster to Benjamin Britten, probably written in early December 1950, *Selected Letters*, vol. 2, letter 394, 242. Forster's italics. See footnote for Crozier quotation.

[11] Ibid., Forster to Lionel Trilling, April 16, 1949, letter 389, 236–37. Forster's italics.

[12] Ibid., Forster to Benjamin Britten, December 9, 1951, letter 398, 246.

[13] Melville, *Billy Budd,* 131.

Selected Bibliography

Abernethy, Bob, and William Bole. *The Life of Meaning: Reflections on Faith, Doubt and Repairing the World* (New York: Seven Stories Press, 2008).

Advani, Rukun. *E. M. Forster as Critic.* London, UK: Croom Helm, 1984.

Aligarh Journal of English Studies 5, no. 1. Aligarh Muslim Univ., Uttar Pradesh, India, 1980.

Annan, Noel. *Leslie Stephen, The Godless Victorian.* New York: Random House, 1984.

Austin, Don. "The Problem of Continuity in Three Novels of E. M. Forster," *Modern Fiction Studies* 7 (Autumn 1961).

Basham, A. L. *The Wonder That Was India.* 1954. New York: Grove, 1959.

Beauman, Nicola. *Morgan: A Biography of E. M. Forster.* London: Hodder and Stoughton, 1993.

Beer, J. B. *The Achievement of E. M. Forster.* London: Chatto and Windus, 1962.

Billy Budd, Opera in Two Acts, revised version 1961, music
by Benjamin Britten, libretto by E. M. Forster and
Eric Crozier, adapted from the story by Herman
Melville (London: Boosey and Hawkes).

Borg, Marcus J. *Meeting Jesus Again for the First Time.* San
Francisco: HarperSanFrancisco, 1994.

Bowen, Elizabeth. *Collected Impressions.* New York: Knopf,
1950.

Brontë, Anne. *Agnes Grey.* New York: Dutton, 1959.

Brown, Robert McAfee, ed. *The Essential Reinhold Niebuhr.*
New Haven, CT: Yale Univ. Press, 1986.

Burra, Peter. "Peter Burra's Introduction to the Everyman
Edition." In Forster, *A Passage to India.* Abinger
edition, vol. 6, appendix B, 316–17. Originally
published as "The Novels of E. M. Forster," in *The
Nineteenth Century and After,* no. 693, November
1934, 581–94.

Buttrick, George Arthur. *The Interpreter's Dictionary of the
Bible.* New York: Abingdon Press, 1962.

Carpenter, Humphrey. *W. H. Auden, A Biography.* Boston:
Houghton Mifflin, 1981.

Chaudhri, Nirad C. "Passage To and From India," *Encounter*
2(6) (June 1954): 15–24.

Chesterton, G. K. *Heretics.* New York: Dodd, Mead, 1927. See
also Chesterton, G. K. *Orthodoxy.*

Colmer, John. *E. M. Forster: The Personal Voice.* London:
Routledge and Kegan Paul, 1975.

Crews, Frederick C. *E. M. Forster: The Perils of Humanism.*
Princeton, NJ: Princeton Univ. Press, 1962.

Cross, J. W. *George Eliot's Life as Related in Her Letters and
Journals.* New York: Harper and Bros., 1885.

Das, G. K. *E. M. Forster's India.* Totowa, NJ: Rowman and
Littlefield, 1977.

Das, G. K. and John Beer, eds. *E. M. Forster: A Human
Exploration.* New York: New York Univ. Press, 1979.

Davidoff, Leonore. "Mastered for Life: Servant and Wife in
Victorian and Edwardian England," *Journal of Social
History* 7 (Summer 1974).

Devi, The Great Goddess. Washington, DC: The Smithsonian
Institution, Arthur M. Sackler Gallery, 1990.

Dickinson, G. Lowes. *The Greek View of Life.* New York:
Macmillan, 1967.

Durrell, Lawrence, ed. *Alexandria,* by E. M. Forster. New
York: Oxford University Press, 1986.

Eliot, George. *Adam Bede.* New York: Houghton Mifflin,
1968.

———. *Middlemarch, An Authoritative Text, Backgrounds, Reviews, and Criticism.* Ed. Bert G. Hornback. New York: W. W. Norton, 1977.

Endo, Shusaku. *A Life of Jesus.* Trans. Richard A. Schuchert. New York: Paulist Press, 1973.

Everdell, William P. *The First Moderns: Profiles in the Origins of Twentieth-Century Thought.* Chicago: Univ. of Chicago Press, 1997.

Farrington, Benjamin. *What Darwin Really Said.* New York: Schocken Books, 1966.

Forster, E. M. *Abinger Harvest and England's Pleasant Land.* Abinger edition, vol. 10, ed. Elizabeth Heine. London: André Deutsch, 1996.

———. *Albergo Empedocle and Other Writings of E. M. Forster.* Ed. George H. Thomson. New York: Liveright, 1971.

———. *Alexandria, A History and a Guide.* Intro. Lawrence Durrell, 1982. Afterword and notes Michael Haag, 1986. New York: Oxford Univ. Press, 1986.

———. *Arctic Summer and Other Fiction.* Abinger edition, vol. 9, ed. Elizabeth Heine and Oliver Stallybrass. London: Edward Arnold, 1980.

———. "The Blue Boy." *Listener* 57, no. 159 (March 14, l957).

———. "The 'Censorship' of Books." *The Nineteenth Century and After*, no. 626 (April 1929).

———. *Commonplace Book.* Ed. Philip Gardner. Stanford, CA: Stanford Univ. Press, 1985.

———. "Credo." *The London Mercury and Bookman* 38, no. 227 (September 1938). This essay is included in Forster, *Two Cheers for Democracy,* Abinger edition, vol. 11, as "What I Believe."

———. "The Gods of India." *The New Weekly* (May 30, 1914).

———. "The Golden Peak." *Athenaeum* (May 14, 1920).

———. *The Hill of Devi.* Abinger edition, vol. 14, ed. Elizabeth Heine. London: Edward Arnold, 1983.

———. *Howards End.* Abinger edition, vol. 4, ed. Oliver Stallybrass. London: Edward Arnold, 1973.

———. "International Congress of Writers." *The New Statesman and Nation*, July 6, 1935.

———. "Letter to *The Twentieth Century*," dated January 1955; Vo 5/4, Forster Archives.

———. *The Life to Come and Other Stories.* Abinger edition, vol. 8, ed. Oliver Stallybrass. London: Edward Arnold, 1972.

———. *The Longest Journey.* Abinger edition, vol. 2, ed. Elizabeth Heine. London: Edward Arnold, 1984.

———. *The Machine Stops and Other Stories,* Abinger
edition, vol. 7, ed. Rod Mengham. London: André
Deutsch, 1997.

———. *Marianne Thornton, A Domestic Biography, 1797–
1887.* New York: Harcourt, Brace, 1956. Abinger
edition, vol. 15, ed. Evelyne Hanquart-Turner.
London: André Deutsch, 2000.

———. *Maurice.* New York: W. W. Norton, 1971. Abinger
edition, vol. 5, ed., intro., and notes by Philip
Gardner. London: André Deutsch, 2nd ed., 1999.

———. "The Mission of Hinduism," *Daily News and Leader,*
April 30, 1915.

———. "Notes on the Way," *Time and Tide,* June 2, 1934.

———. *A Passage to India.* Abinger edition, vol. 6, ed. Oliver
Stallybrass. New York: Holmes and Meier, 1979.

———. Presidential Address, E. M. Forster Archives, Modern
Archives of King's College Library, Cambridge
University, Cambridge, UK, Vo 8/22 at fo 135.

———. *The Prince's Tale and Other Uncollected Writings.*
Abinger edition, vol. 17, ed. P. N. Furbank. London:
André Deutsch, 1998.

———. *A Room With a View.* Abinger edition, vol. 3, ed.
Oliver Stallybrass. London: Edward Arnold, 1977.

———. *Selected Letters of E. M. Forster*, vol. 1, *1879–1920*. Vol. 2, *1921–1970*. Ed. Mary Lago and P. N. Furbank. Cambridge, MA: The Belknap Press of Harvard Univ. Press, 1983.

———. "Still the Sedition Bill!" *Time and Tide* 15, no. 43 (October 27, 1934).

———. "Three Countries," E. M. Forster, Essays, Lectures, etc., Series #2, vol. 1 in bound volume 8/22, Forster Archives, King's College Library, Cambridge University, England.

———. *Two Cheers for Democracy*. Abinger edition, vol. 11, ed. Oliver Stallybrass. London: Edward Arnold, 1972.

———. "The University and the Universe." *Spectator* (March 17, 1933).

———. *Where Angels Fear to Tread*. Abinger edition, vol. 1, ed. Oliver Stallybrass. London: Edward Arnold, 1975.

Fraser, Rebecca. *The Brontës—Charlotte Brontë and Her Family*. New York: Fawcett Columbine, 1988.

Funk, Robert W., Roy W. Hoover, and the Jesus Seminar. *The Five Gospels: The Search for the Authentic Words of Jesus: New Translation and Commentary*. New York: Macmillan, 1993.

Furbank, P. N. *E. M. Forster: A Life*, vol. 1, *The Growth of the Novelist (1879–1914)*; vol. 2, *Polycrates Ring (1914–1970)*. New York: Harcourt Brace Jovanovich, 1978.

———. "The Personality of E. M. Forster," *Encounter* 35, no. 5 (November 1970).

Furbank, P. N. and F. J. H. Haskell. "E. M. Forster." In Malcolm Cowley, ed., *Paris Review, Writers at Work*. New York: Viking, 1958.

Gardner, Philip. *E. M. Forster, the Critical Heritage*. London: Routledge and Kegan Paul, 1973.

Garnett, Angelica. *The Eternal Moment*. Orono, ME: Puckerbrush Press, 1998.

Gaskell, Elizabeth Cleghorn. *The Life of Charlotte Brontë*. New York: Dutton, 1966.

Gay, Peter. *The Tender Passion*. New York: Oxford Univ. Press, 1986.

Gerber, Helmut E. "E. M. Forster: An Annotated Checklist of Writings about Him," *English Fiction in Transition* 2 (Spring 1959): 4–27, bound in *English Literature in Transition,* vols. 1–3 (1957–60).

Glover, T. R. *The Jesus of History*. New York: Association Press, 1917.

Grandsden, K. W. *E. M. Forster*. New York: Grove, 1962.

———. "E. M. Forster at Eighty." *Encounter* 12, no. 1 (January 1959).

Hall, James. *The Tragic Comedians, Seven Modern British Novelists.* Bloomington: Indiana Univ. Press, 1963.

Hall, N. John. *Trollope, A Biography.* Oxford: Clarendon, 1991.

Hatfield, C. W., ed., *The Complete Poems of Emily Jane Brontë.* New York: Columbia Univ. Press, 1941.

Henry, Patrick. *The Ironic Christian's Companion: Finding the Marks of God's Grace in the World.* New York: Riverhead Books, 1999.

Herz, Judith Scherer. "Forster's Three Experiments in Autobiographical Biography," *Studies in the Literary Imagination* 13 (Spring 1980).

Herz, Judith Scherer, and Robert K. Martin, eds., *E. M. Forster: Centenary Revaluations.* Toronto, ON: Univ. of Toronto Press, 1982.

Hochschild, Adam. *King Leopold's Ghost.* Boston: Houghton Mifflin, 1998.

Hornback, Bert. G., ed. *George Eliot, Middlemarch, An Authoritative Text, Backgrounds, Reviews, and Criticism.* New York: W. W. Norton, 1977. Including also Hornback's essay, "The Moral Imagination of George Eliot."

Hussey, L. M. "The Wit of the Carpenter," *American Mercury* 5, no. 19 (July 1925).

Isherwood, Christopher. *Christopher and His Kind, 1929–1949*. New York: Farrar Strauss Giroux, 1976.

———. *Down There on a Visit*. New York: Simon and Schuster, 1962.

Jesus Seminar, see Robert W. Funk. *The Five Gospels*.

Kant, Immanuel. *Critique of Judgment* (1790). Trans. Werner S. Pluhar. Indianapolis, IN: Hackett, 1987.

Kazin, Alfred. "Howards End Revisited." *Partisan Review* 59, no. 1 (Winter 1992): 29–43; reprinted in *Twentieth Century Literary Criticism* 125 (2003): 114–20.

Kennedy, Pagan. *Black Livingstone*. New York: Viking, 2002.

Kermode, Frank. *Concerning E. M. Forster*. New York: Farrar, Straus and Giroux, 2009.

Küng, Hans. *On Being a Christian*. Trans. Edward Quinn. New York: Doubleday, 1984.

Livingston, James C. *Religious Thought in the Victorian Age: Challenges and Reconceptions*. London: Continuum, 2007.

Mahood, M. M. "Amritsar to Chandrapore, E. M. Forster and the Massacre." *Encounter* 41, no. 3 (September 1973): 26–29.

Martin, Robert K., and George Piggford, eds. *Queer Forster.* Chicago: Univ. of Chicago Press, 1997.

McBride, Theresa M. *The Domestic Revolution.* New York: Holmes and Meier, 1976.

McConkey, James. *The Novels of E. M. Forster.* Ithaca, NY: Cornell Univ. Press, 1957.

McDowell, Frederick P. W. *E. M. Forster, an Annotated Bibliography of Writings about Him.* DeKalb: Northern Illinois Univ. Press, 1976.

———. "E. M. Forster: Recent Extended Studies," *English Literature in Transition* 9 (Fall 1966): 156–68.

———. "Bibliography, News, and Notes: E. M. Forster," *English Literature in Transition* 10 (Spring 1967): 47–64.

———. "Recent Books on Forster and on Bloomsbury," *English Literature in Transition* 12 (Fall 1969): 135–50.

Melville, Herman. *Billy Budd, Sailor: An Inside Narrative.* Chicago: Univ. of Chicago Press, 1962.

Moffat, Wendy. *A Great Unrecorded History: A New Life of E. M. Forster.* New York: Farrar, Straus and Giroux, 2010.

Morison, D. N. *The Humour of Christ.* London, 1931.

Naylor, Gillian. *Bloomsbury: Its Artists, Authors and Designers.* Boston: Little, Brown, 1990.

Norris, Kathleen. *Amazing Grace.* New York: Penguin Putnam, 1998.

Olson, Jeane N. "E. M. Forster's Prophetic Vision of the Modern Family in *Howards End." Texas Studies in Literature and Language* 35, no. 3 (Fall 1993): 347–62; reprinted in *Twentieth-Century Literary Criticism* 125 (2003): 120–28.

———. "The 'Noble Peasant' in E. M. Forster's Fiction." *Studies in the Novel* 20, no. 4 (Winter 1988): 389–403.

O'Mealy, Joseph H. "Scenes of Professional Life: Mrs. Oliphant and the New Victorian Clergyman." *Studies in the Novel* 23, no. 2 (Summer 1992): 245–61.

Orange, Michael. "Language and Silence in *A Passage to India."* In G. K. Das and John Beer, eds., *E. M. Forster: A Human Exploration.* New York: New York Univ. Press, 1979.

Pagels, Elaine. *Beyond Belief, The Sacred Gospel of Thomas.* New York: Random House, 2003.

———. *The Gnostic Gospels.* New York: Random House, 1979.

Parker, Peter. *Ackerley: A Life of J. R. Ackerley.* New York: Farrar Strauss Giroux, 1989.

Partridge, Frances. *Everything to Lose, Diaries 1945–1960.* Boston: Little, Brown, 1985.

Pittenger, Norman. "E. M. Forster, Homosexuality and Christian Morality," *Christian Century* 88 (December 15, 1971): 168–71.

Plomer, William. *Introduction to* Billy Budd. London: John Lehmann, 1946.

Pollock, Linda. *A Lasting Relationship: Parents and Children over Three Centuries.* Hanover, NH: Univ. Press of New England, 1987.

Price, Reynolds. *Three Gospels.* New York: Scribner, 1996.

Richards, I. A. "A Passage to Forster: Reflections on a Novelist." *Forum* 78 (December 1927).

Rynne, Xavier. *Letters from Vatican City*, Vatican Council II (First Session): Background and Debates. New York: Farrar Straus, 1963.

Sahni, Chaman L. "The Marabar Caves in the Light of Indian Thought." In V. A. Shahane, ed., *Focus on Forster's "A Passage to India."* Bombay: Orient Longman, 1975.

Savary, Louis M., S. J., and Thomas J. O'Connor, eds., *The Heart Has Its Seasons: Reflections on the Human Condition.* New York: Regina Press, 1970.

Schillebeecks, Eduard. *The Real Achievement of Vatican II.* Trans. H.J.J. Vaughan. New York: Herder and Herder, 1967.

Sen, K. M. *Hinduism.* 1961. Reprint, New York: Penguin Books, 1991.

Sennett, Richard. *Flesh and Stone: The Body and the City in Western Civilization.* New York: W. W. Norton, 1994.

Sethi, Rajeev, ed., *Aditi: The Living Arts of India.* Washington, DC: Smithsonian Institution Press, 1985.

Shahane, V. A., ed. *Focus on Forster's "A Passage to India."* Bombay: Orient Longman, 1975.

———. "Symbolism in E. M. Forster's *A Passage to India:* 'Temple,'" *English Studies* 44, no. 6, December 1963.

Spear, Percival. *A History of India.* vol. 2. 1965. Reprint, London: Penguin Books, 1990.

Spender, Stephen. *Letters to Christopher Isherwood.* Ed. Lee Bartlett. Santa Barbara, CA: Black Sparrow Press, 1980.

———. *World Within World: The Autobiography of Stephen Spender.* Berkeley: Univ. of California Press, 1966.

Stone, Lawrence. *The Family, Sex and Marriage in England, 1500–1800.* Abridged ed. New York: Harper and Row, 1979.

Stone, Wilfred. *The Cave and the Mountain: A Study of E. M. Forster.* Stanford, CA: Stanford Univ. Press, 1966.

———. "'Overleaping Class': Forster's Problems in Connection," *Modern Language Quarterly* 39, no. 4 (December 1978): 386–404.

Summers, Claude J. *E. M. Forster.* New York: Ungar, 1983. Reprint, 1987.

Thompson, F.M.L. *The Rise of Respectable Society.* Cambridge, MA: Harvard Univ. Press, 1988.

Thomson, George H. *The Fiction of E. M. Forster.* Detroit, MI: Wayne State Univ. Press, 1967.

Trilling, Lionel. *E. M. Forster.* New York: Harcourt Brace Jovanovich, 1963.

Trollope, Anthony. *Clergymen of the Church of England.* London: Chapman and Hall, 1866.

Trueblood, Elton. *The Humor of Christ.* New York: Harper and Row, 1964.

Vaidyanathan, T. G. "In Defence of Professor Godbole." In V. A. Shahane, ed., *Focus on Forster's "A Passage to India."* Bombay: Orient Longman, 1975.

Webster, Gary. *Laughter in the Bible.* St. Louis: Bethany Press, 1960.

Weeks, Jeffrey. *Coming Out: Homosexual Politics in Britain from the Nineteenth Century to the Present.* 1977. Rev. ed., London: Quartet Books, 1990.

Wilde, Alan. *Art and Order: A Study of E. M. Forster.* New York: New York Univ. Press, 1964.

Wills, Garry. *Why I Am a Catholic.* Boston: Houghton Mifflin, 2002.

Wilson, Angus. "A Conversation with E. M. Forster," *Encounter* 9, no. 5 (November 1957).

Wolfenden Report. *Committee on Homosexual Offenses and Prostitution.* New York: Stein and Day, 1963. Authorized America edition, intro. Karl Menninger, M.D.

Yarrow, Alexandra. "Sympathy in the Novels of E. M. Forster." In *Aspects of E. M. Forster*, ed. Heiko Zimmermann. http://emforster.de/pdf/yarrow.pdf.

Zeikowitz, Richard E., ed., *Letters between Forster and Isherwood on Homosexuality and Literature.* New York: Palgrave Macmillan, 2008.

Zuver, Dudley. *Salvation by Laughter.* New York: Harper and Brothers, 1933.

Index